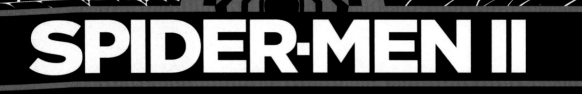

SPIDER-MEN II

BOTH SPIDER-MEN MET FOR THE FIRST TIME WHEN A VILLAIN BROKE THROUGH THE DIMENSIONAL WALL BETWEEN THEIR WORLDS. BOTH PETER AND MILES HAD A PROFOUND EXPERIENCE SEEING HOW EACH OTHER LIVED AS SPIDER-MAN.

SINCE THEN, THEIR WORLDS HAVE MERGED AND MILES HAS CONTINUED FIGHTING CRIME AS SPIDER-MAN WITH PETER'S ENTHUSIASTIC BLESSING.

BUT WHEN PETER RETURNED HOME AFTER THEIR FIRST MEETING, HE WONDERED IF HIS NATIVE REALITY HAD ITS OWN MILES MORALES.

WHAT DID PETER PARKER DISCOVER?!

BRIAN MICHAEL BENDIS WRITER

SARA PICHELLI WITH **MARK BAGLEY** & **JOHN DELL** (#5) ARTISTS

ELISABETTA D'AMICO INKING ASSISTANT

JUSTIN PONSOR COLOR ARTIST

VC's CHRIS ELIOPOULOS (#1) & **CORY PETIT** (#2-5) LETTERERS

SARA PICHELLI WITH **JUSTIN PONSOR** (#1, #5), **JASON KEITH** (#2) & **MORRY HOLLOWELL** (#3-4) COVER ART

KATHLEEN WISNESKI ASSISTANT EDITOR

DEVIN LEWIS ASSOCIATE EDITOR

NICK LOWE EDITOR

SPIDER-MAN CREATED BY **STAN LEE** & **STEVE DITKO**

JENNIFER GRÜNWALD COLLECTION EDITOR
CAITLIN O'CONNELL ASSISTANT EDITOR
KATERI WOODY ASSOCIATE MANAGING EDITOR
MARK D. BEAZLEY EDITOR, SPECIAL PROJECTS
JEFF YOUNGQUIST VP PRODUCTION & SPECIAL PROJECTS
DAVID GABRIEL SVP PRINT, SALES & MARKETING
ADAM DEL RE BOOK DESIGNER

C.B. CEBULSKI EDITOR IN CHIEF
JOE QUESADA CHIEF CREATIVE OFFICER
DAN BUCKLEY PRESIDENT
ALAN FINE EXECUTIVE PRODUCER

SPIDER-MEN II. Contains material originally published in magazine form as SPIDER-MEN II #1-5. First printing 2018. ISBN 978-1-302-90883-6. Published by MARVEL WORLDWIDE, INC., a subsidiary of MARVEL ENTERTAINMENT, LLC. OFFICE OF PUBLICATION: 135 West 50th Street, New York, NY 10020.

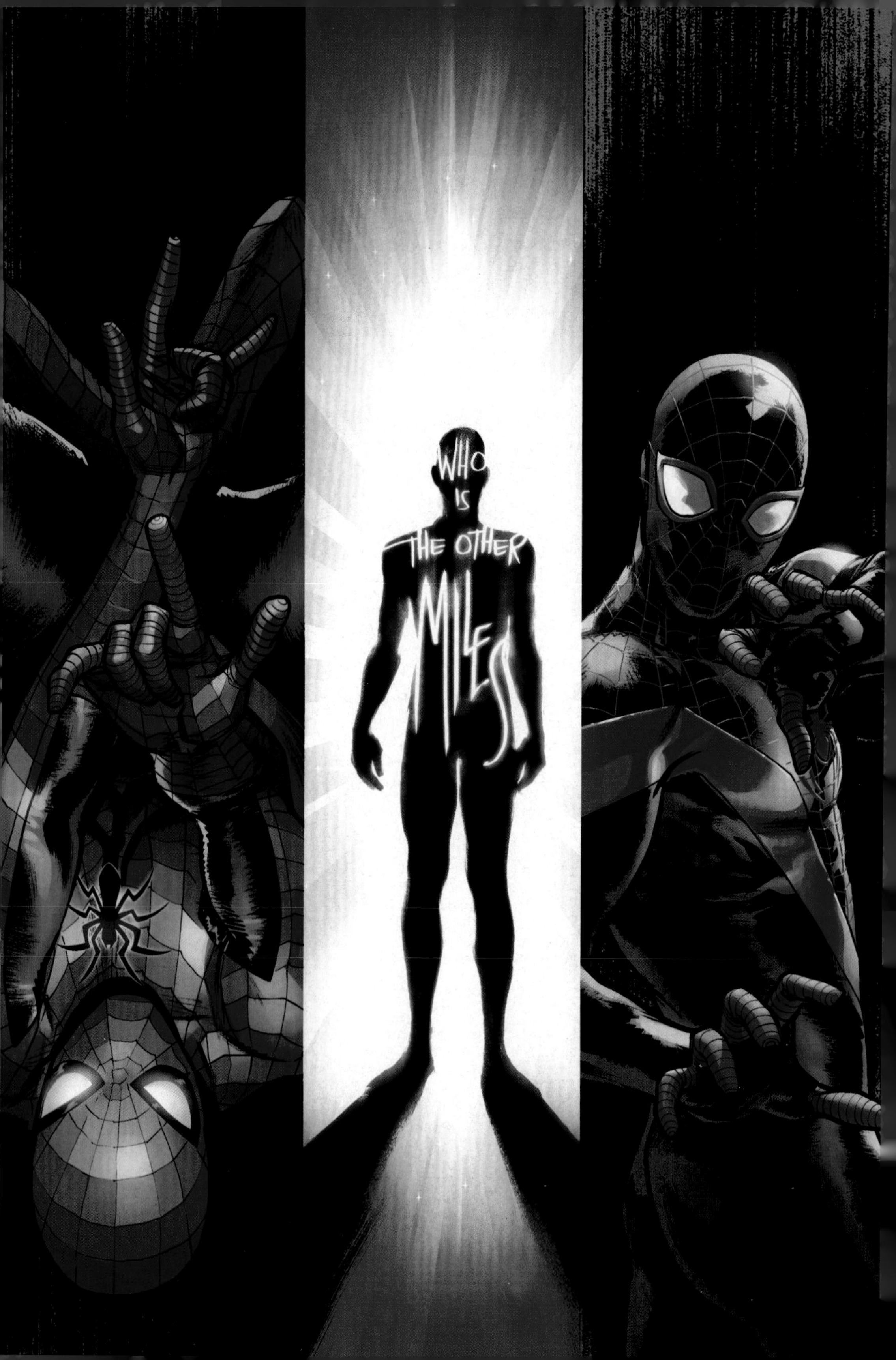
WHO
IS
THE OTHER
MILES

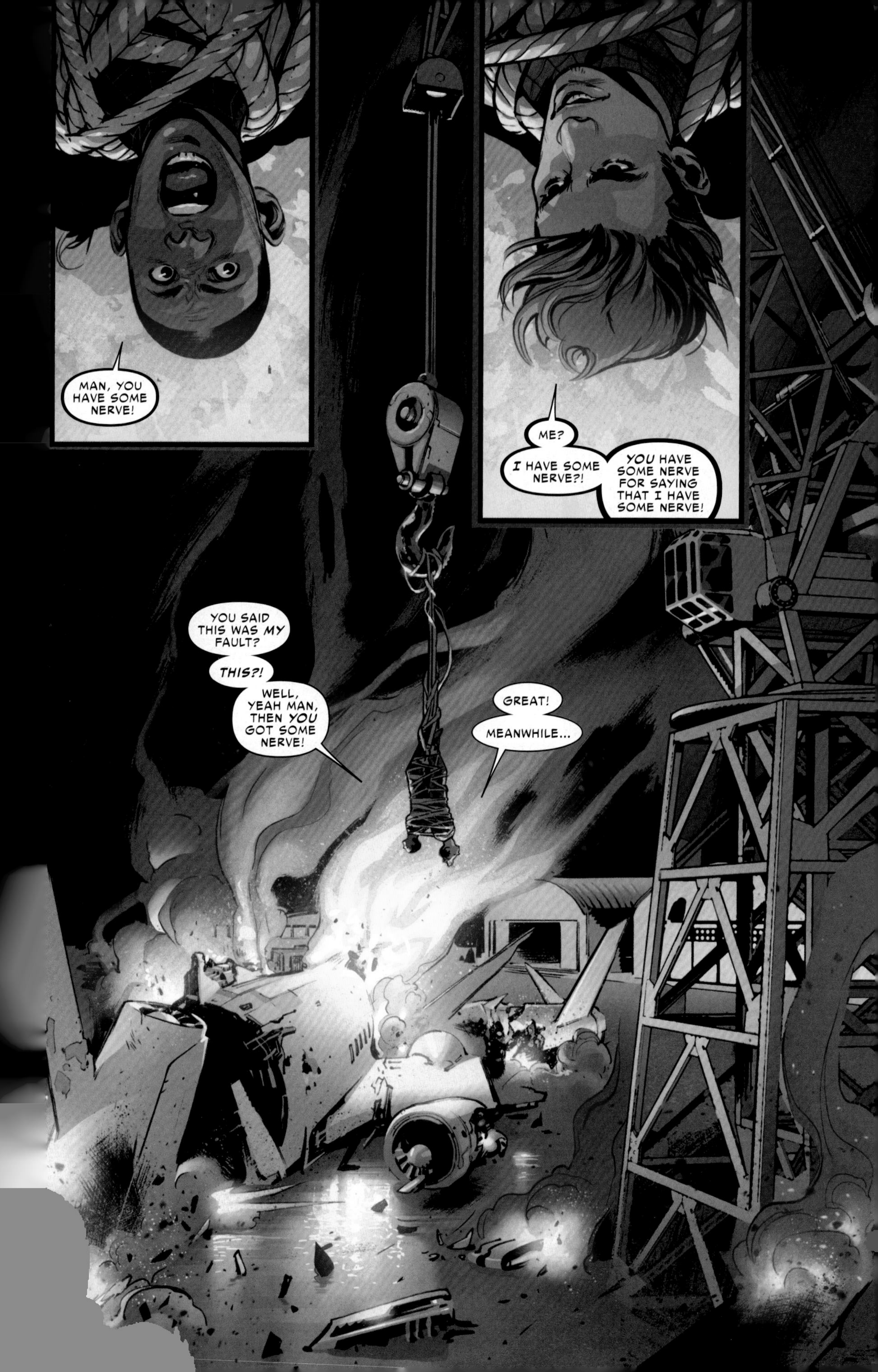
MAN, YOU HAVE SOME NERVE!
ME?
I HAVE SOME NERVE?!
YOU HAVE SOME NERVE FOR SAYING THAT I HAVE SOME NERVE!
YOU SAID THIS WAS MY FAULT?
THIS?!
WELL, YEAH MAN, THEN YOU GOT SOME NERVE!
GREAT!
MEANWHILE...

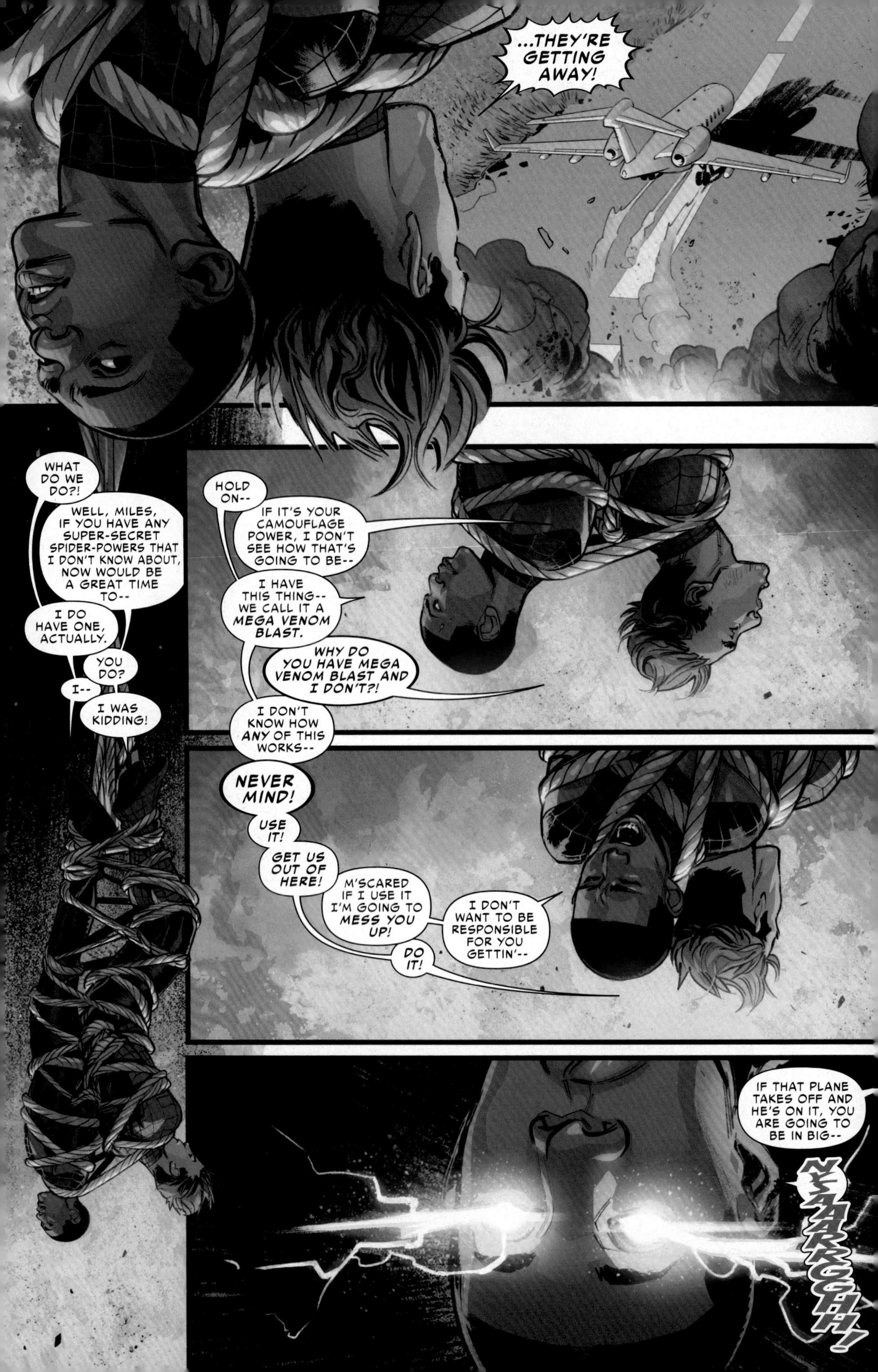

...THEY'RE GETTING AWAY!
WHAT DO WE DO?!
WELL, MILES, IF YOU HAVE ANY SUPER-SECRET SPIDER-POWERS THAT I DON'T KNOW ABOUT, NOW WOULD BE A GREAT TIME TO--
I DO HAVE ONE, ACTUALLY.
YOU DO?
I--
I WAS KIDDING!
HOLD ON--
IF IT'S YOUR CAMOUFLAGE POWER, I DON'T SEE HOW THAT'S GOING TO BE--
I HAVE THIS THING-- WE CALL IT A MEGA VENOM BLAST.
WHY DO YOU HAVE MEGA VENOM BLAST AND I DON'T?!
I DON'T KNOW HOW ANY OF THIS WORKS--
NEVER MIND!
USE IT!
GET US OUT OF HERE!
M'SCARED IF I USE IT I'M GOING TO MESS YOU UP!
I DON'T WANT TO BE RESPONSIBLE FOR YOU GETTIN'--
DO IT!
IF THAT PLANE TAKES OFF AND HE'S ON IT, YOU ARE GOING TO BE IN BIG--
NYAARRGGHH!

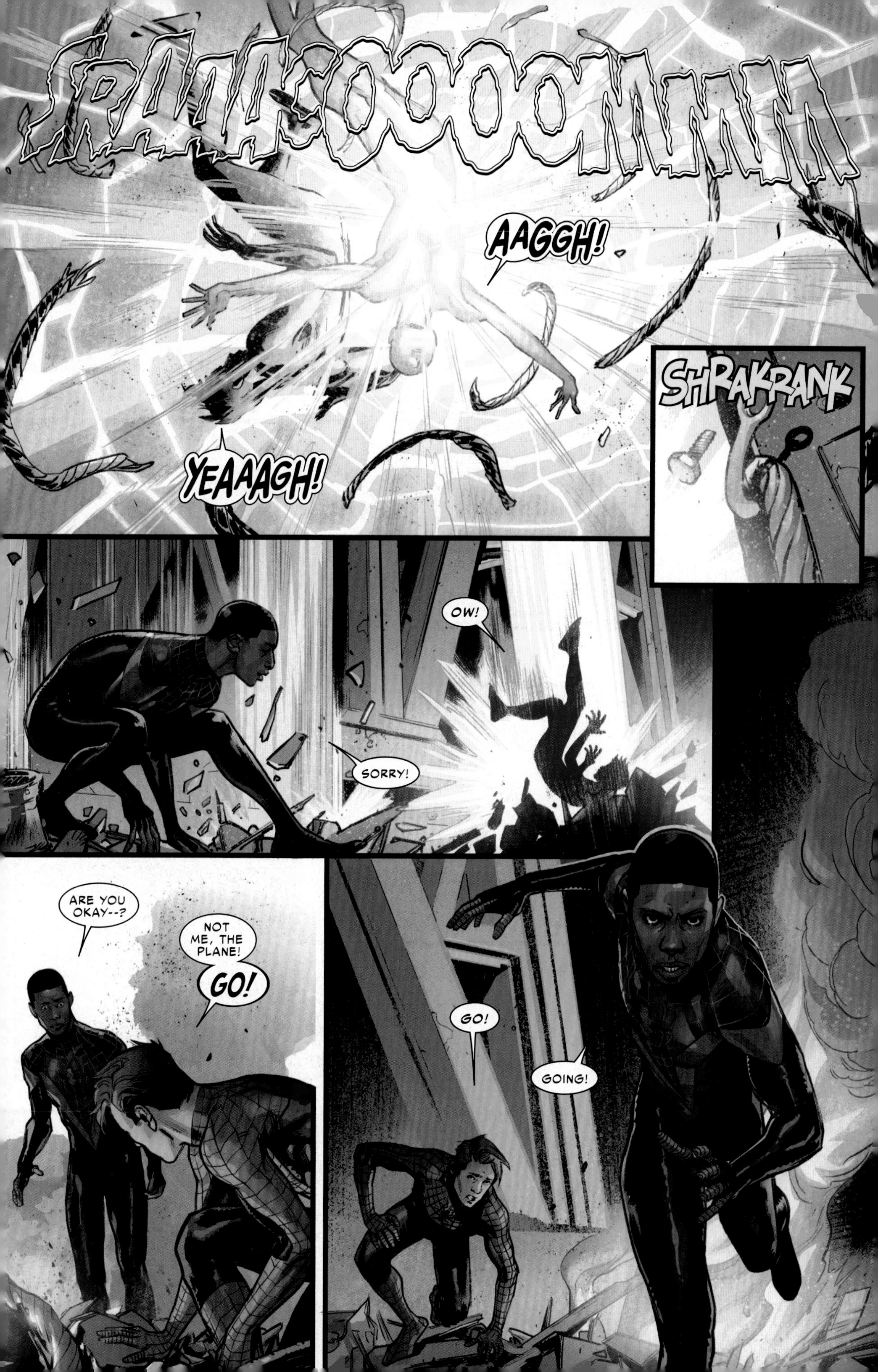

AAGGH!
YEAAAGH!
SHRAKRANK
OW!
SORRY!
ARE YOU OKAY--?
NOT ME, THE PLANE!
GO!
GO!
GOING!

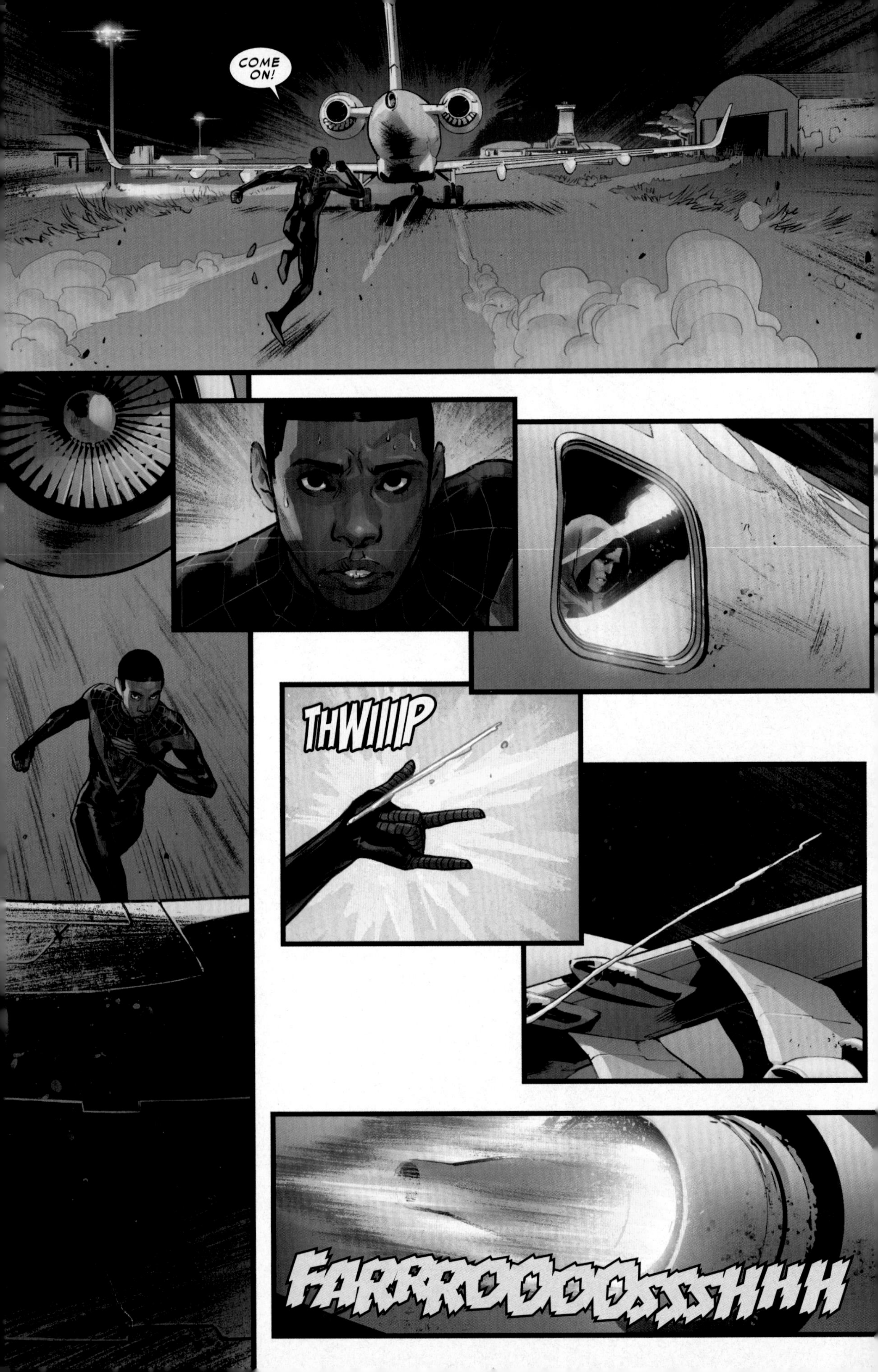
COME ON!
THWIIIIP
FARRROOOOSSHHH

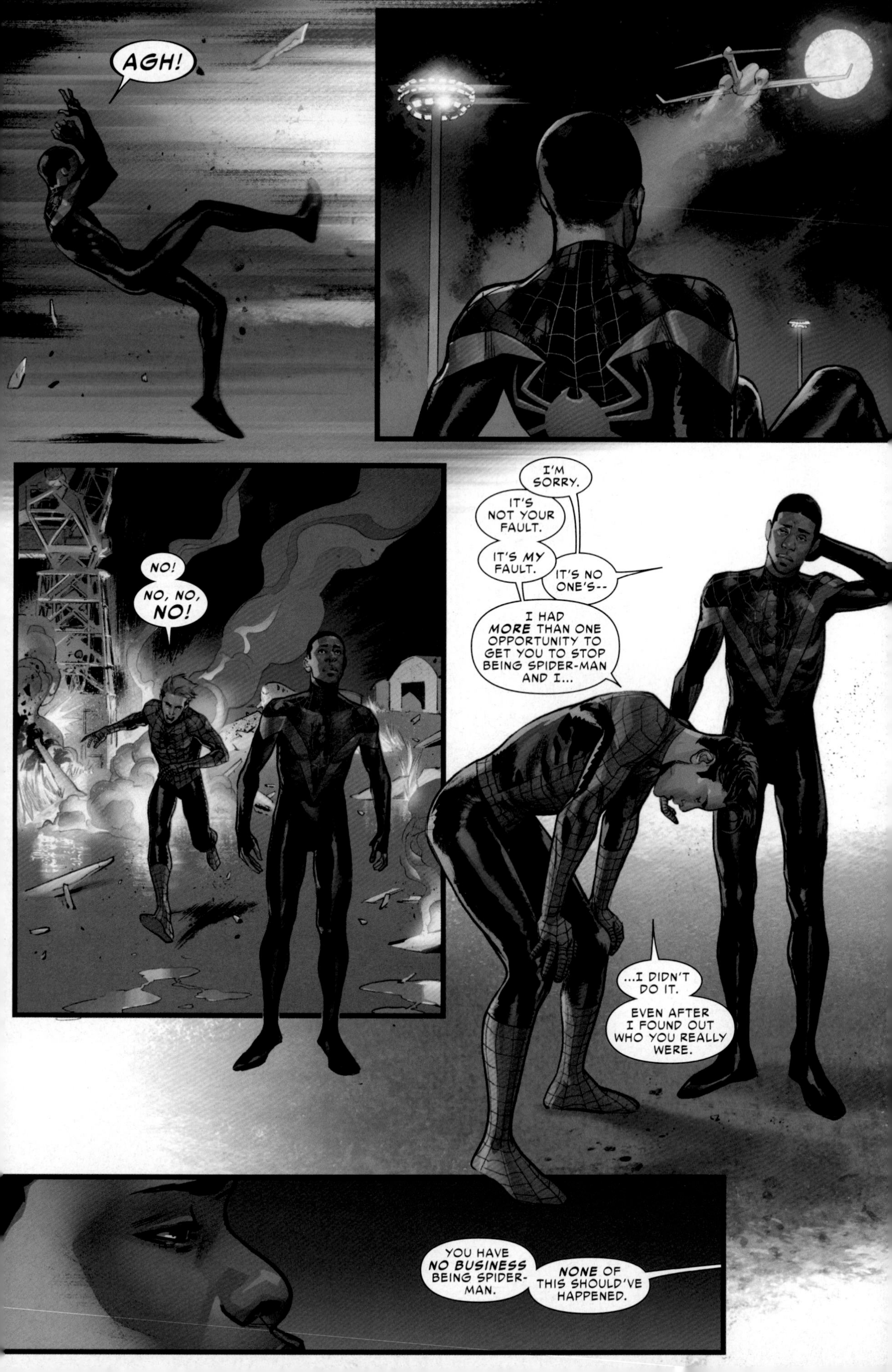
AGH!
NO!
NO, NO, NO!
I'M SORRY.
IT'S NOT YOUR FAULT.
IT'S MY FAULT.
IT'S NO ONE'S--
I HAD MORE THAN ONE OPPORTUNITY TO GET YOU TO STOP BEING SPIDER-MAN AND I...
...I DIDN'T DO IT.
EVEN AFTER I FOUND OUT WHO YOU REALLY WERE.
YOU HAVE NO BUSINESS BEING SPIDER-MAN.
NONE OF THIS SHOULD'VE HAPPENED.

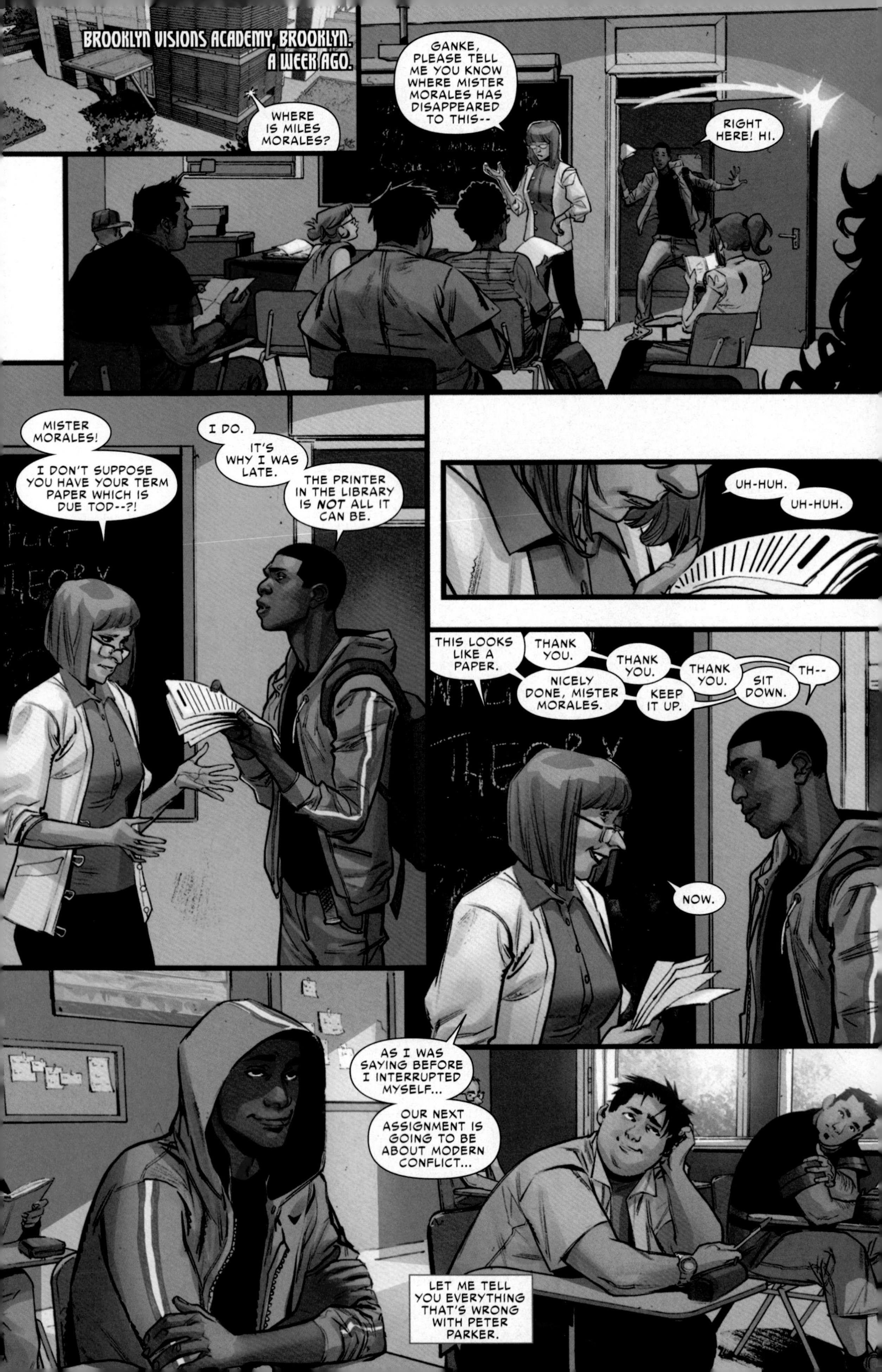
BROOKLYN VISIONS ACADEMY, BROOKLYN. A WEEK AGO.
WHERE IS MILES MORALES?
GANKE, PLEASE TELL ME YOU KNOW WHERE MISTER MORALES HAS DISAPPEARED TO THIS--
RIGHT HERE! HI.
MISTER MORALES!
I DON'T SUPPOSE YOU HAVE YOUR TERM PAPER WHICH IS DUE TOD--?!
I DO.
IT'S WHY I WAS LATE.
THE PRINTER IN THE LIBRARY IS NOT ALL IT CAN BE.
UH-HUH.
UH-HUH.
THIS LOOKS LIKE A PAPER.
THANK YOU.
NICELY DONE, MISTER MORALES.
THANK YOU.
KEEP IT UP.
THANK YOU.
SIT DOWN.
TH--
NOW.
AS I WAS SAYING BEFORE I INTERRUPTED MYSELF...
OUR NEXT ASSIGNMENT IS GOING TO BE ABOUT MODERN CONFLICT...
LET ME TELL YOU EVERYTHING THAT'S WRONG WITH PETER PARKER.

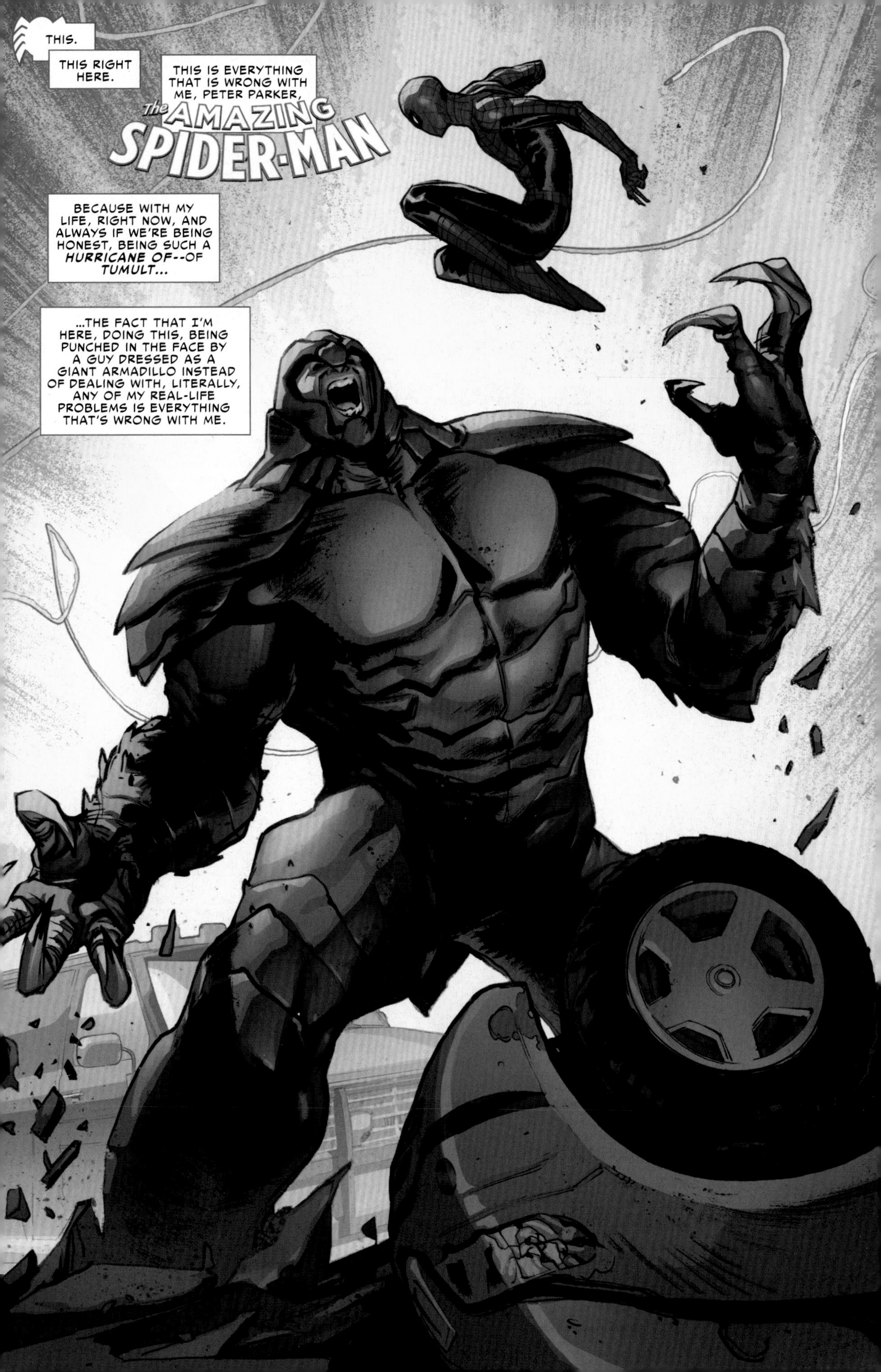
THIS.
THIS RIGHT HERE.
THIS IS EVERYTHING THAT IS WRONG WITH ME, PETER PARKER,
The AMAZING SPIDER-MAN
BECAUSE WITH MY LIFE, RIGHT NOW, AND ALWAYS IF WE'RE BEING HONEST, BEING SUCH A HURRICANE OF--OF TUMULT...
...THE FACT THAT I'M HERE, DOING THIS, BEING PUNCHED IN THE FACE BY A GIANT ARMADILLO INSTEAD OF DEALING WITH, LITERALLY, ANY OF MY REAL-LIFE PROBLEMS IS EVERYTHING THAT'S WRONG WITH ME.

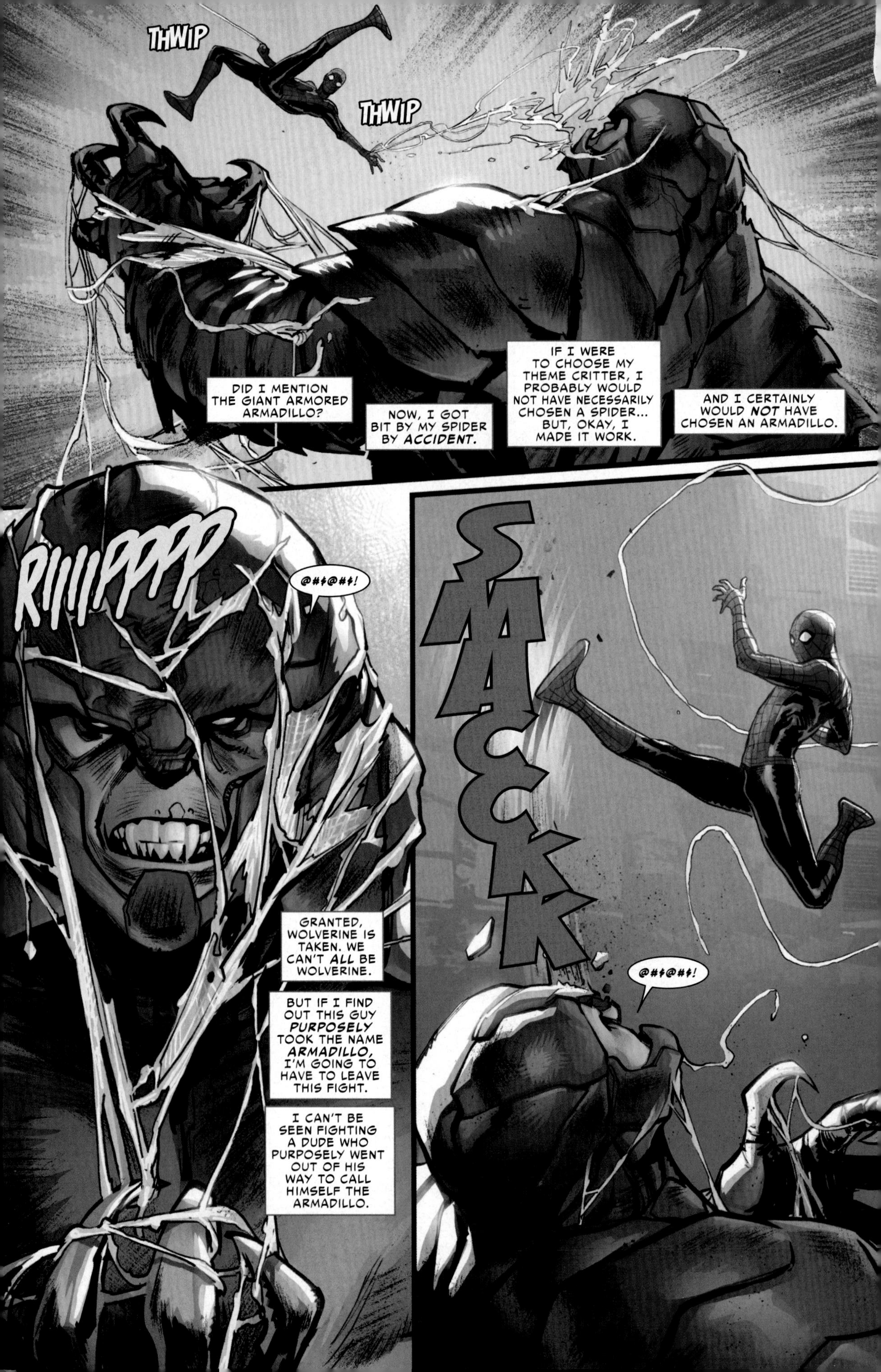
THWIP
THWIP
DID I MENTION THE GIANT ARMORED ARMADILLO?
NOW, I GOT BIT BY MY SPIDER BY ACCIDENT.
IF I WERE TO CHOOSE MY THEME CRITTER, I PROBABLY WOULD NOT HAVE NECESSARILY CHOSEN A SPIDER... BUT, OKAY, I MADE IT WORK.
AND I CERTAINLY WOULD NOT HAVE CHOSEN AN ARMADILLO.
RIIIIPPPP
@#$@#$!
GRANTED, WOLVERINE IS TAKEN. WE CAN'T ALL BE WOLVERINE.
BUT IF I FIND OUT THIS GUY PURPOSELY TOOK THE NAME ARMADILLO, I'M GOING TO HAVE TO LEAVE THIS FIGHT.
I CAN'T BE SEEN FIGHTING A DUDE WHO PURPOSELY WENT OUT OF HIS WAY TO CALL HIMSELF THE ARMADILLO.
SMACK
@#$@#$!

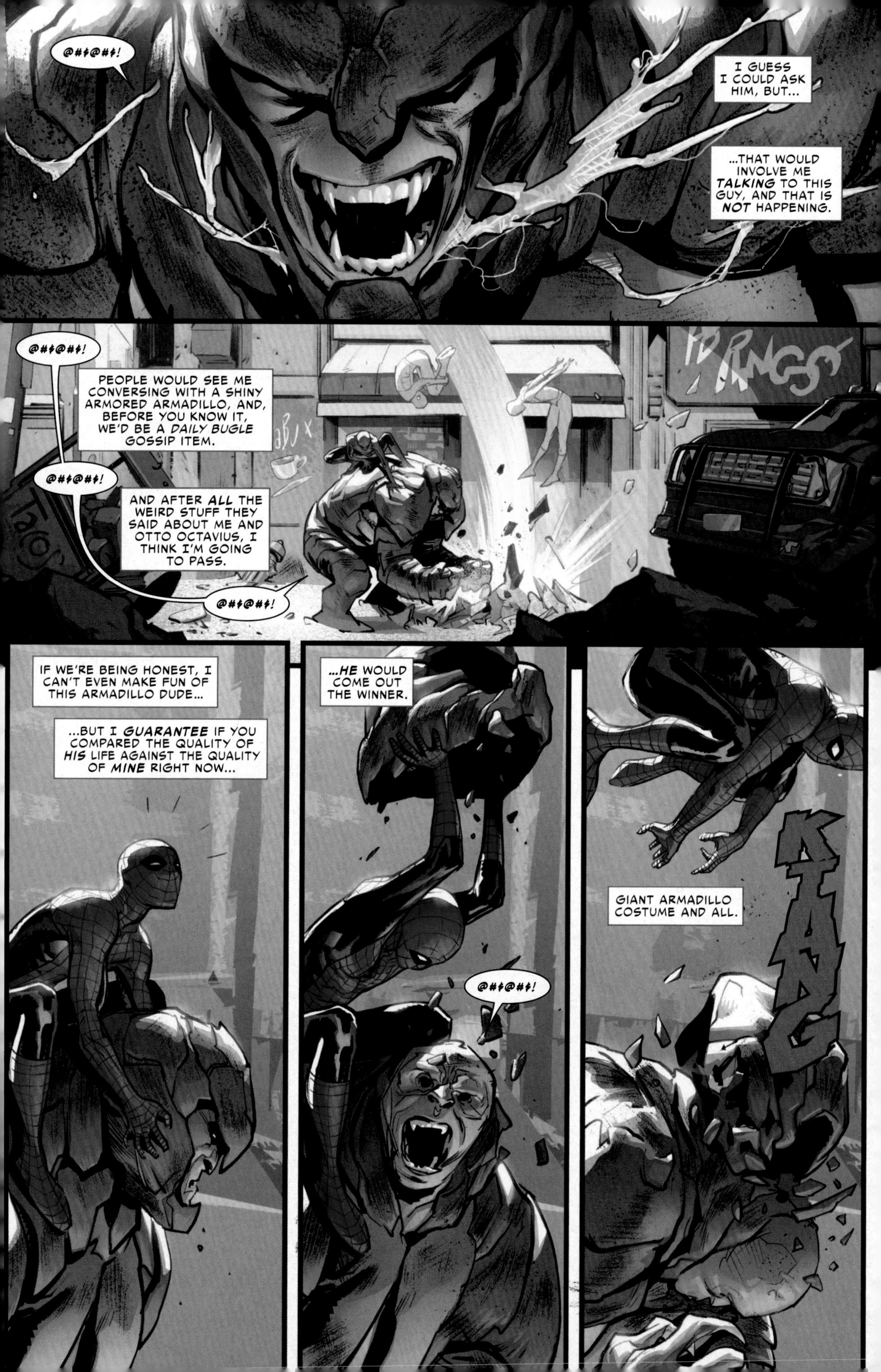
@#$@#$!
I GUESS I COULD ASK HIM, BUT...
...THAT WOULD INVOLVE ME TALKING TO THIS GUY, AND THAT IS NOT HAPPENING.
@#$@#$!
PEOPLE WOULD SEE ME CONVERSING WITH A SHINY ARMORED ARMADILLO, AND, BEFORE YOU KNOW IT, WE'D BE A DAILY BUGLE GOSSIP ITEM.
@#$@#$!
AND AFTER ALL THE WEIRD STUFF THEY SAID ABOUT ME AND OTTO OCTAVIUS, I THINK I'M GOING TO PASS.
@#$@#$!
IF WE'RE BEING HONEST, I CAN'T EVEN MAKE FUN OF THIS ARMADILLO DUDE...
...BUT I GUARANTEE IF YOU COMPARED THE QUALITY OF HIS LIFE AGAINST THE QUALITY OF MINE RIGHT NOW...
...HE WOULD COME OUT THE WINNER.
@#$@#$!
GIANT ARMADILLO COSTUME AND ALL.
KRAAG

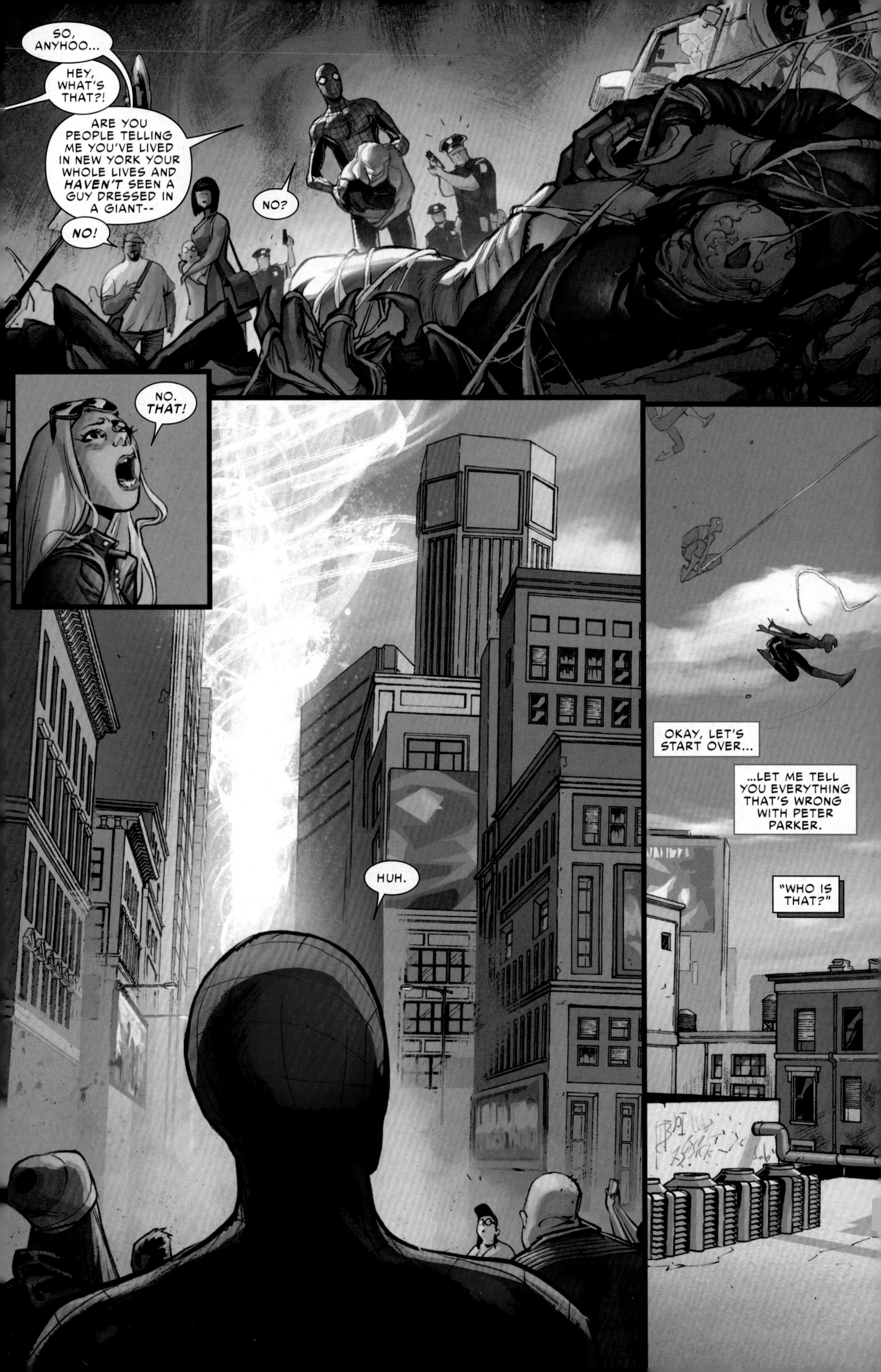
SO, ANYHOO...
HEY, WHAT'S THAT?!
ARE YOU PEOPLE TELLING ME YOU'VE LIVED IN NEW YORK YOUR WHOLE LIVES AND HAVEN'T SEEN A GUY DRESSED IN A GIANT--
NO?
NO!
NO. THAT!
HUH.
OKAY, LET'S START OVER...
...LET ME TELL YOU EVERYTHING THAT'S WRONG WITH PETER PARKER.
"WHO IS THAT?"

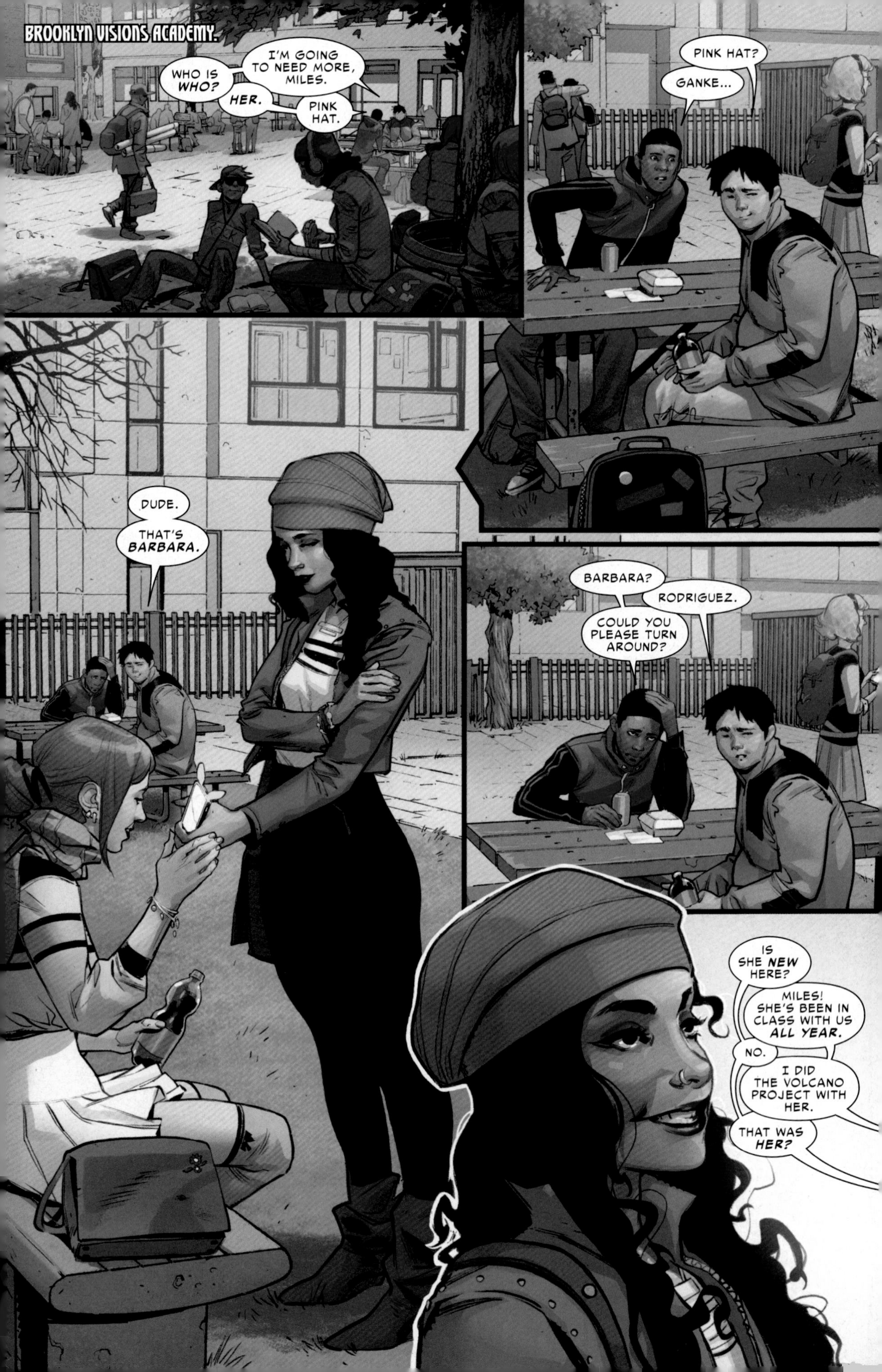
BROOKLYN VISIONS ACADEMY.
I'M GOING TO NEED MORE, MILES.
WHO IS WHO?
HER.
PINK HAT.
PINK HAT?
GANKE...
DUDE.
THAT'S BARBARA.
BARBARA?
RODRIGUEZ.
COULD YOU PLEASE TURN AROUND?
IS SHE NEW HERE?
MILES! SHE'S BEEN IN CLASS WITH US ALL YEAR.
NO.
I DID THE VOLCANO PROJECT WITH HER.
THAT WAS HER?

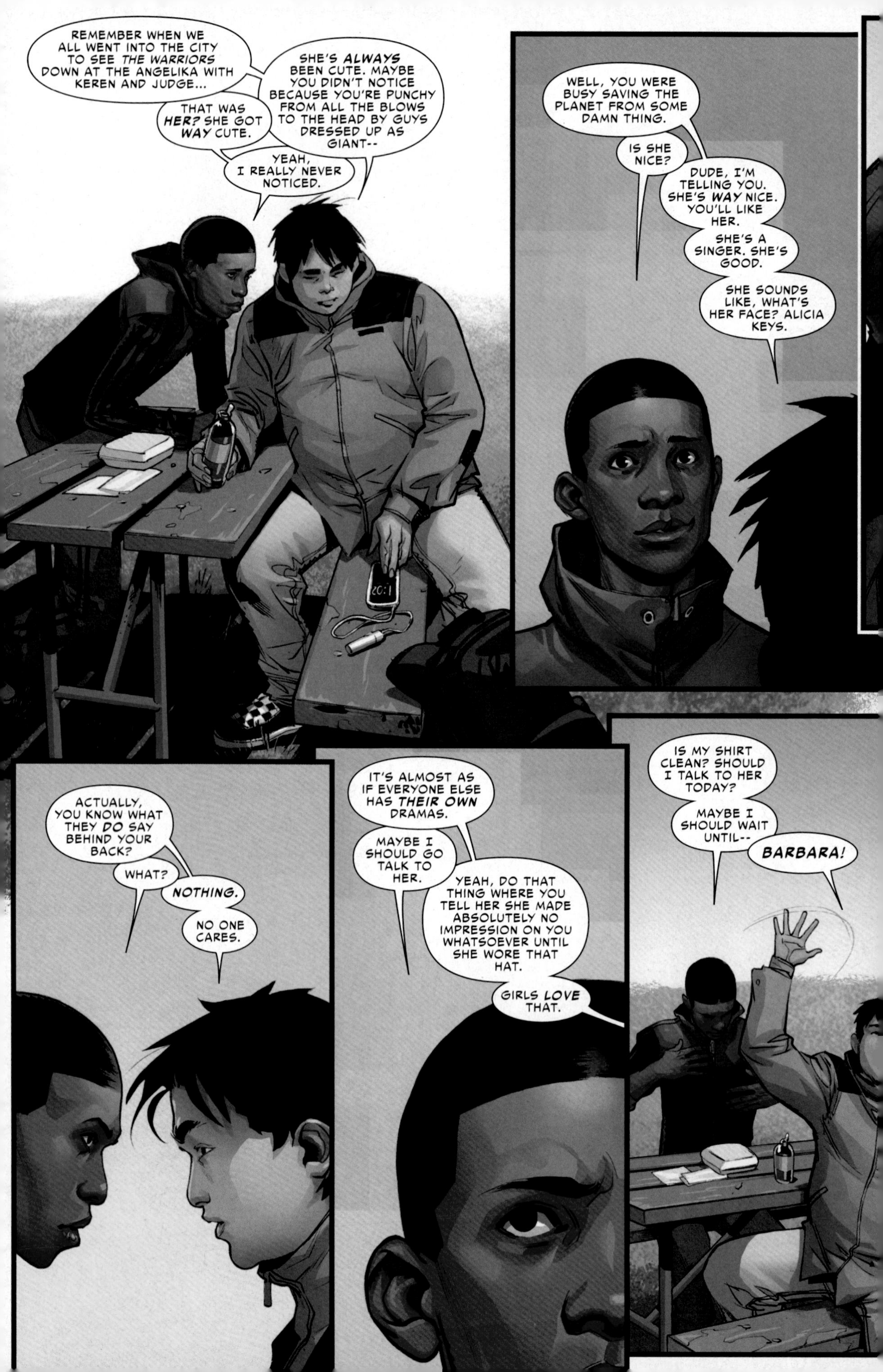

REMEMBER WHEN WE ALL WENT INTO THE CITY TO SEE *THE WARRIORS* DOWN AT THE ANGELIKA WITH KEREN AND JUDGE...
THAT WAS *HER?* SHE GOT *WAY* CUTE.
SHE'S *ALWAYS* BEEN CUTE. MAYBE YOU DIDN'T NOTICE BECAUSE YOU'RE PUNCHY FROM ALL THE BLOWS TO THE HEAD BY GUYS DRESSED UP AS GIANT--
YEAH, I REALLY NEVER NOTICED.
WELL, YOU WERE BUSY SAVING THE PLANET FROM SOME DAMN THING.
IS SHE NICE?
DUDE, I'M TELLING YOU. SHE'S *WAY* NICE. YOU'LL LIKE HER.
SHE'S A SINGER. SHE'S GOOD.
SHE SOUNDS LIKE, WHAT'S HER FACE? ALICIA KEYS.
ACTUALLY, YOU KNOW WHAT THEY *DO* SAY BEHIND YOUR BACK?
WHAT?
NOTHING.
NO ONE CARES.
IT'S ALMOST AS IF EVERYONE ELSE HAS *THEIR OWN* DRAMAS.
MAYBE I SHOULD GO TALK TO HER.
YEAH, DO THAT THING WHERE YOU TELL HER SHE MADE ABSOLUTELY NO IMPRESSION ON YOU WHATSOEVER UNTIL SHE WORE THAT HAT.
GIRLS *LOVE* THAT.
IS MY SHIRT CLEAN? SHOULD I TALK TO HER TODAY?
MAYBE I SHOULD WAIT UNTIL--
BARBARA!

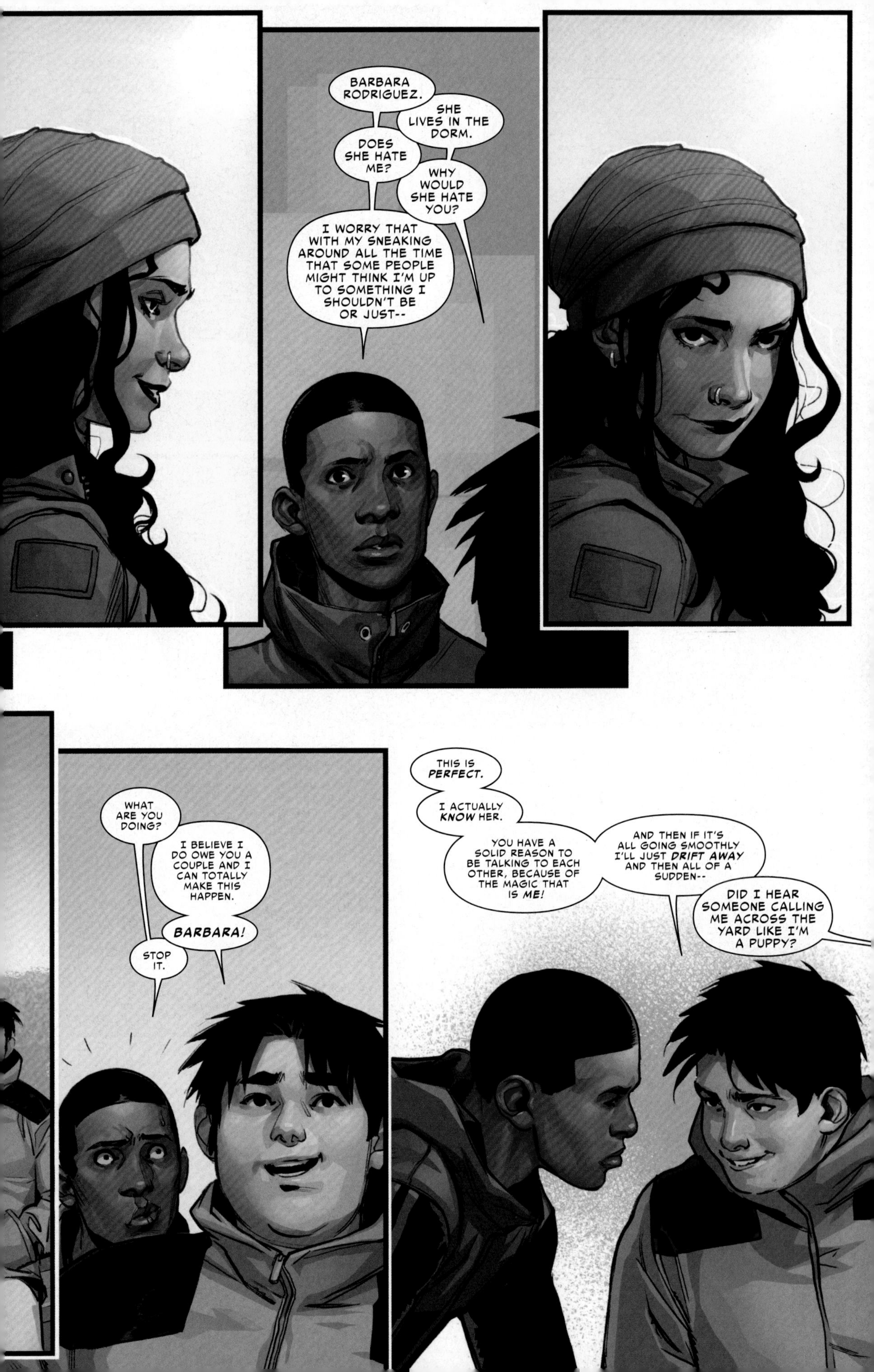
BARBARA RODRIGUEZ.
SHE LIVES IN THE DORM.
DOES SHE HATE ME?
WHY WOULD SHE HATE YOU?
I WORRY THAT WITH MY SNEAKING AROUND ALL THE TIME THAT SOME PEOPLE MIGHT THINK I'M UP TO SOMETHING I SHOULDN'T BE OR JUST--
WHAT ARE YOU DOING?
I BELIEVE I DO OWE YOU A COUPLE AND I CAN TOTALLY MAKE THIS HAPPEN.
BARBARA!
STOP IT.
THIS IS PERFECT.
I ACTUALLY KNOW HER.
YOU HAVE A SOLID REASON TO BE TALKING TO EACH OTHER, BECAUSE OF THE MAGIC THAT IS ME!
AND THEN IF IT'S ALL GOING SMOOTHLY I'LL JUST DRIFT AWAY AND THEN ALL OF A SUDDEN--
DID I HEAR SOMEONE CALLING ME ACROSS THE YARD LIKE I'M A PUPPY?

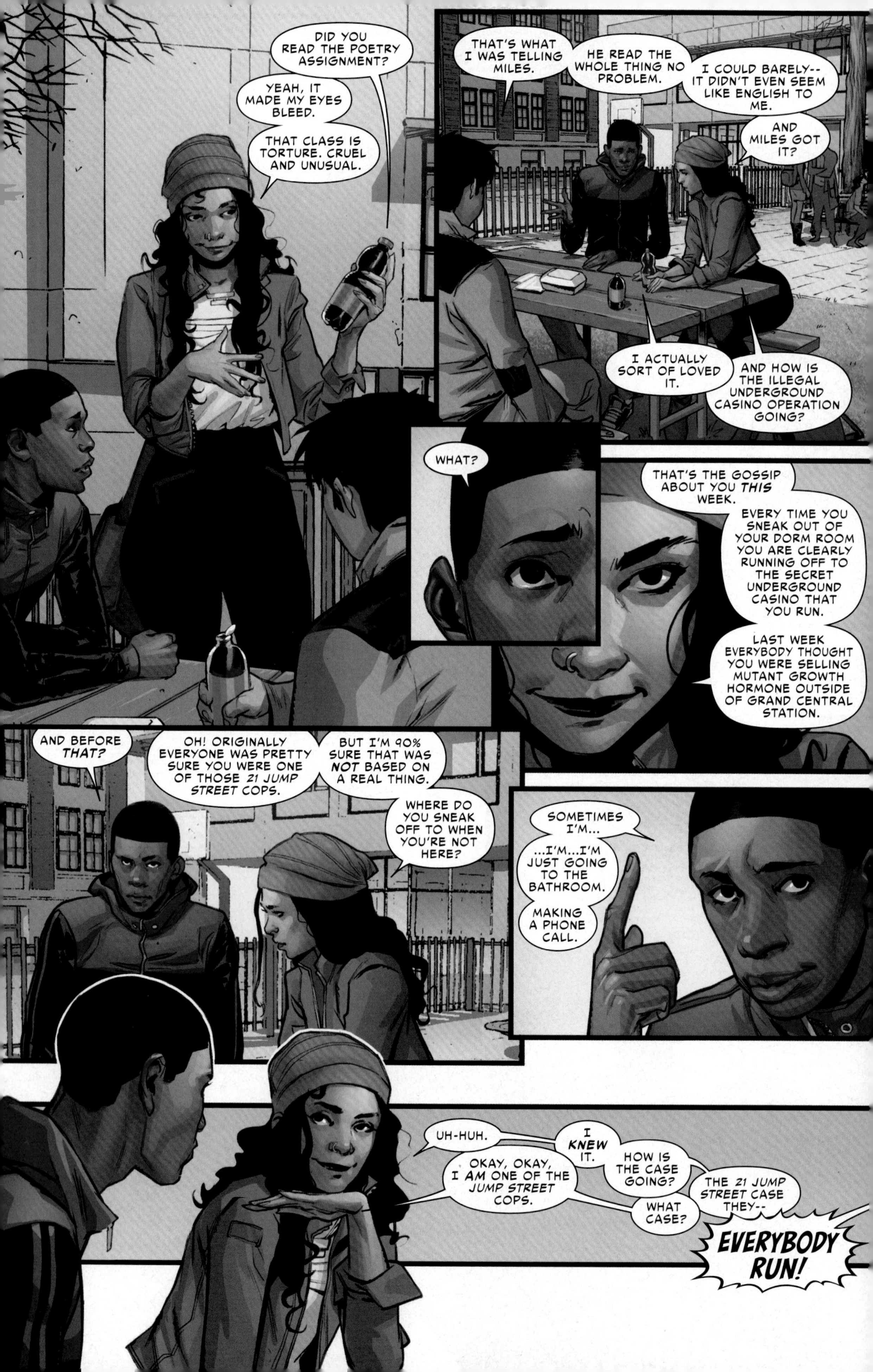
DID YOU READ THE POETRY ASSIGNMENT?
YEAH, IT MADE MY EYES BLEED.
THAT CLASS IS TORTURE. CRUEL AND UNUSUAL.
THAT'S WHAT I WAS TELLING MILES.
HE READ THE WHOLE THING NO PROBLEM.
I COULD BARELY-- IT DIDN'T EVEN SEEM LIKE ENGLISH TO ME.
AND MILES GOT IT?
I ACTUALLY SORT OF LOVED IT.
AND HOW IS THE ILLEGAL UNDERGROUND CASINO OPERATION GOING?
WHAT?
THAT'S THE GOSSIP ABOUT YOU *THIS* WEEK.
EVERY TIME YOU SNEAK OUT OF YOUR DORM ROOM YOU ARE CLEARLY RUNNING OFF TO THE SECRET UNDERGROUND CASINO THAT YOU RUN.
LAST WEEK EVERYBODY THOUGHT YOU WERE SELLING MUTANT GROWTH HORMONE OUTSIDE OF GRAND CENTRAL STATION.
AND BEFORE *THAT?*
OH! ORIGINALLY EVERYONE WAS PRETTY SURE YOU WERE ONE OF THOSE *21 JUMP STREET* COPS.
BUT I'M 90% SURE THAT WAS *NOT* BASED ON A REAL THING.
WHERE DO YOU SNEAK OFF TO WHEN YOU'RE NOT HERE?
SOMETIMES I'M...
...I'M...I'M JUST GOING TO THE BATHROOM.
MAKING A PHONE CALL.
UH-HUH.
OKAY, OKAY, I *AM* ONE OF THE *JUMP STREET* COPS.
I *KNEW* IT.
HOW IS THE CASE GOING?
WHAT CASE?
THE *21 JUMP STREET* CASE THEY--
EVERYBODY RUN!

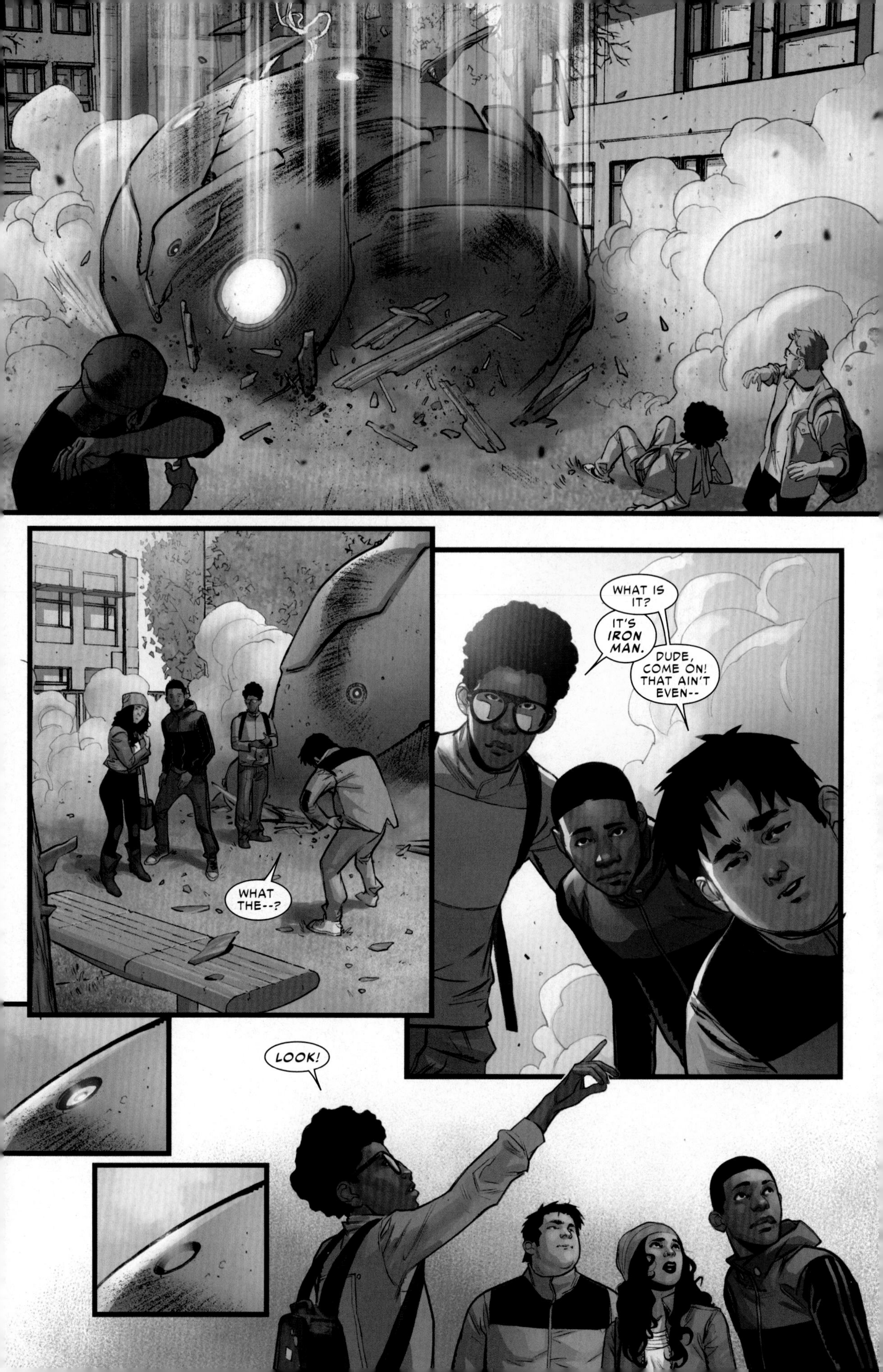
WHAT THE--?
WHAT IS IT?
IT'S IRON MAN.
DUDE, COME ON! THAT AIN'T EVEN--
LOOK!

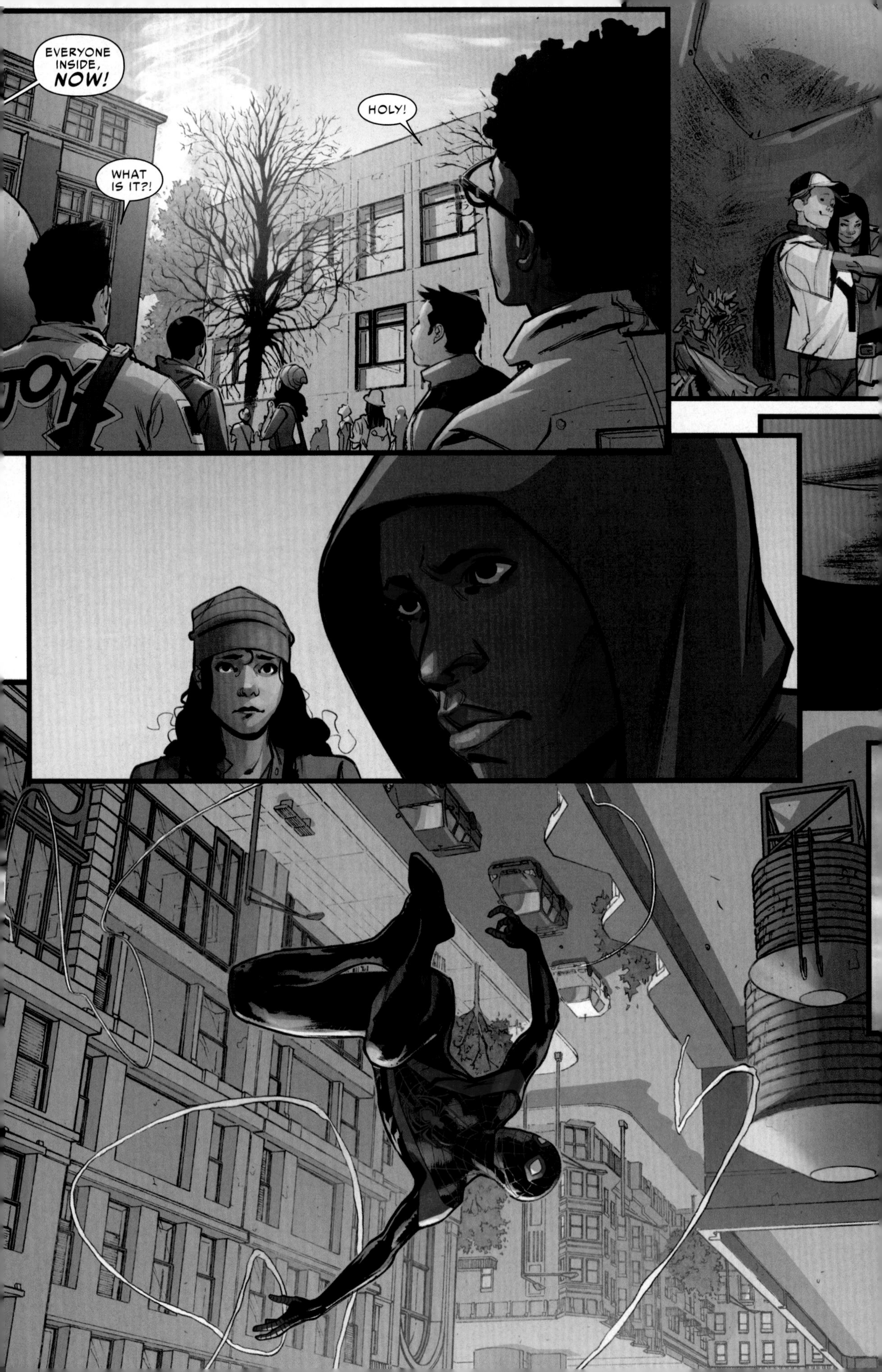

EVERYONE INSIDE, NOW!
WHAT IS IT?!
HOLY!
JOY

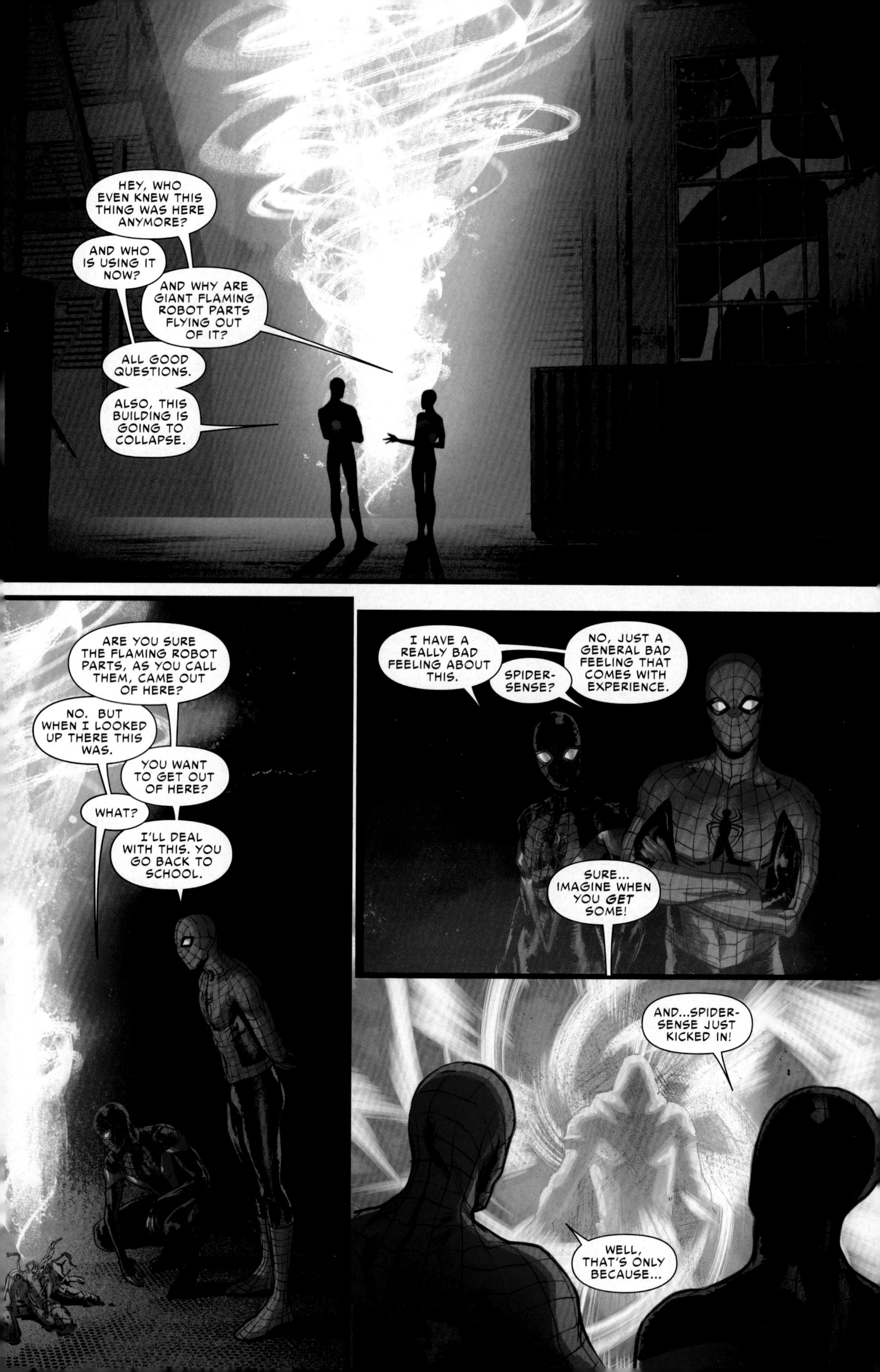
HEY, WHO EVEN KNEW THIS THING WAS HERE ANYMORE?
AND WHO IS USING IT NOW?
AND WHY ARE GIANT FLAMING ROBOT PARTS FLYING OUT OF IT?
ALL GOOD QUESTIONS.
ALSO, THIS BUILDING IS GOING TO COLLAPSE.
ARE YOU SURE THE FLAMING ROBOT PARTS, AS YOU CALL THEM, CAME OUT OF HERE?
NO. BUT WHEN I LOOKED UP THERE THIS WAS.
YOU WANT TO GET OUT OF HERE?
WHAT?
I'LL DEAL WITH THIS. YOU GO BACK TO SCHOOL.
I HAVE A REALLY BAD FEELING ABOUT THIS.
SPIDER-SENSE?
NO, JUST A GENERAL BAD FEELING THAT COMES WITH EXPERIENCE.
SURE... IMAGINE WHEN YOU GET SOME!
AND...SPIDER-SENSE JUST KICKED IN!
WELL, THAT'S ONLY BECAUSE...

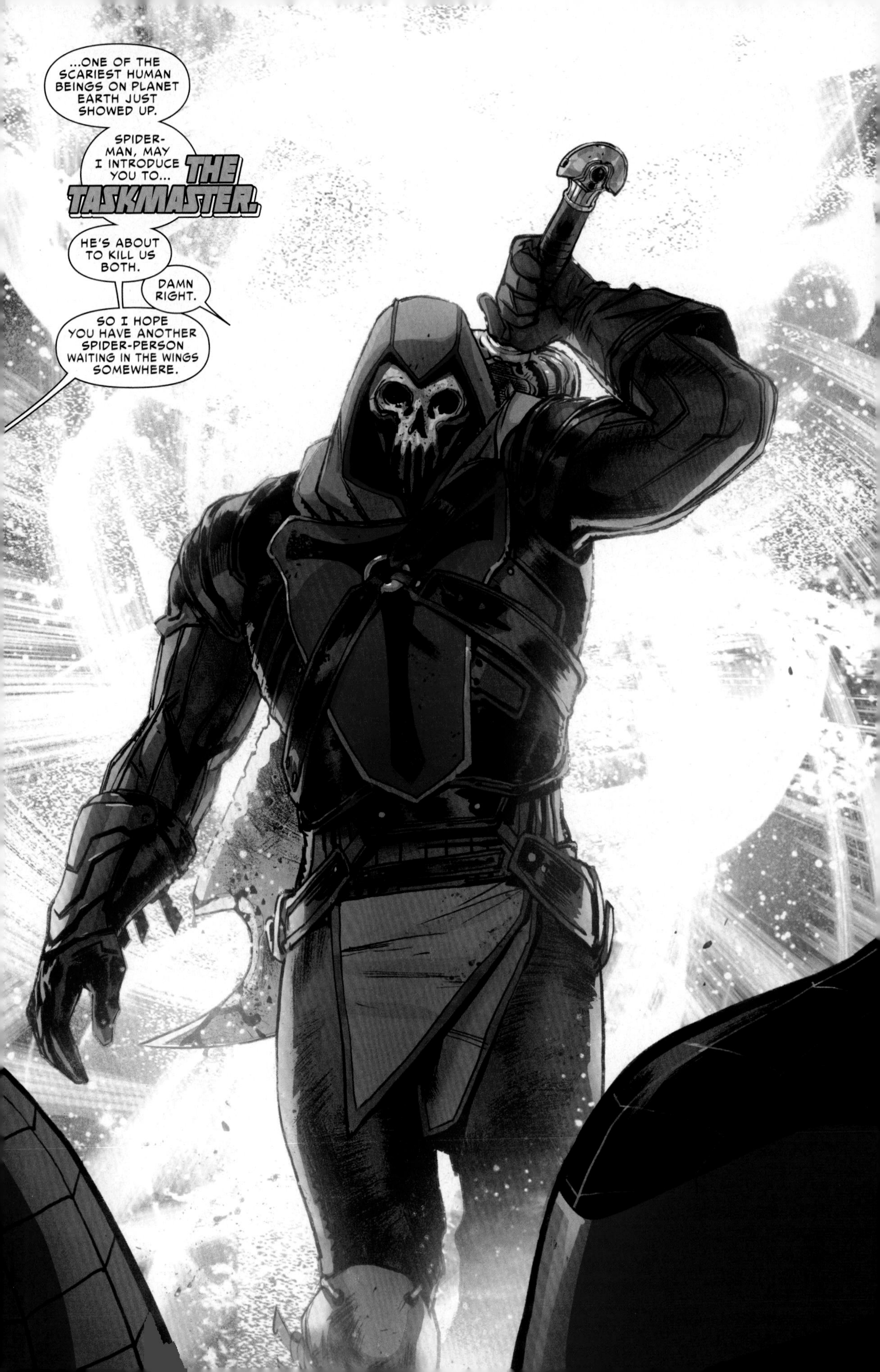
...ONE OF THE SCARIEST HUMAN BEINGS ON PLANET EARTH JUST SHOWED UP.
SPIDER-MAN, MAY I INTRODUCE YOU TO... THE TASKMASTER.
HE'S ABOUT TO KILL US BOTH.
DAMN RIGHT.
SO I HOPE YOU HAVE ANOTHER SPIDER-PERSON WAITING IN THE WINGS SOMEWHERE.

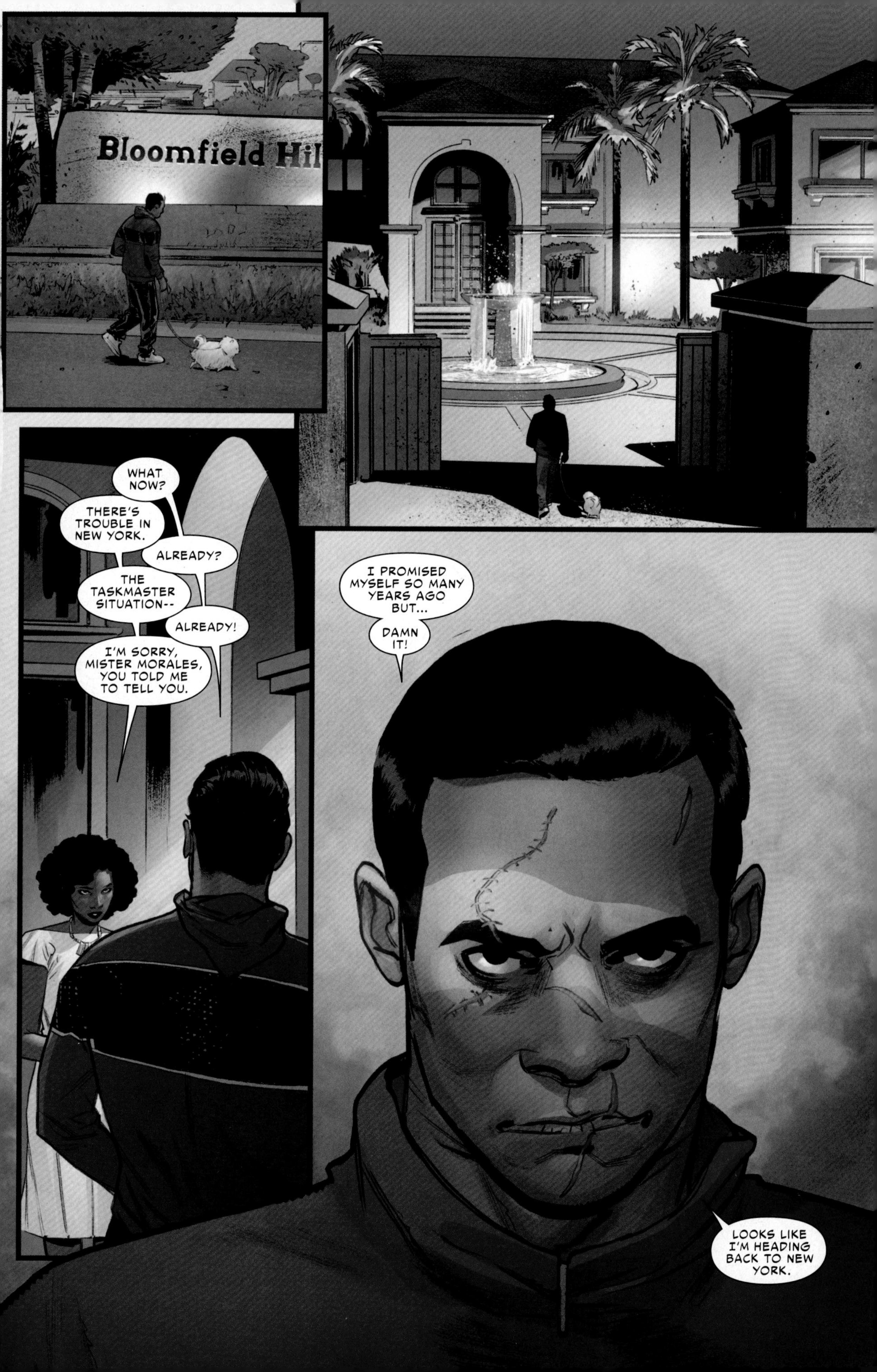
Bloomfield Hil
WHAT NOW?
THERE'S TROUBLE IN NEW YORK.
ALREADY?
THE TASKMASTER SITUATION--
ALREADY!
I'M SORRY, MISTER MORALES, YOU TOLD ME TO TELL YOU.
I PROMISED MYSELF SO MANY YEARS AGO BUT...
DAMN IT!
LOOKS LIKE I'M HEADING BACK TO NEW YORK.

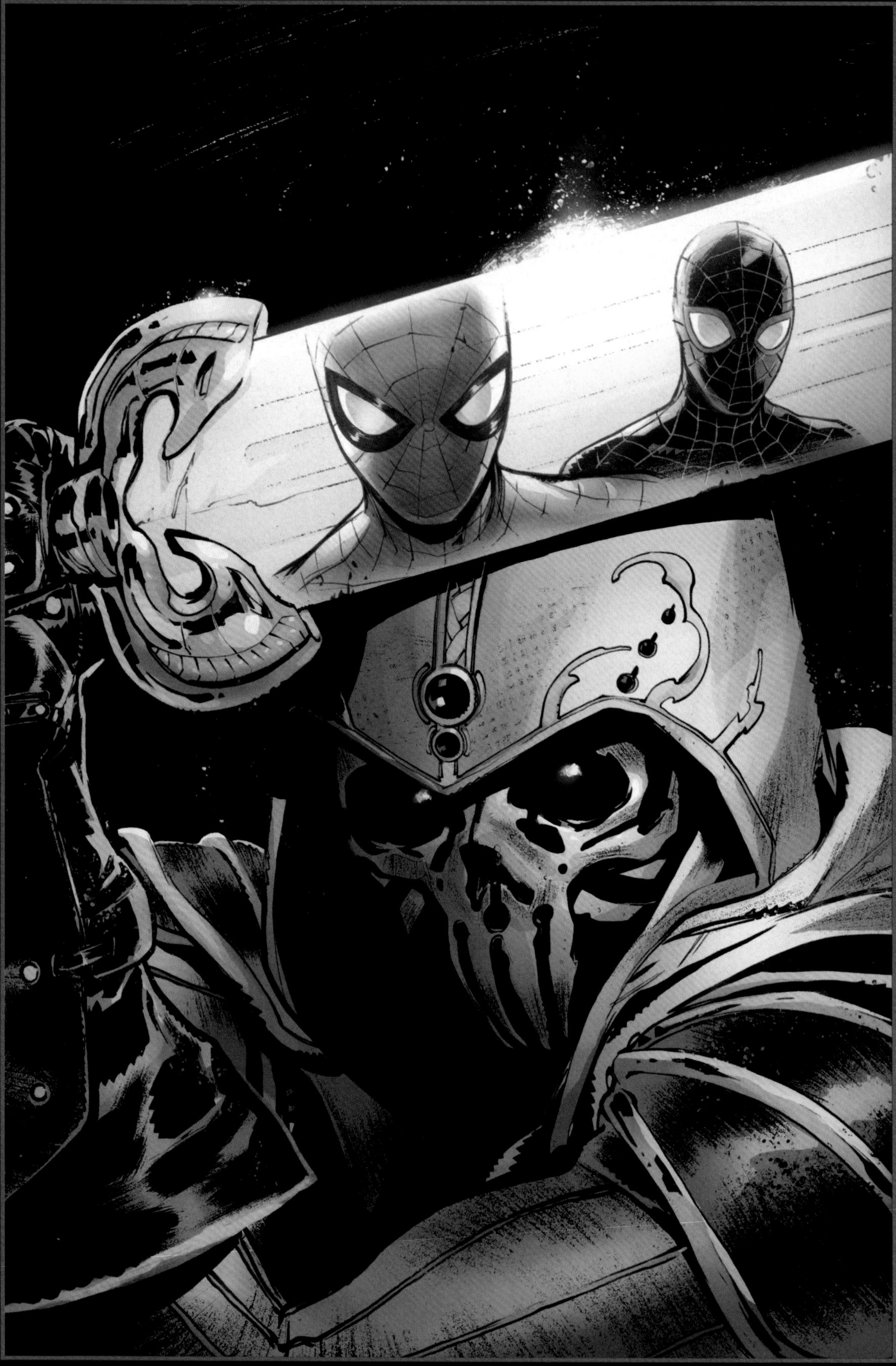

II

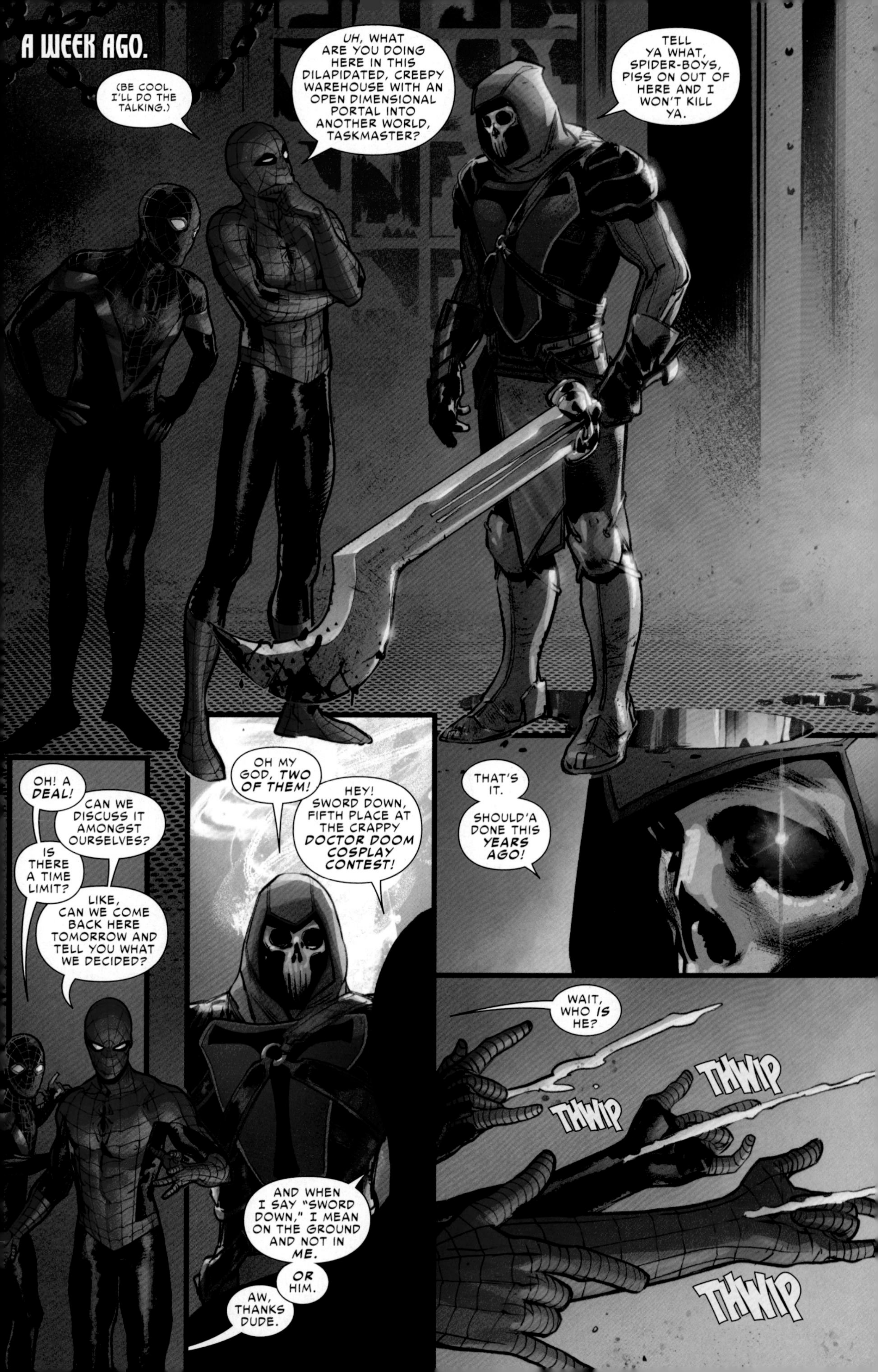
A WEEK AGO.
(BE COOL. I'LL DO THE TALKING.)
UH, WHAT ARE YOU DOING HERE IN THIS DILAPIDATED, CREEPY WAREHOUSE WITH AN OPEN DIMENSIONAL PORTAL INTO ANOTHER WORLD, TASKMASTER?
TELL YA WHAT, SPIDER-BOYS, PISS ON OUT OF HERE AND I WON'T KILL YA.
OH! A DEAL!
CAN WE DISCUSS IT AMONGST OURSELVES?
IS THERE A TIME LIMIT?
LIKE, CAN WE COME BACK HERE TOMORROW AND TELL YOU WHAT WE DECIDED?
OH MY GOD, TWO OF THEM!
HEY! SWORD DOWN, FIFTH PLACE AT THE CRAPPY DOCTOR DOOM COSPLAY CONTEST!
AND WHEN I SAY "SWORD DOWN," I MEAN ON THE GROUND AND NOT IN ME.
OR HIM.
AW, THANKS DUDE.
THAT'S IT.
SHOULD'A DONE THIS YEARS AGO!
WAIT, WHO IS HE?
THWIP
THWIP
THWIP

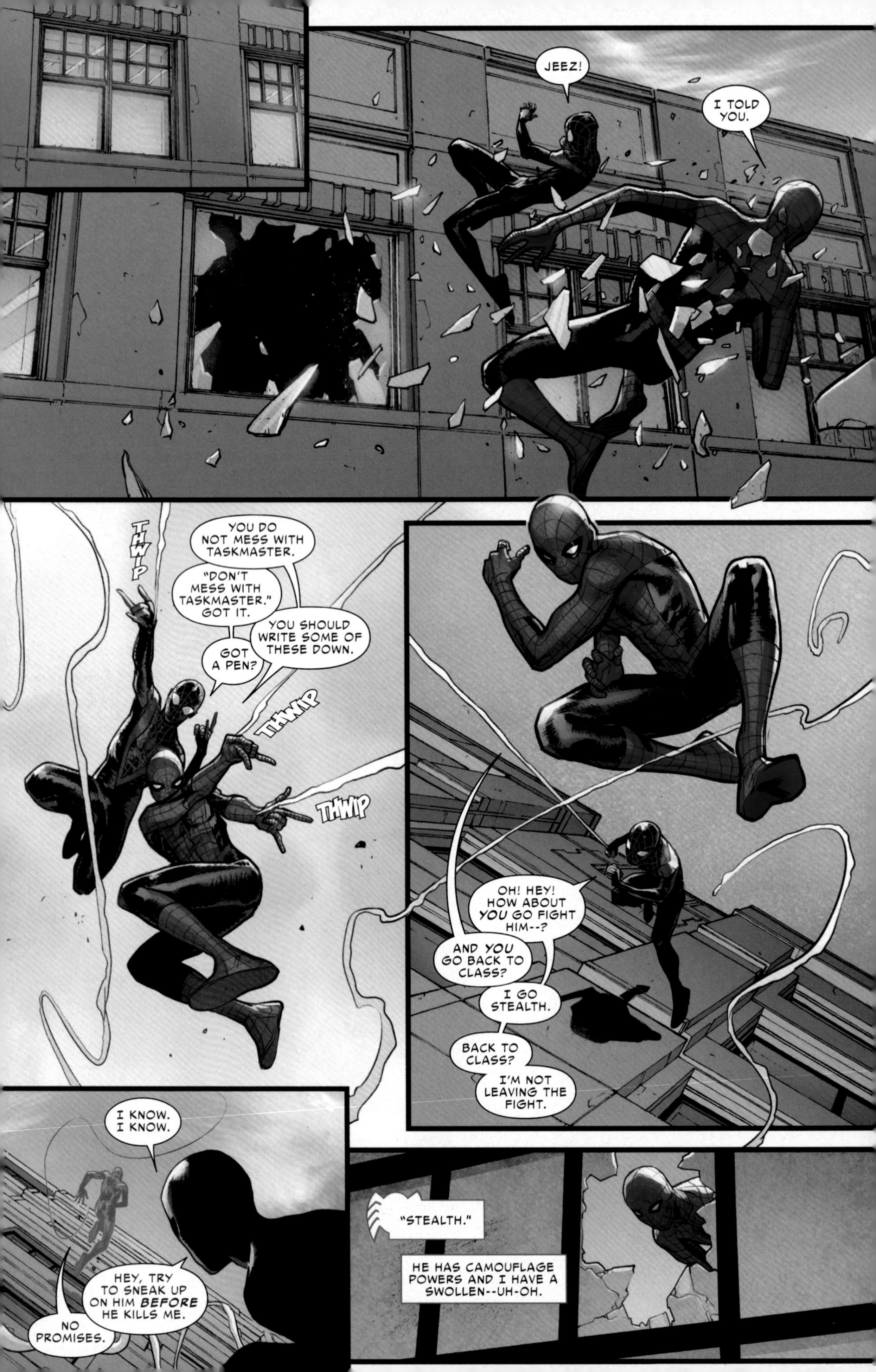
JEEZ!
I TOLD YOU.
THWIP
YOU DO NOT MESS WITH TASKMASTER.
"DON'T MESS WITH TASKMASTER." GOT IT.
YOU SHOULD WRITE SOME OF THESE DOWN.
GOT A PEN?
THWIP
THWIP
OH! HEY! HOW ABOUT *YOU* GO FIGHT HIM--?
AND *YOU* GO BACK TO CLASS?
I GO STEALTH.
BACK TO CLASS?
I'M NOT LEAVING THE FIGHT.
I KNOW. I KNOW.
HEY, TRY TO SNEAK UP ON HIM *BEFORE* HE KILLS ME.
NO PROMISES.
"STEALTH."
HE HAS CAMOUFLAGE POWERS AND I HAVE A SWOLLEN--UH-OH.

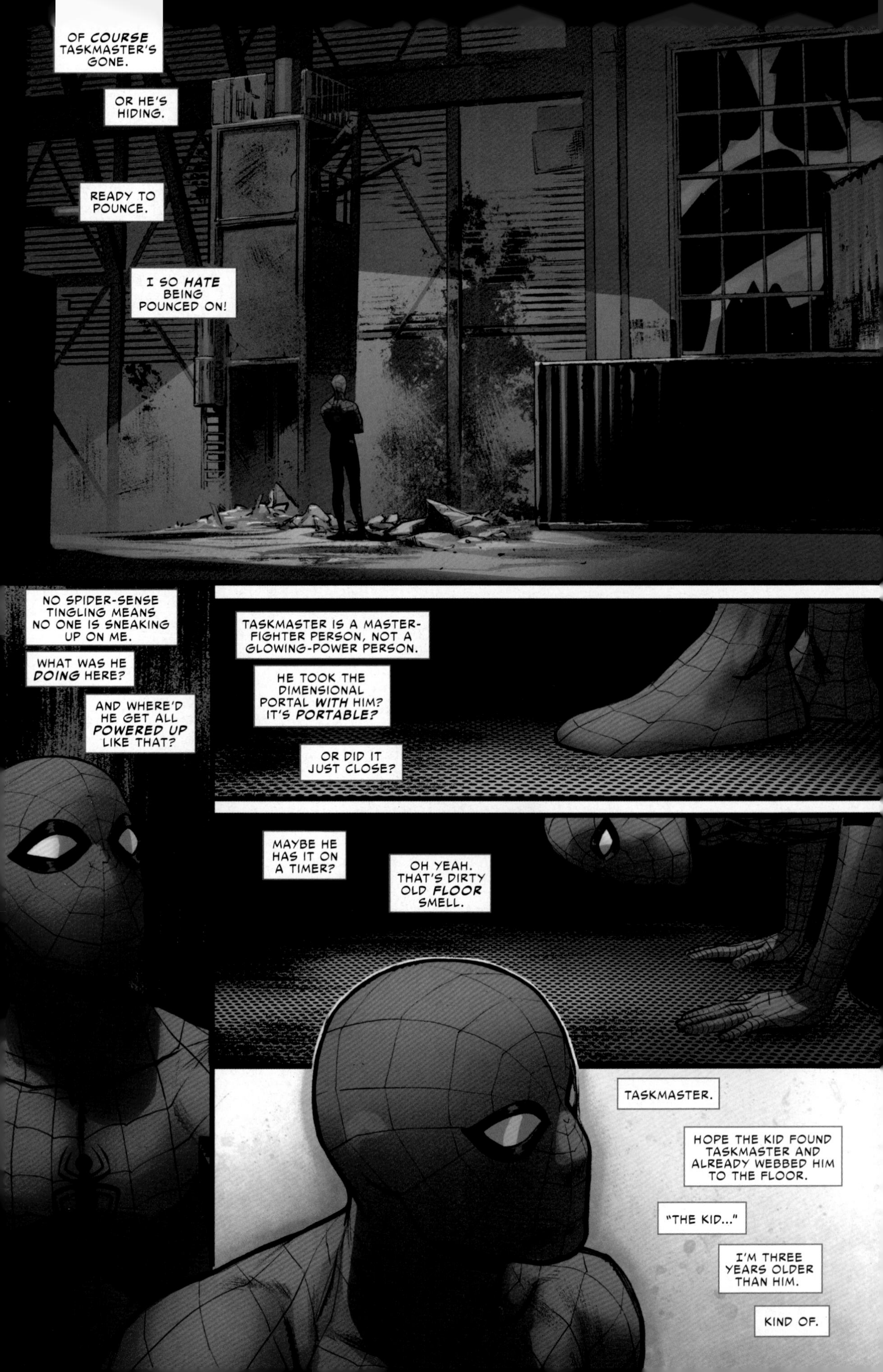
OF COURSE TASKMASTER'S GONE.
OR HE'S HIDING.
READY TO POUNCE.
I SO HATE BEING POUNCED ON!
NO SPIDER-SENSE TINGLING MEANS NO ONE IS SNEAKING UP ON ME.
WHAT WAS HE DOING HERE?
AND WHERE'D HE GET ALL POWERED UP LIKE THAT?
TASKMASTER IS A MASTER-FIGHTER PERSON, NOT A GLOWING-POWER PERSON.
HE TOOK THE DIMENSIONAL PORTAL WITH HIM? IT'S PORTABLE?
OR DID IT JUST CLOSE?
MAYBE HE HAS IT ON A TIMER?
OH YEAH. THAT'S DIRTY OLD FLOOR SMELL.
TASKMASTER.
HOPE THE KID FOUND TASKMASTER AND ALREADY WEBBED HIM TO THE FLOOR.
"THE KID..."
I'M THREE YEARS OLDER THAN HIM.
KIND OF.

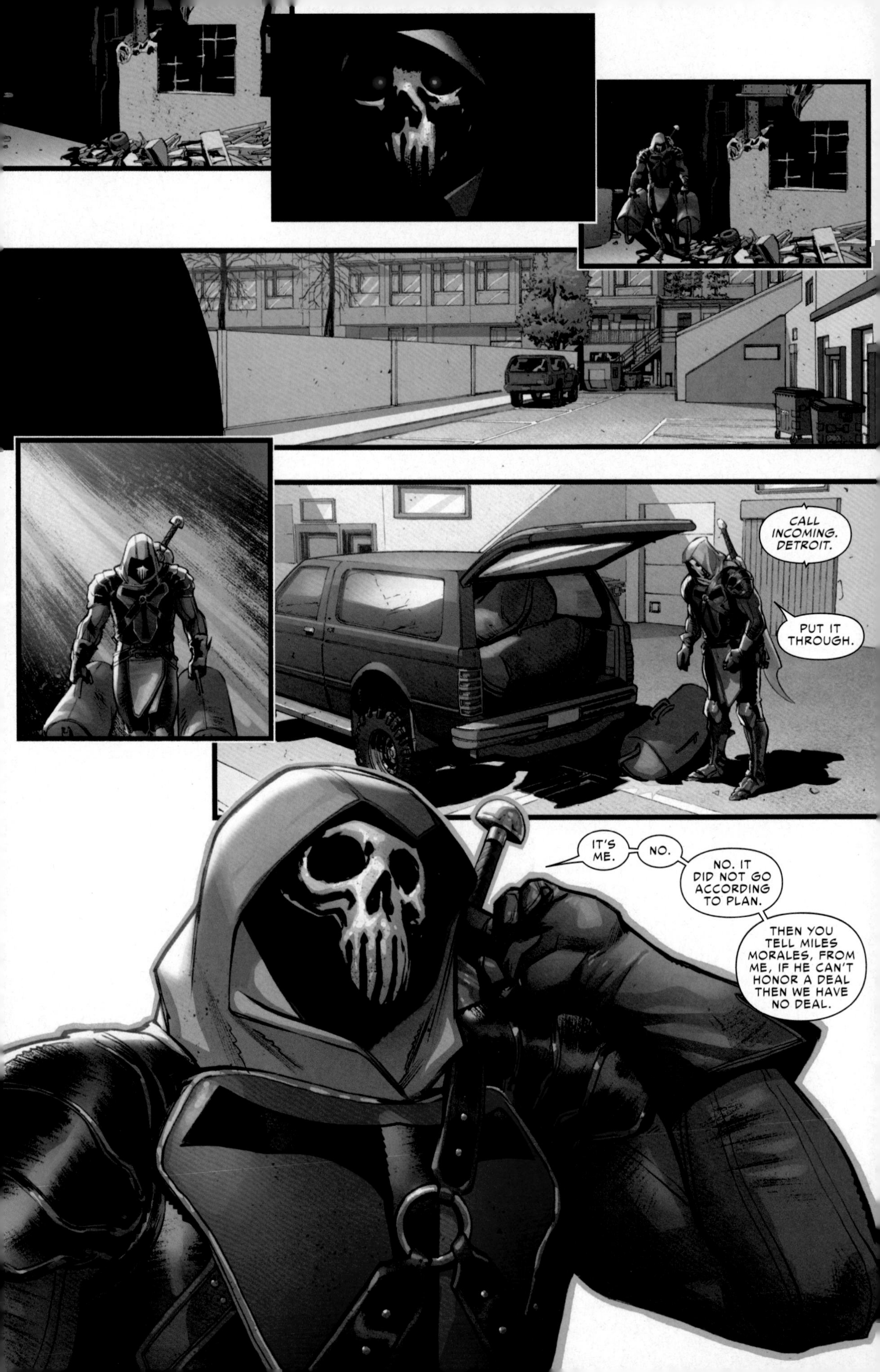
CALL INCOMING. DETROIT.
PUT IT THROUGH.
IT'S ME.
NO.
NO. IT DID NOT GO ACCORDING TO PLAN.
THEN YOU TELL MILES MORALES, FROM ME, IF HE CAN'T HONOR A DEAL THEN WE HAVE NO DEAL.

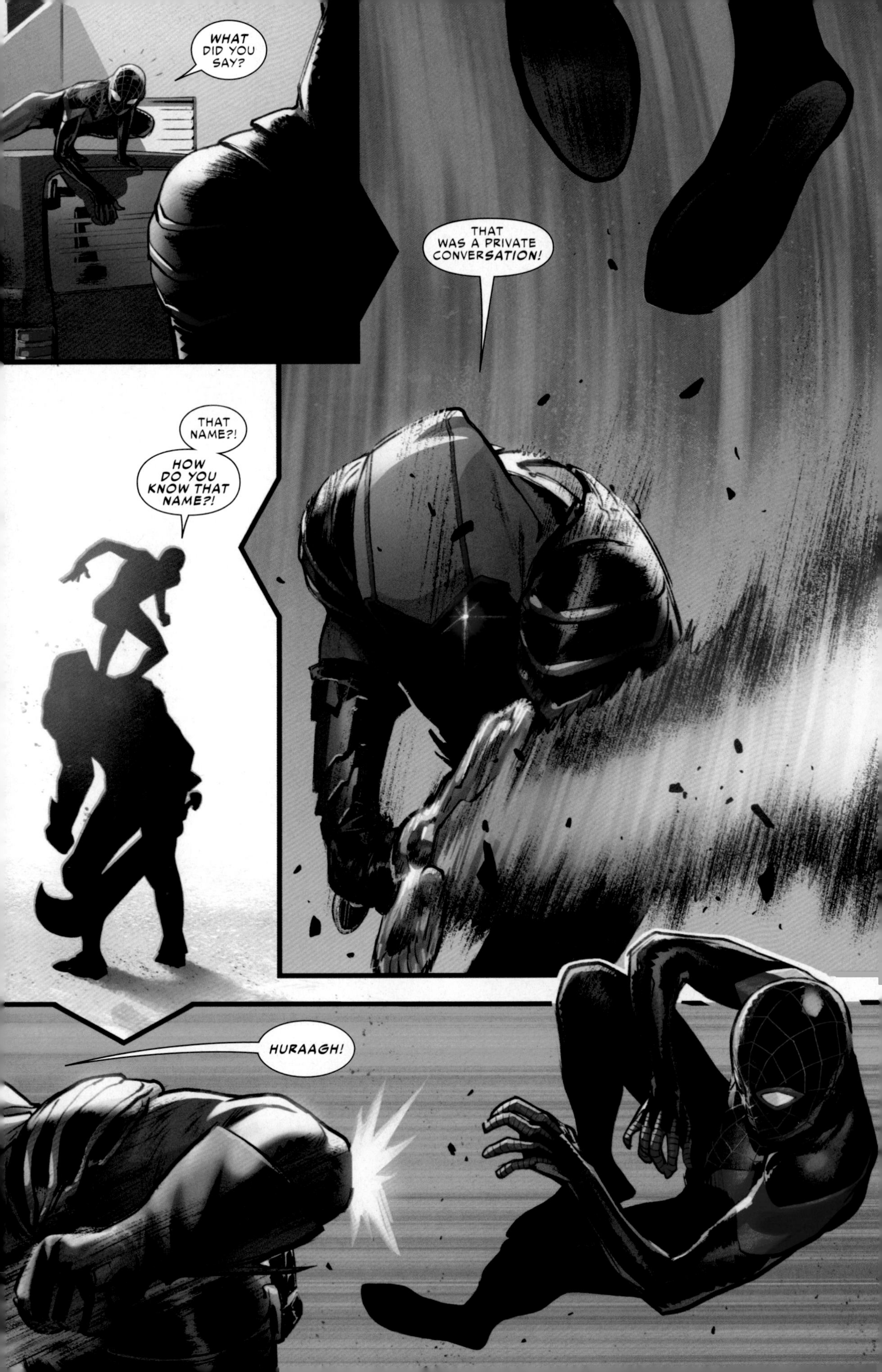
WHAT DID YOU SAY?
THAT WAS A PRIVATE CONVERSATION!
THAT NAME?!
HOW DO YOU KNOW THAT NAME?!
HURAAGH!

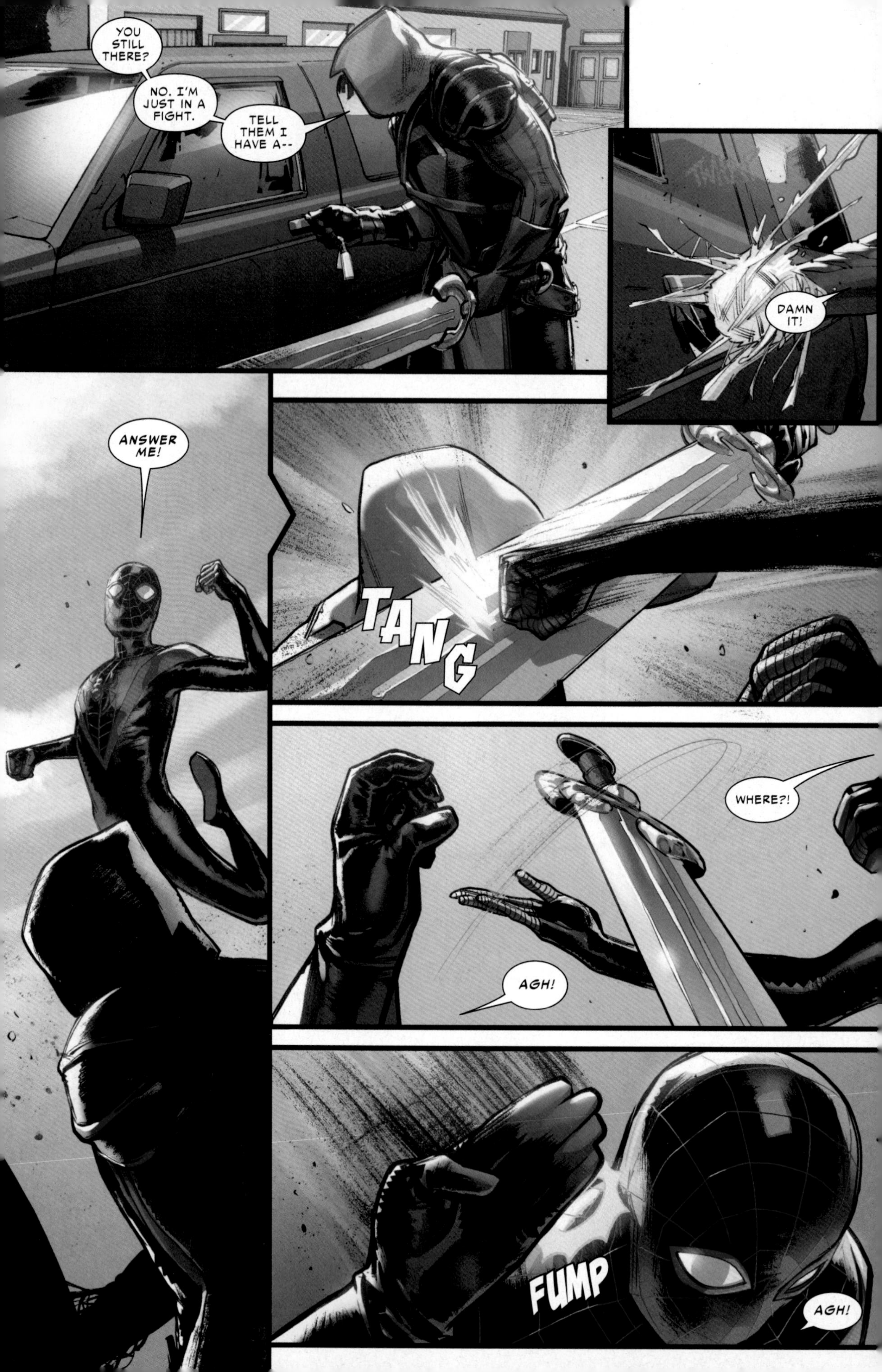
YOU STILL THERE?
NO. I'M JUST IN A FIGHT.
TELL THEM I HAVE A--
DAMN IT!
ANSWER ME!
TANG
WHERE?!
AGH!
FUMP
AGH!

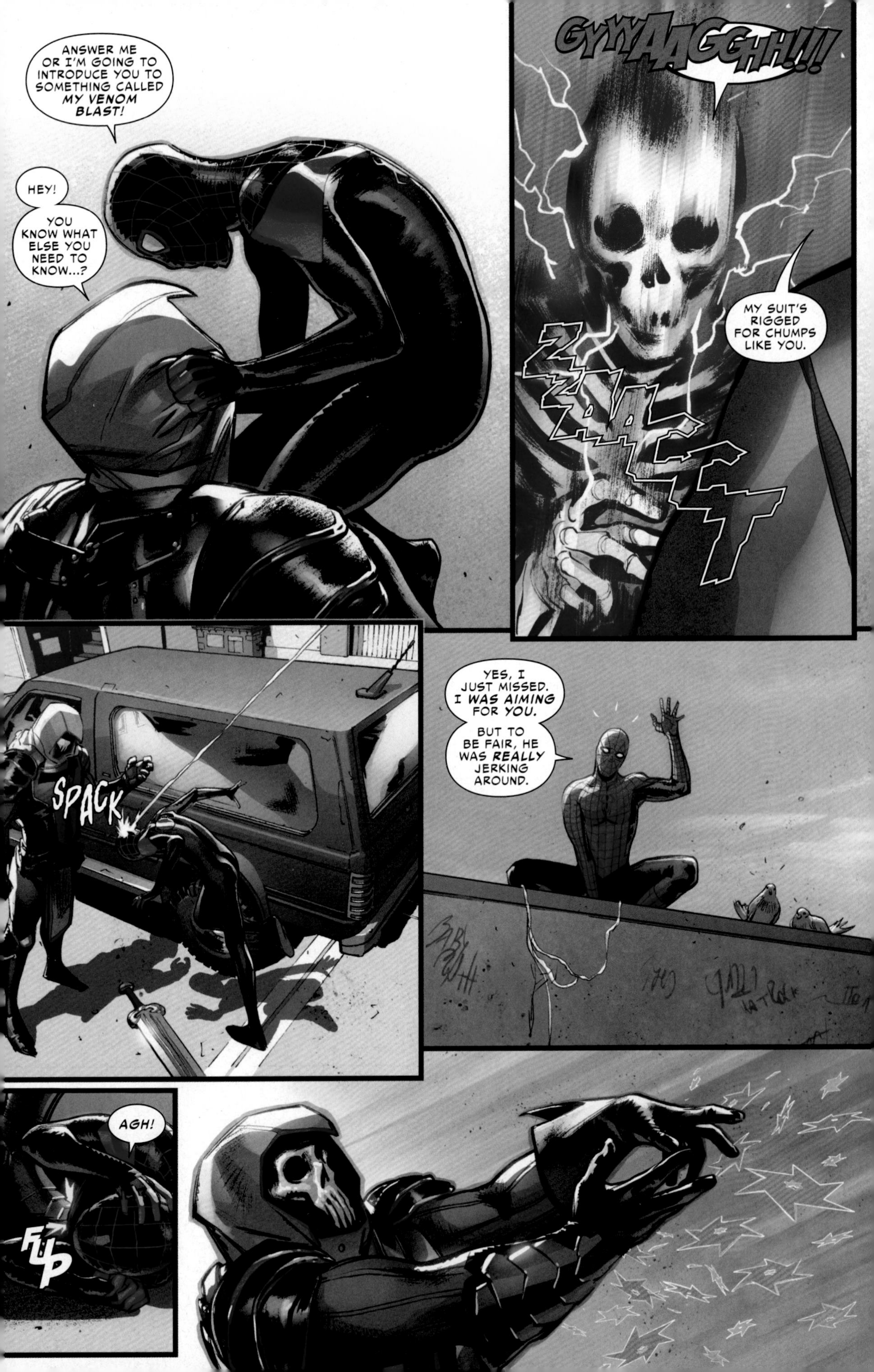
ANSWER ME OR I'M GOING TO INTRODUCE YOU TO SOMETHING CALLED *MY VENOM BLAST!*
HEY!
YOU KNOW WHAT ELSE YOU NEED TO KNOW...?
GYYYAAAGGHH!!!
MY SUIT'S RIGGED FOR CHUMPS LIKE YOU.
ZZAKT
SPACK
YES, I JUST MISSED. I *WAS AIMING* FOR *YOU.*
BUT TO BE FAIR, HE WAS *REALLY* JERKING AROUND.
AGH!
FLIP

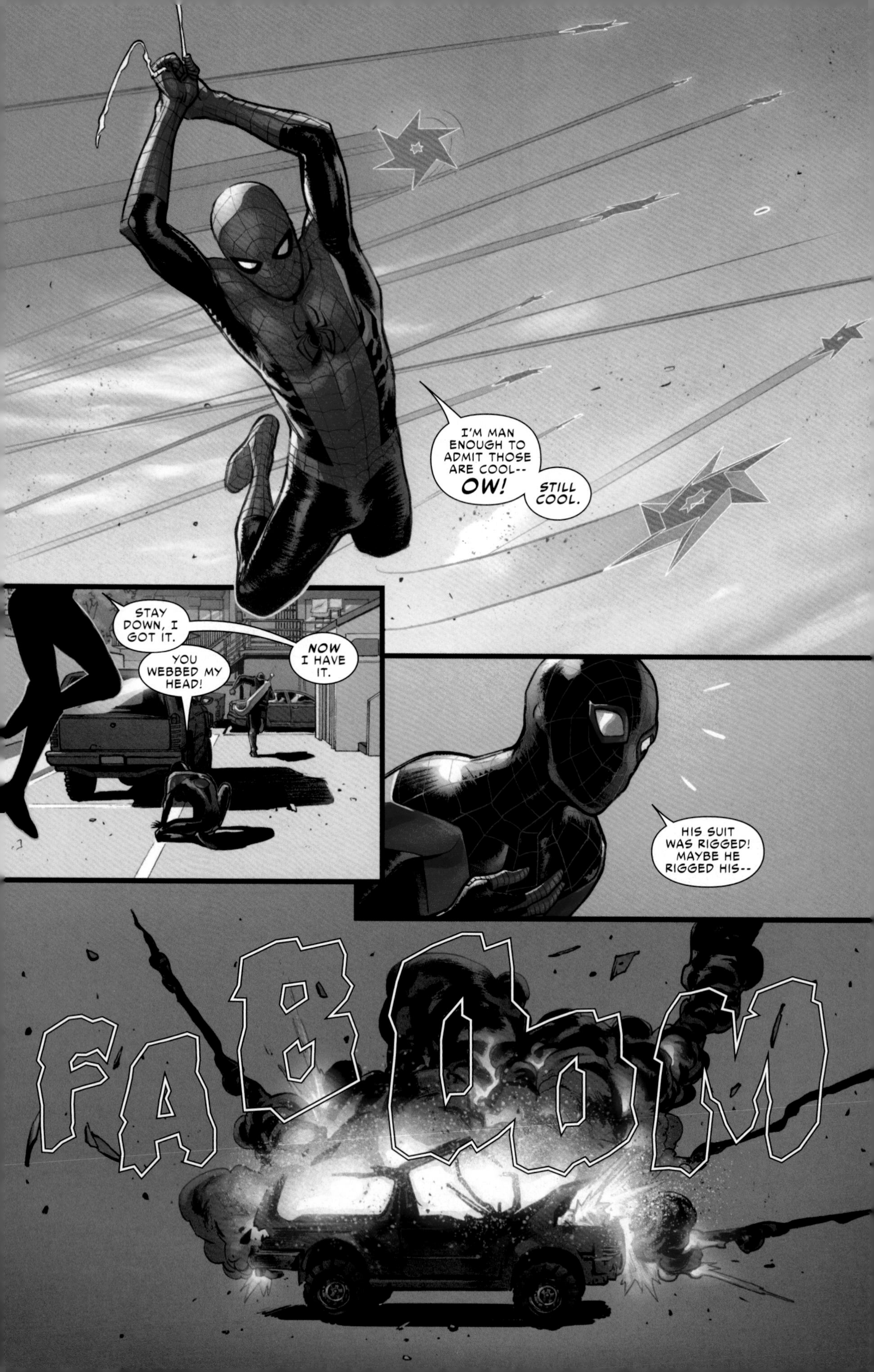

I'M MAN ENOUGH TO ADMIT THOSE ARE COOL-- OW!
STILL COOL.
STAY DOWN, I GOT IT.
YOU WEBBED MY HEAD!
NOW I HAVE IT.
HIS SUIT WAS RIGGED! MAYBE HE RIGGED HIS--
FABOOM

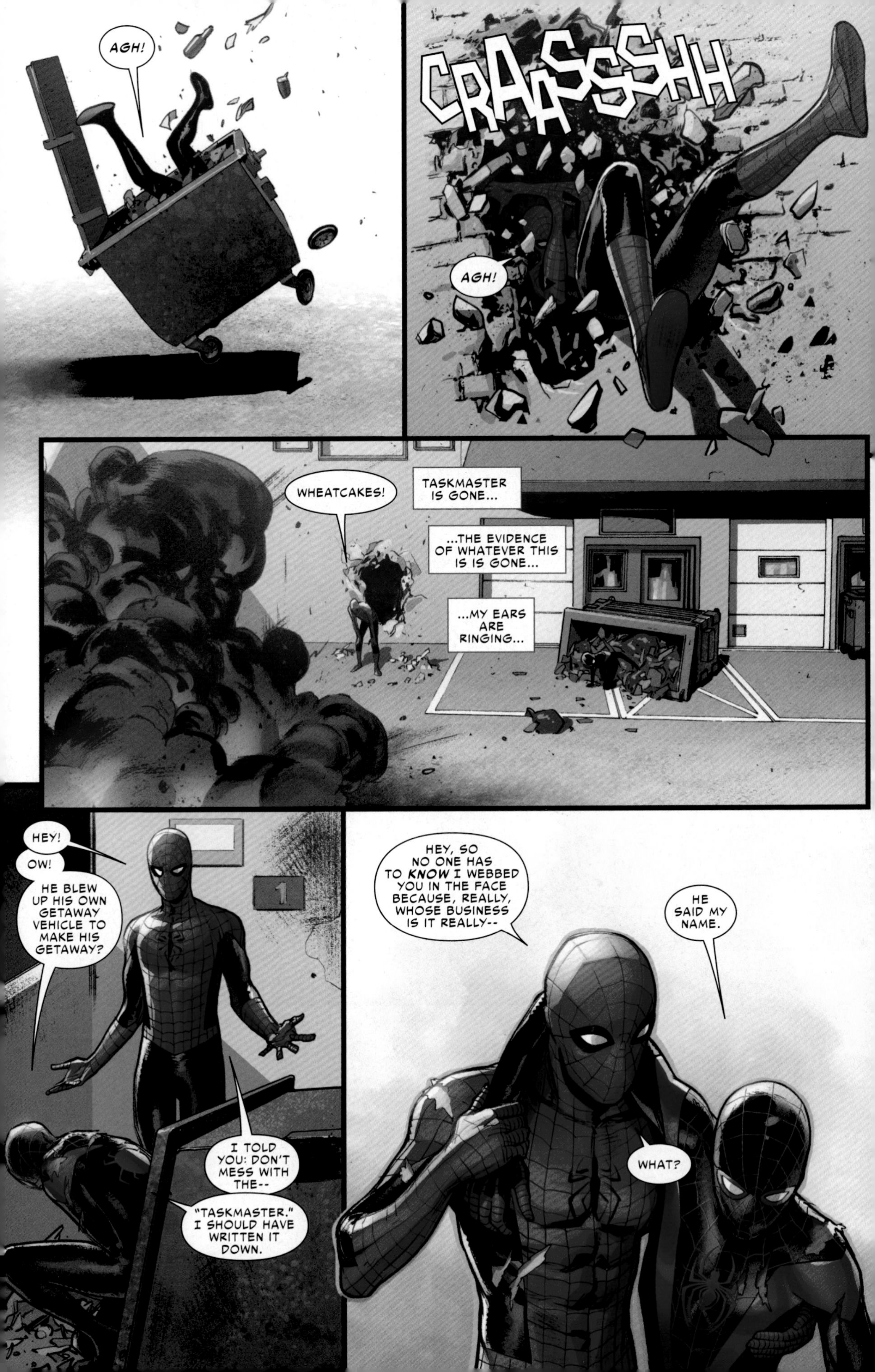
AGH!
CRAASSSHH
AGH!
WHEATCAKES!
TASKMASTER IS GONE...
...THE EVIDENCE OF WHATEVER THIS IS IS GONE...
...MY EARS ARE RINGING...
HEY!
OW!
HE BLEW UP HIS OWN GETAWAY VEHICLE TO MAKE HIS GETAWAY?
I TOLD YOU: DON'T MESS WITH THE--
"TASKMASTER." I SHOULD HAVE WRITTEN IT DOWN.
HEY, SO NO ONE HAS TO KNOW I WEBBED YOU IN THE FACE BECAUSE, REALLY, WHOSE BUSINESS IS IT REALLY--
HE SAID MY NAME.
WHAT?

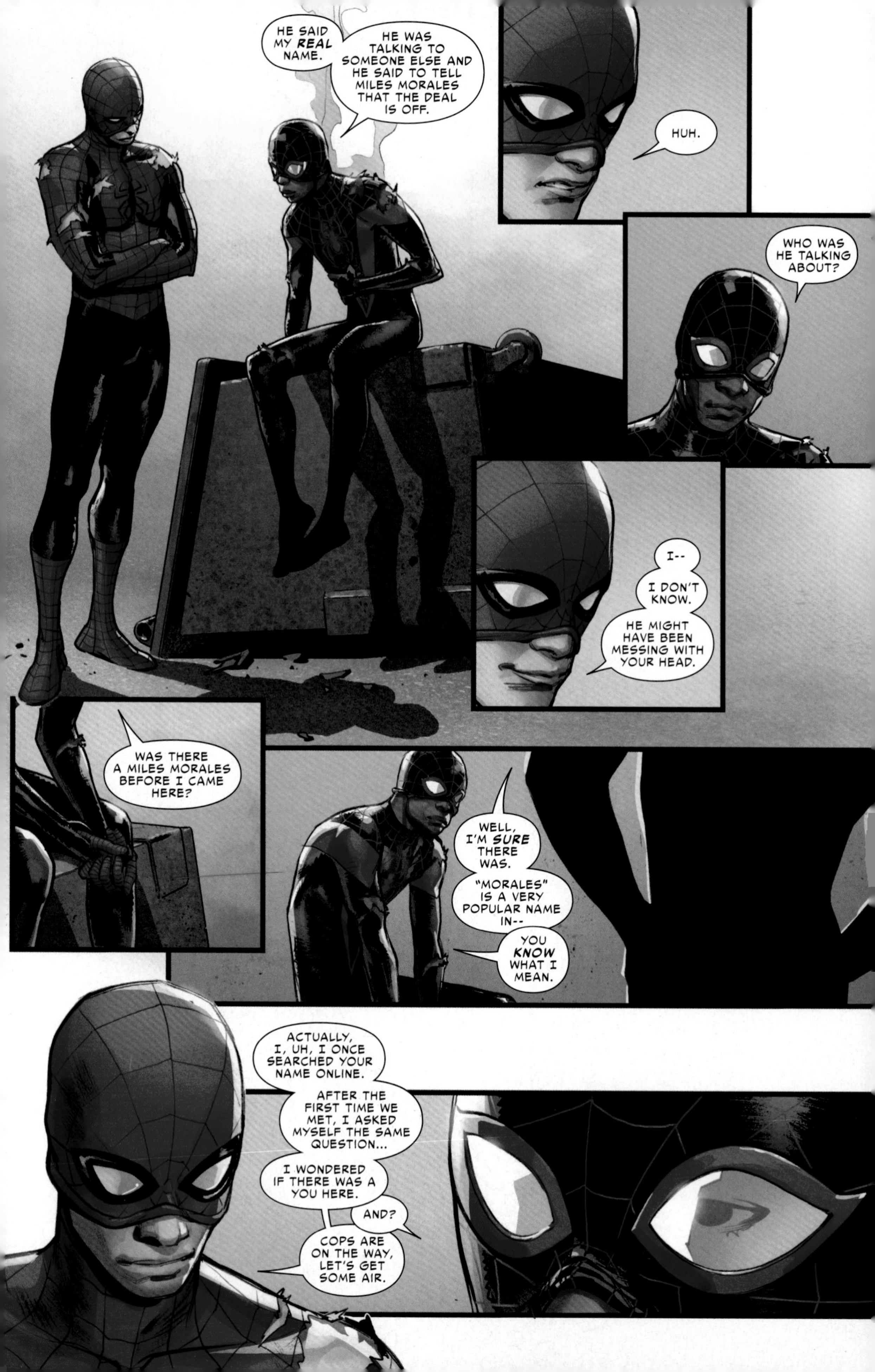
HE SAID MY REAL NAME.
HE WAS TALKING TO SOMEONE ELSE AND HE SAID TO TELL MILES MORALES THAT THE DEAL IS OFF.
HUH.
WHO WAS HE TALKING ABOUT?
I--
I DON'T KNOW.
HE MIGHT HAVE BEEN MESSING WITH YOUR HEAD.
WAS THERE A MILES MORALES BEFORE I CAME HERE?
WELL, I'M SURE THERE WAS.
"MORALES" IS A VERY POPULAR NAME IN--
YOU KNOW WHAT I MEAN.
ACTUALLY, I, UH, I ONCE SEARCHED YOUR NAME ONLINE.
AFTER THE FIRST TIME WE MET, I ASKED MYSELF THE SAME QUESTION...
I WONDERED IF THERE WAS A YOU HERE.
AND?
COPS ARE ON THE WAY, LET'S GET SOME AIR.

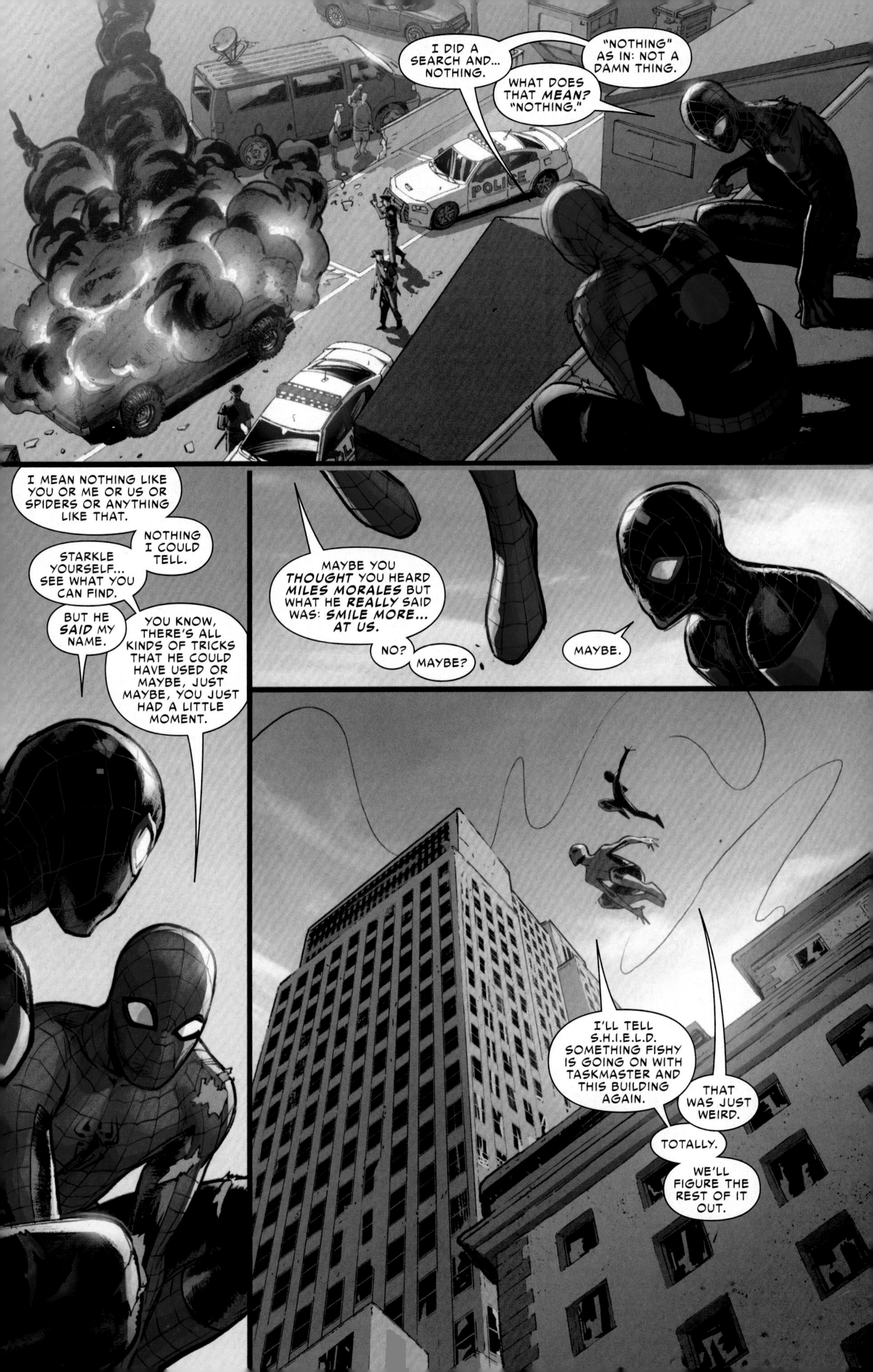
I DID A SEARCH AND... NOTHING.
WHAT DOES THAT MEAN? "NOTHING."
"NOTHING" AS IN: NOT A DAMN THING.
I MEAN NOTHING LIKE YOU OR ME OR US OR SPIDERS OR ANYTHING LIKE THAT.
NOTHING I COULD TELL.
STARKLE YOURSELF... SEE WHAT YOU CAN FIND.
BUT HE SAID MY NAME.
YOU KNOW, THERE'S ALL KINDS OF TRICKS THAT HE COULD HAVE USED OR MAYBE, JUST MAYBE, YOU JUST HAD A LITTLE MOMENT.
MAYBE YOU THOUGHT YOU HEARD MILES MORALES BUT WHAT HE REALLY SAID WAS: SMILE MORE... AT US.
NO?
MAYBE?
MAYBE.
I'LL TELL S.H.I.E.L.D. SOMETHING FISHY IS GOING ON WITH TASKMASTER AND THIS BUILDING AGAIN.
THAT WAS JUST WEIRD.
TOTALLY.
WE'LL FIGURE THE REST OF IT OUT.

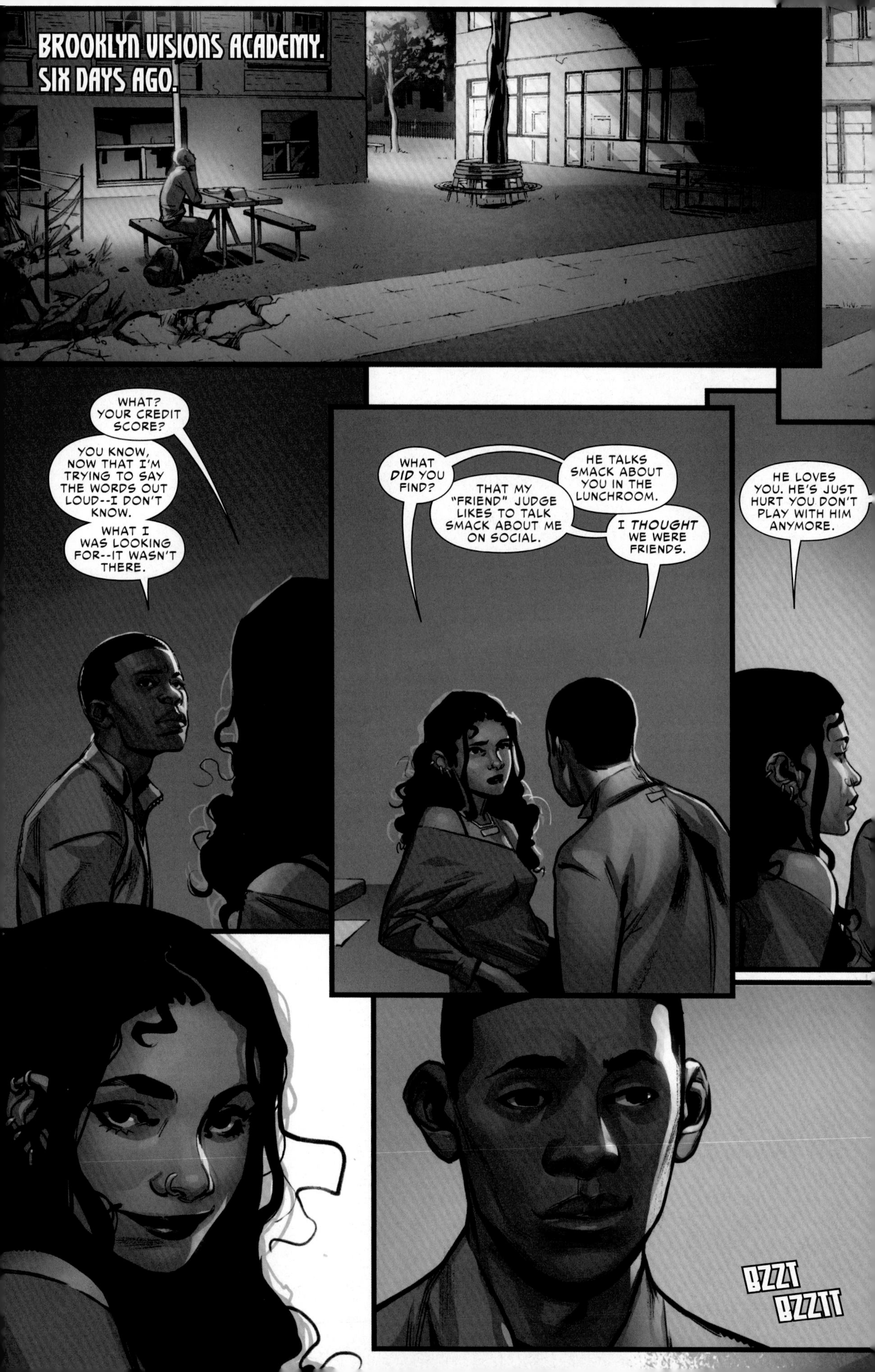
BROOKLYN VISIONS ACADEMY. SIX DAYS AGO.
WHAT? YOUR CREDIT SCORE?
YOU KNOW, NOW THAT I'M TRYING TO SAY THE WORDS OUT LOUD--I DON'T KNOW.
WHAT I WAS LOOKING FOR--IT WASN'T THERE.
WHAT DID YOU FIND?
THAT MY "FRIEND" JUDGE LIKES TO TALK SMACK ABOUT ME ON SOCIAL.
HE TALKS SMACK ABOUT YOU IN THE LUNCHROOM.
I THOUGHT WE WERE FRIENDS.
HE LOVES YOU. HE'S JUST HURT YOU DON'T PLAY WITH HIM ANYMORE.
BZZT BZZTT

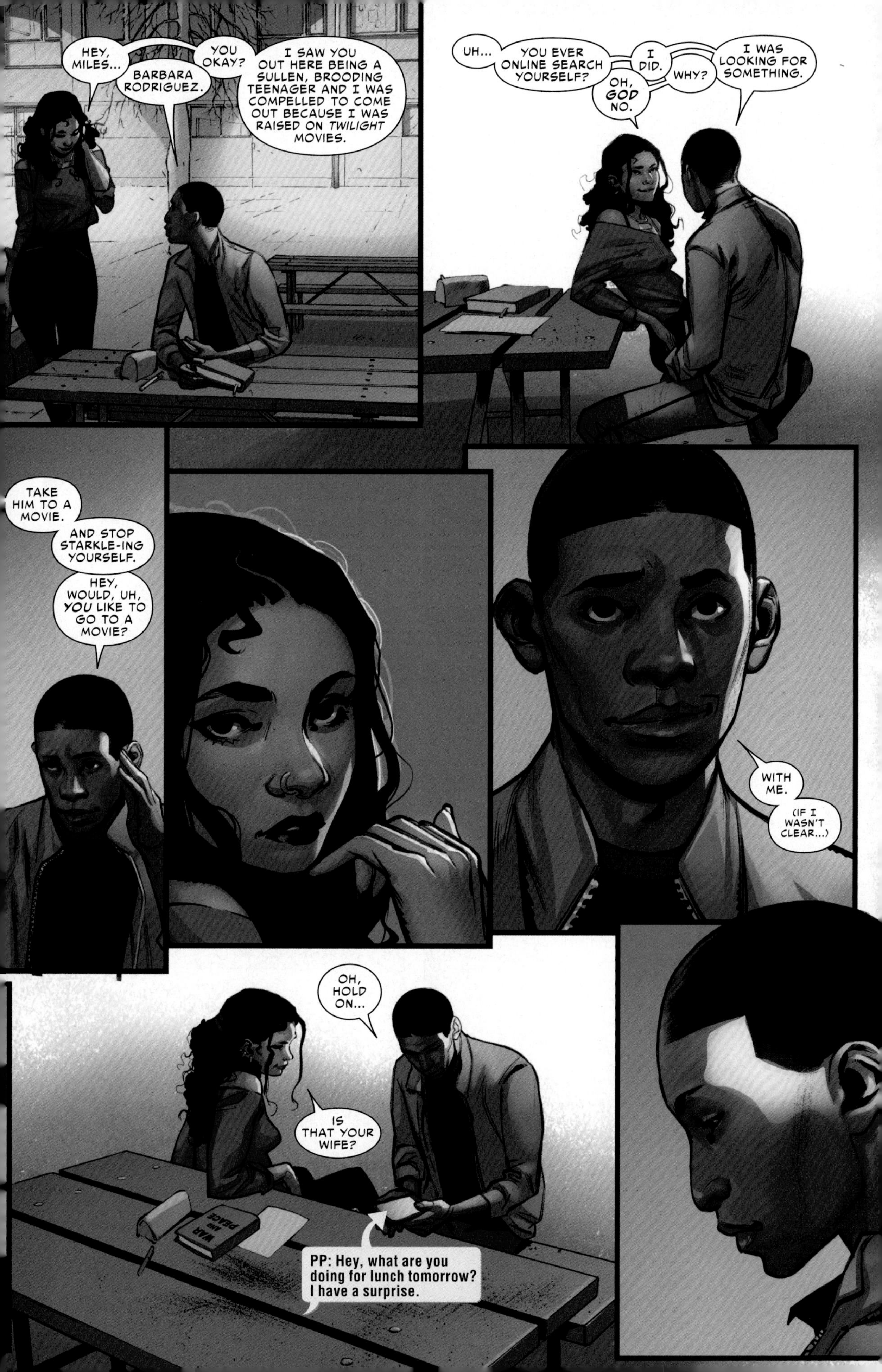

HEY, MILES...
BARBARA RODRIGUEZ.
YOU OKAY?
I SAW YOU OUT HERE BEING A SULLEN, BROODING TEENAGER AND I WAS COMPELLED TO COME OUT BECAUSE I WAS RAISED ON TWILIGHT MOVIES.
UH...
YOU EVER ONLINE SEARCH YOURSELF?
I DID.
OH, GOD NO.
WHY?
I WAS LOOKING FOR SOMETHING.
TAKE HIM TO A MOVIE.
AND STOP STARKLE-ING YOURSELF.
HEY, WOULD, UH, YOU LIKE TO GO TO A MOVIE?
WITH ME.
(IF I WASN'T CLEAR...)
OH, HOLD ON...
IS THAT YOUR WIFE?
WAR AND PEACE
PP: Hey, what are you doing for lunch tomorrow? I have a surprise.

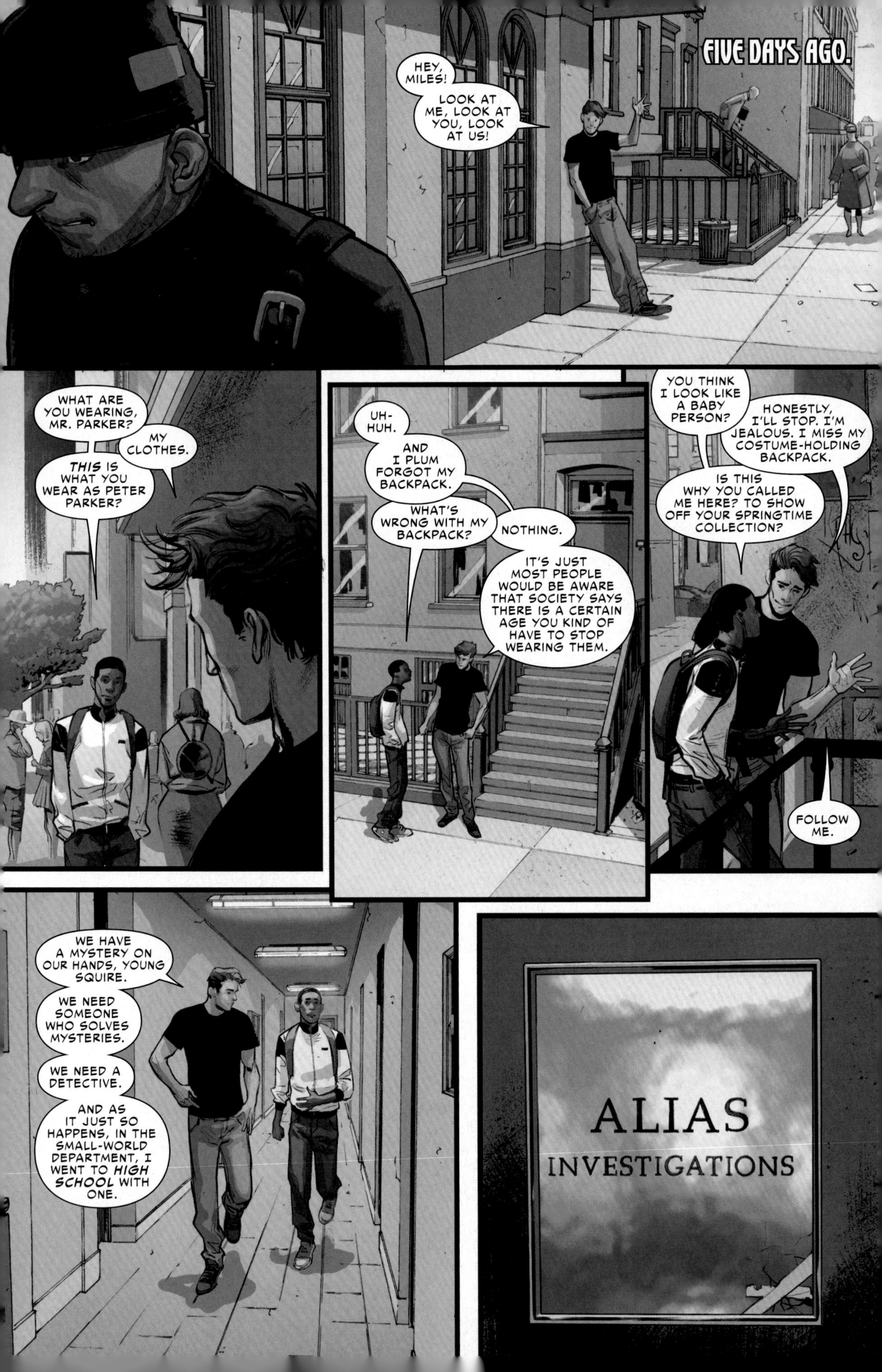
FIVE DAYS AGO.
HEY, MILES!
LOOK AT ME, LOOK AT YOU, LOOK AT US!
WHAT ARE YOU WEARING, MR. PARKER?
MY CLOTHES.
THIS IS WHAT YOU WEAR AS PETER PARKER?
UH-HUH.
AND I PLUM FORGOT MY BACKPACK.
WHAT'S WRONG WITH MY BACKPACK?
NOTHING.
IT'S JUST MOST PEOPLE WOULD BE AWARE THAT SOCIETY SAYS THERE IS A CERTAIN AGE YOU KIND OF HAVE TO STOP WEARING THEM.
YOU THINK I LOOK LIKE A BABY PERSON?
HONESTLY, I'LL STOP. I'M JEALOUS. I MISS MY COSTUME-HOLDING BACKPACK.
IS THIS WHY YOU CALLED ME HERE? TO SHOW OFF YOUR SPRINGTIME COLLECTION?
FOLLOW ME.
WE HAVE A MYSTERY ON OUR HANDS, YOUNG SQUIRE.
WE NEED SOMEONE WHO SOLVES MYSTERIES.
WE NEED A DETECTIVE.
AND AS IT JUST SO HAPPENS, IN THE SMALL-WORLD DEPARTMENT, I WENT TO HIGH SCHOOL WITH ONE.
ALIAS INVESTIGATIONS

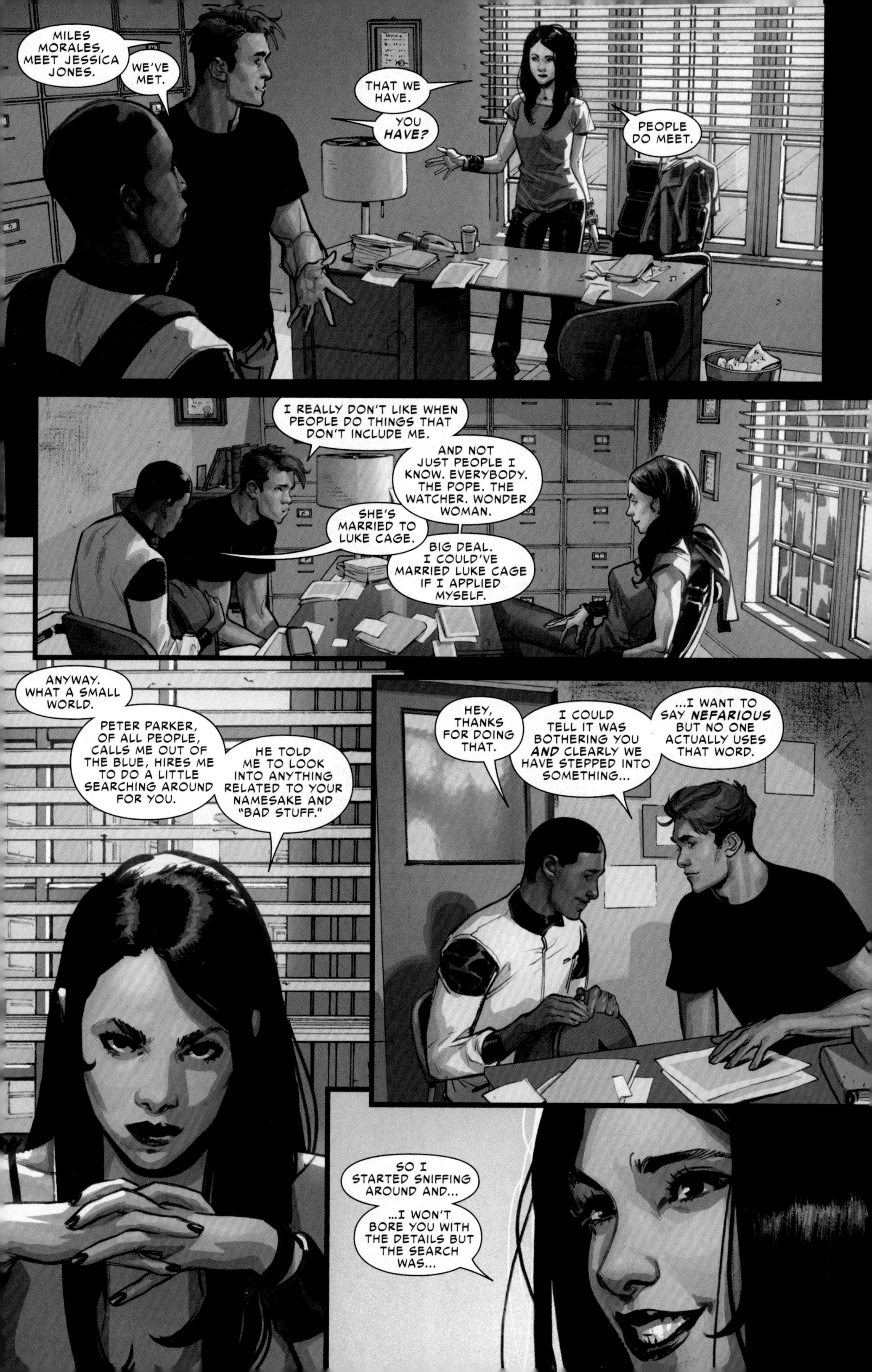
MILES MORALES, MEET JESSICA JONES.
WE'VE MET.
THAT WE HAVE.
YOU *HAVE?*
PEOPLE DO MEET.
I REALLY DON'T LIKE WHEN PEOPLE DO THINGS THAT DON'T INCLUDE ME.
AND NOT JUST PEOPLE I KNOW. EVERYBODY. THE POPE. THE WATCHER. WONDER WOMAN.
SHE'S MARRIED TO LUKE CAGE.
BIG DEAL. I COULD'VE MARRIED LUKE CAGE IF I APPLIED MYSELF.
ANYWAY. WHAT A SMALL WORLD.
PETER PARKER, OF ALL PEOPLE, CALLS ME OUT OF THE BLUE, HIRES ME TO DO A LITTLE SEARCHING AROUND FOR YOU.
HE TOLD ME TO LOOK INTO ANYTHING RELATED TO YOUR NAMESAKE AND "BAD STUFF."
HEY, THANKS FOR DOING THAT.
I COULD TELL IT WAS BOTHERING YOU *AND* CLEARLY WE HAVE STEPPED INTO SOMETHING...
...I WANT TO SAY *NEFARIOUS* BUT NO ONE ACTUALLY USES THAT WORD.
SO I STARTED SNIFFING AROUND AND...
...I WON'T BORE YOU WITH THE DETAILS BUT THE SEARCH WAS...

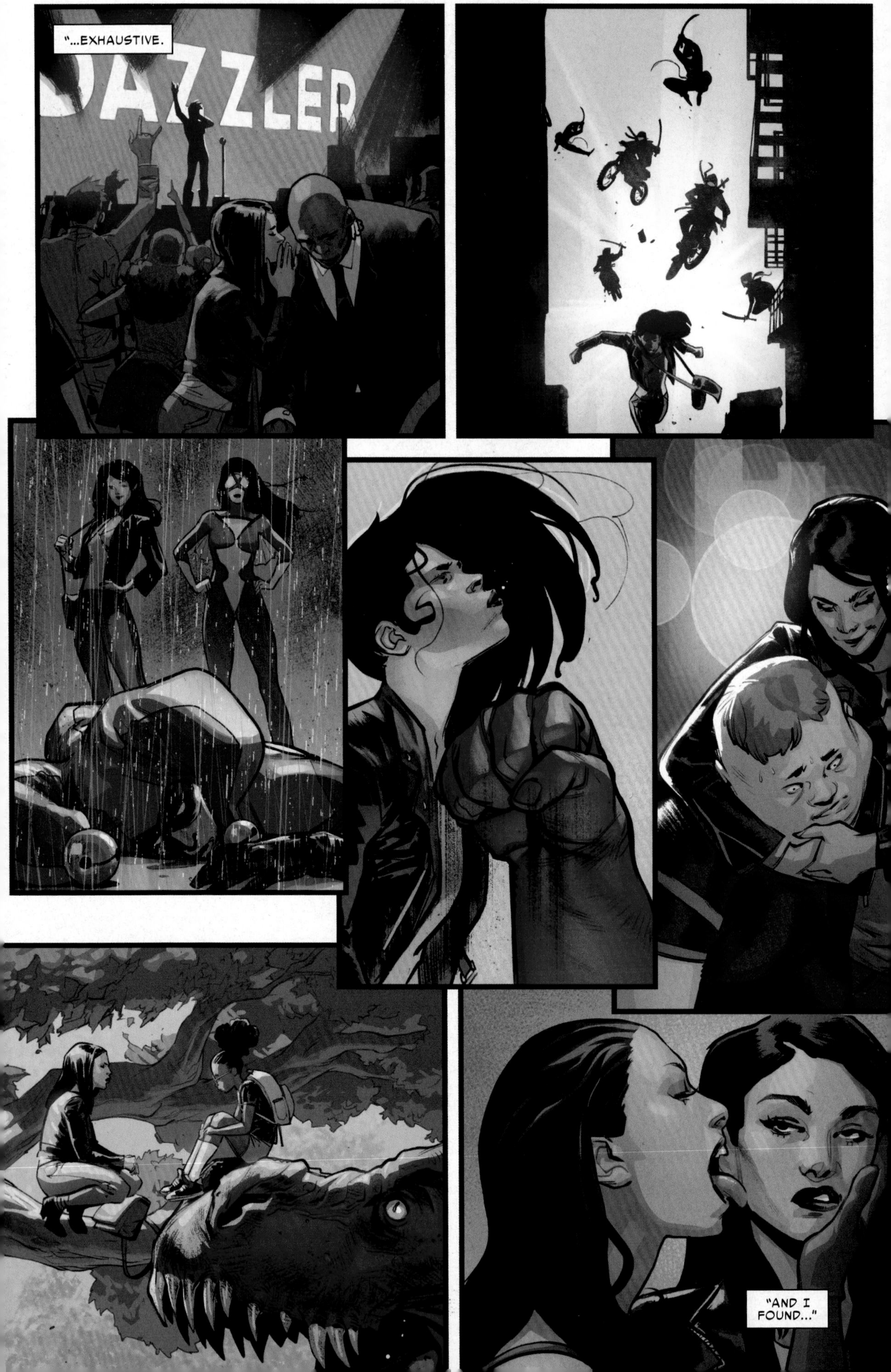
"...EXHAUSTIVE.
DAZZLER
"AND I FOUND..."

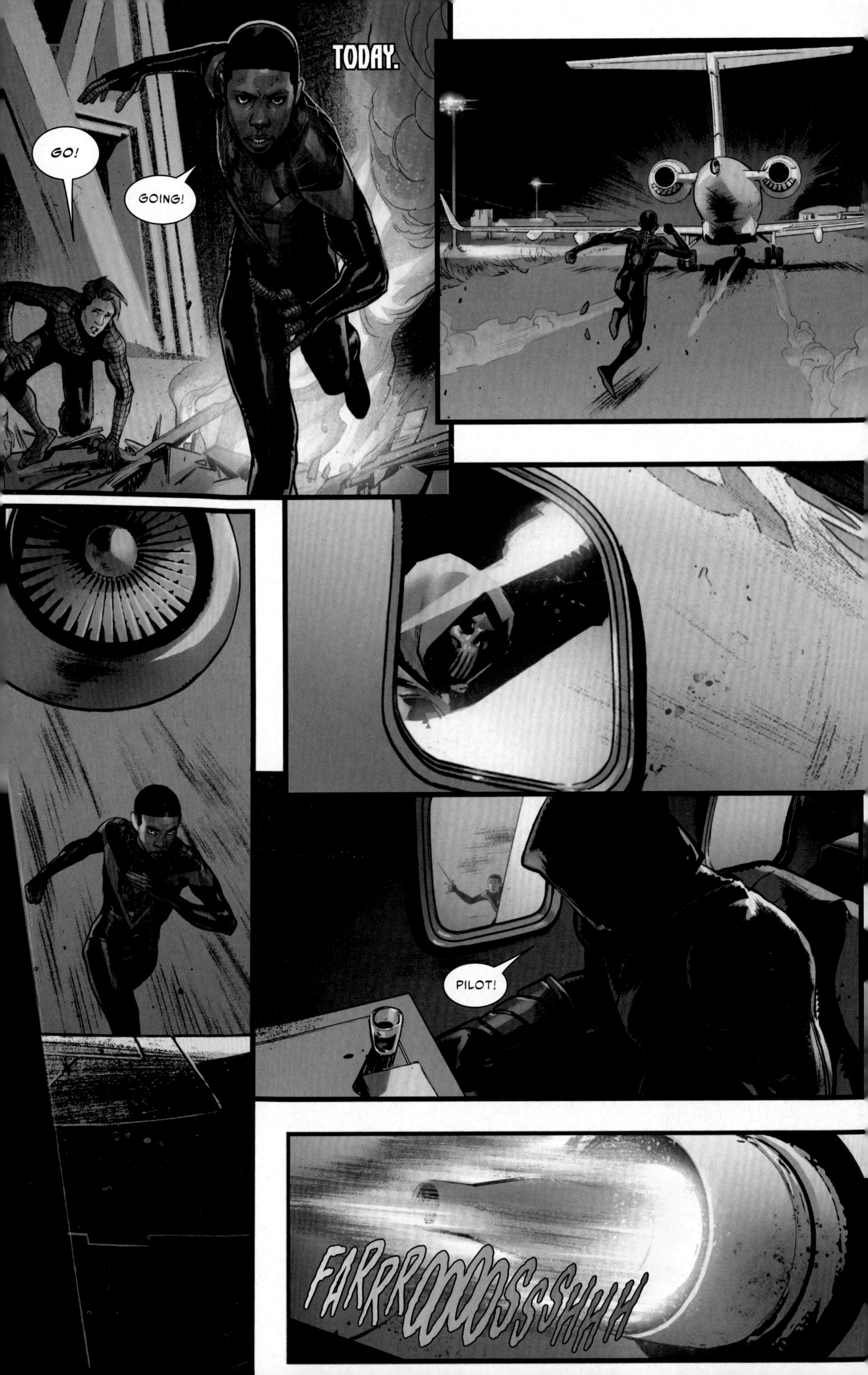
TODAY.
GO!
GOING!
PILOT!
FARRROOOOSSSHHH

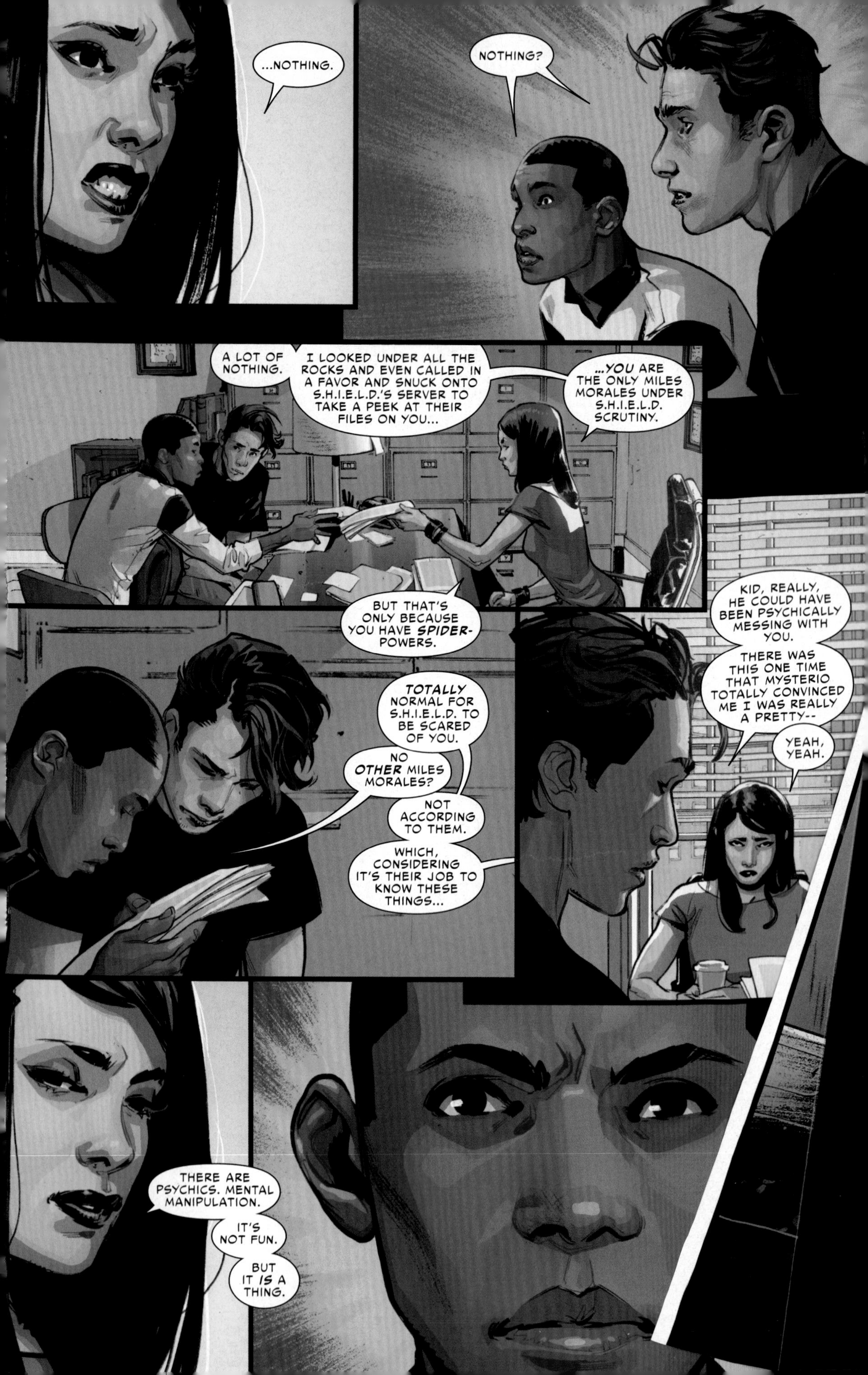
...NOTHING.
NOTHING?
A LOT OF NOTHING.
I LOOKED UNDER ALL THE ROCKS AND EVEN CALLED IN A FAVOR AND SNUCK ONTO S.H.I.E.L.D.'S SERVER TO TAKE A PEEK AT THEIR FILES ON YOU...
...YOU ARE THE ONLY MILES MORALES UNDER S.H.I.E.L.D. SCRUTINY.
BUT THAT'S ONLY BECAUSE YOU HAVE SPIDER-POWERS.
TOTALLY NORMAL FOR S.H.I.E.L.D. TO BE SCARED OF YOU.
NO OTHER MILES MORALES?
NOT ACCORDING TO THEM.
WHICH, CONSIDERING IT'S THEIR JOB TO KNOW THESE THINGS...
KID, REALLY, HE COULD HAVE BEEN PSYCHICALLY MESSING WITH YOU.
THERE WAS THIS ONE TIME THAT MYSTERIO TOTALLY CONVINCED ME I WAS REALLY A PRETTY--
YEAH, YEAH.
THERE ARE PSYCHICS. MENTAL MANIPULATION.
IT'S NOT FUN.
BUT IT IS A THING.

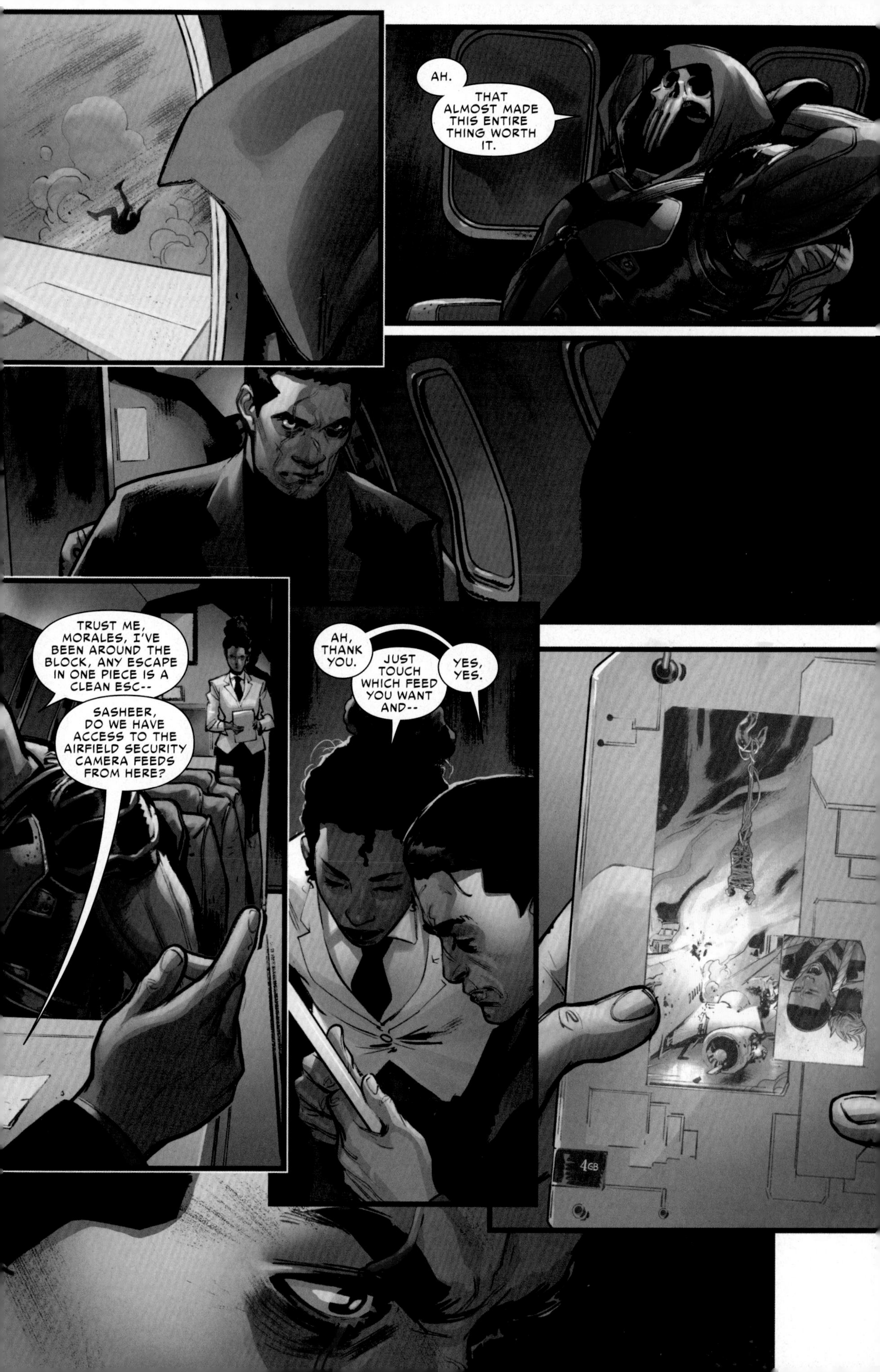
AH.
THAT ALMOST MADE THIS ENTIRE THING WORTH IT.
TRUST ME, MORALES, I'VE BEEN AROUND THE BLOCK, ANY ESCAPE IN ONE PIECE IS A CLEAN ESC--
SASHEER, DO WE HAVE ACCESS TO THE AIRFIELD SECURITY CAMERA FEEDS FROM HERE?
AH, THANK YOU.
JUST TOUCH WHICH FEED YOU WANT AND--
YES, YES.
4GB

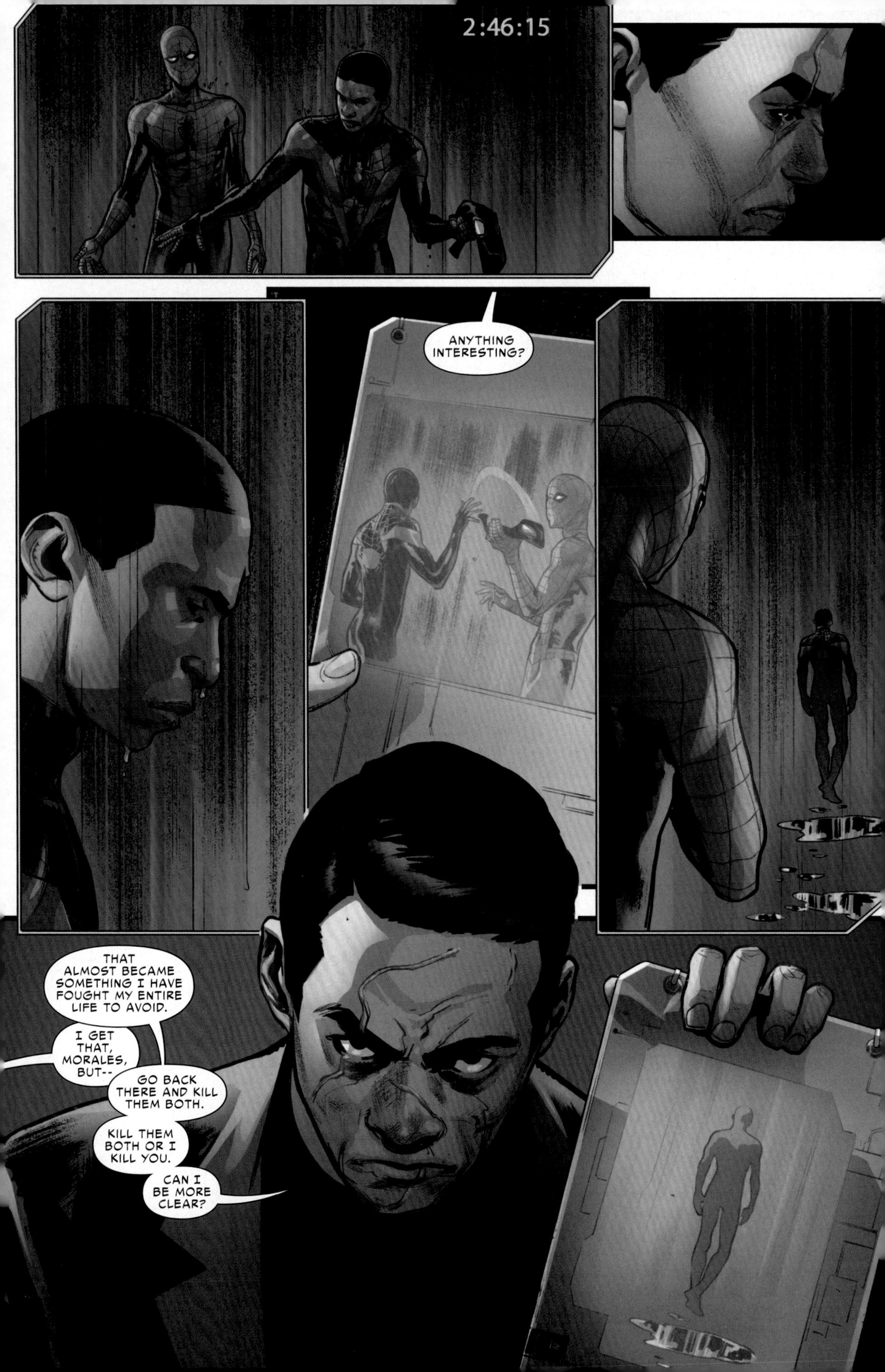
2:46:15
ANYTHING INTERESTING?
THAT ALMOST BECAME SOMETHING I HAVE FOUGHT MY ENTIRE LIFE TO AVOID.
I GET THAT, MORALES, BUT--
GO BACK THERE AND KILL THEM BOTH.
KILL THEM BOTH OR I KILL YOU.
CAN I BE MORE CLEAR?

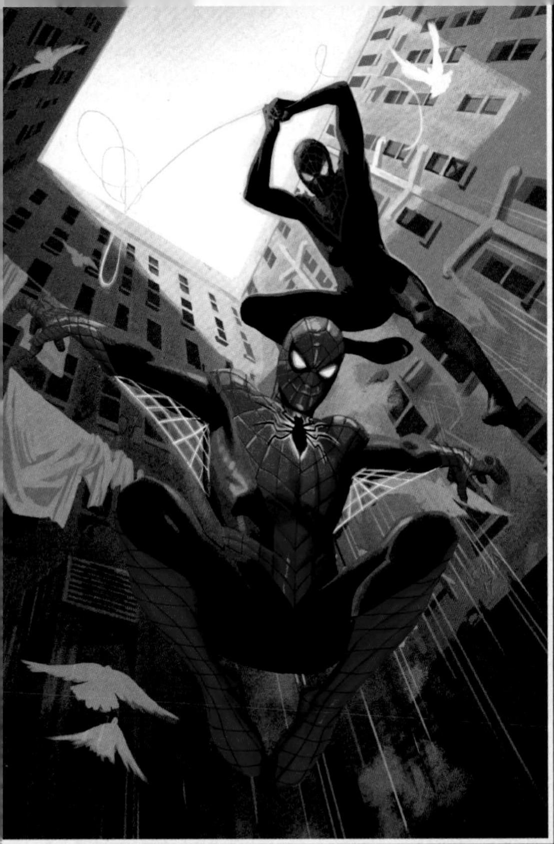

#1 VARIANT BY **DANIEL ACUÑA**

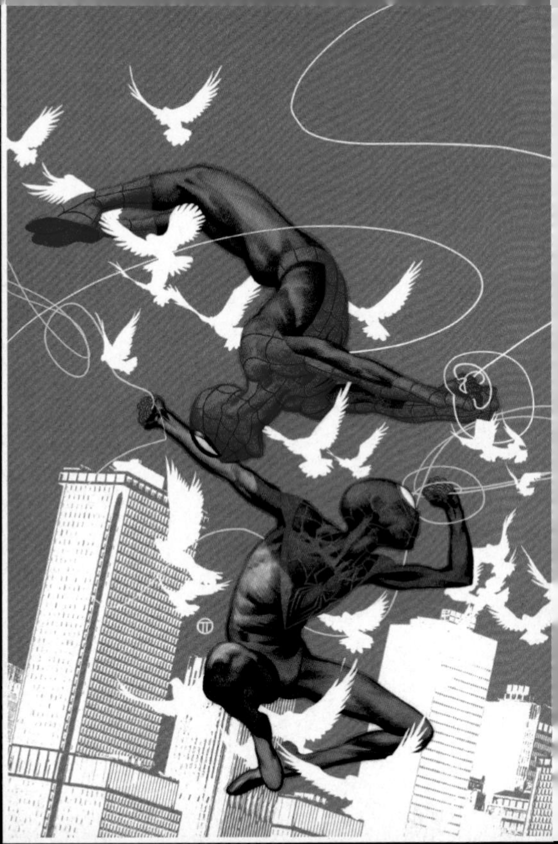

#1 VARIANT BY **JULIAN TOTINO TEDESCO**

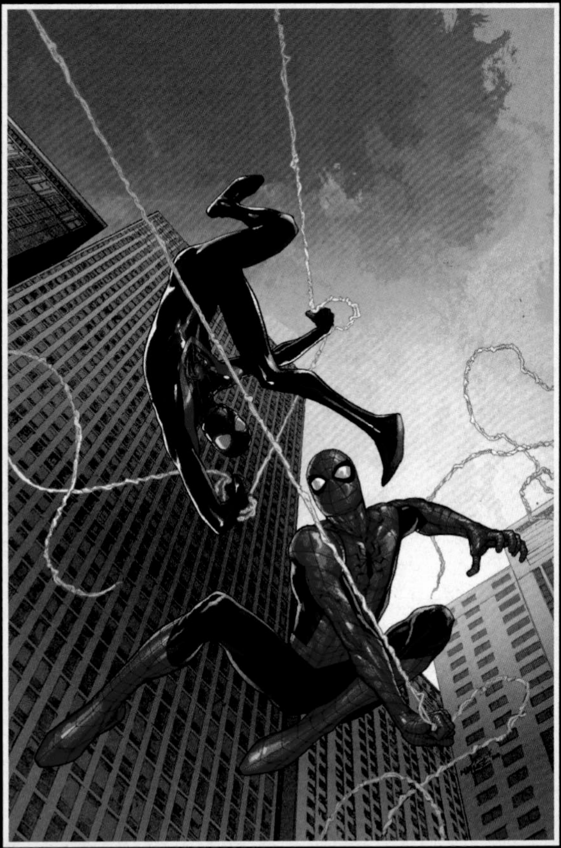

#1 VARIANT BY **DAVID MARQUEZ** & **RAIN BEREDO**

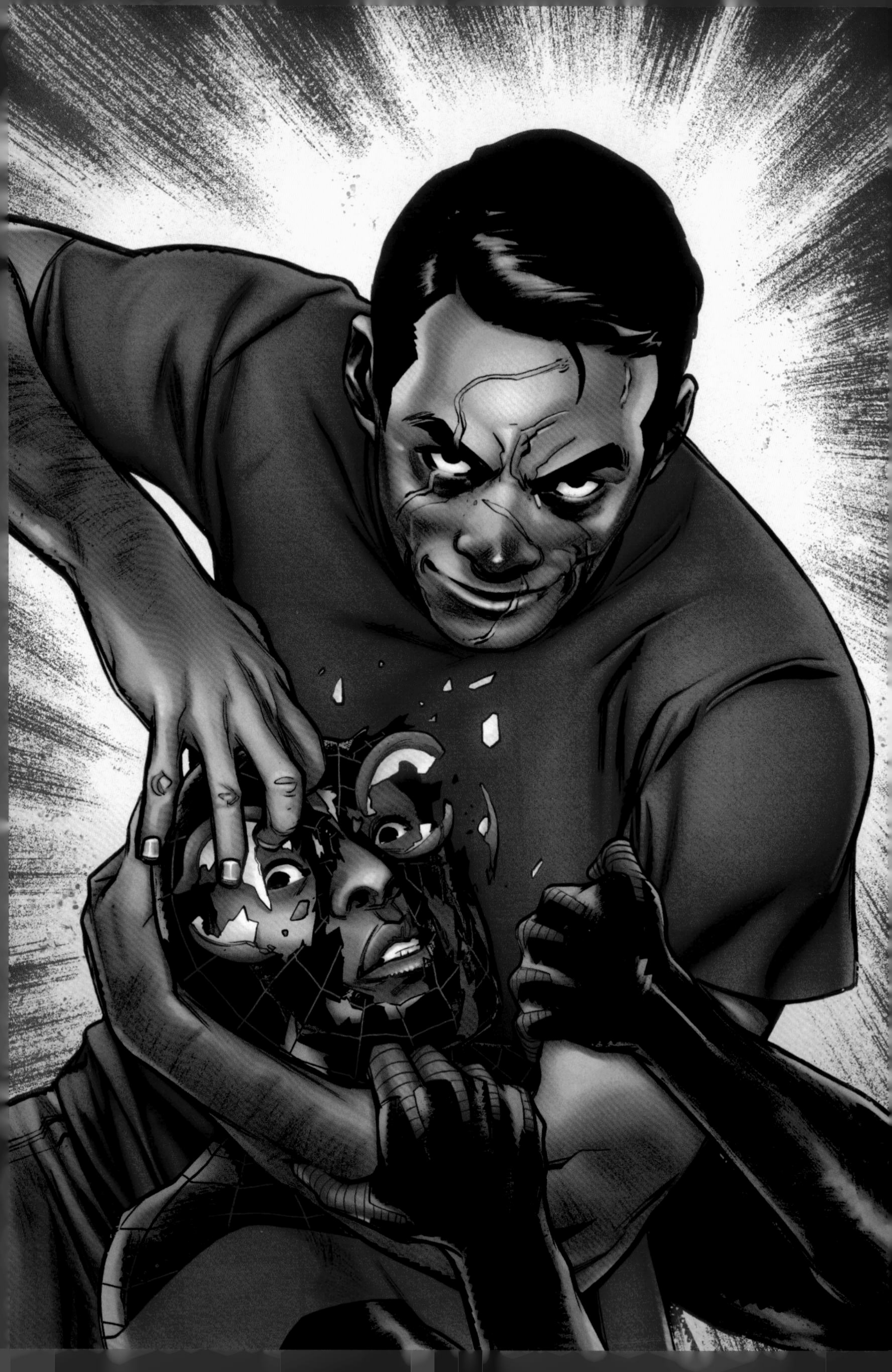

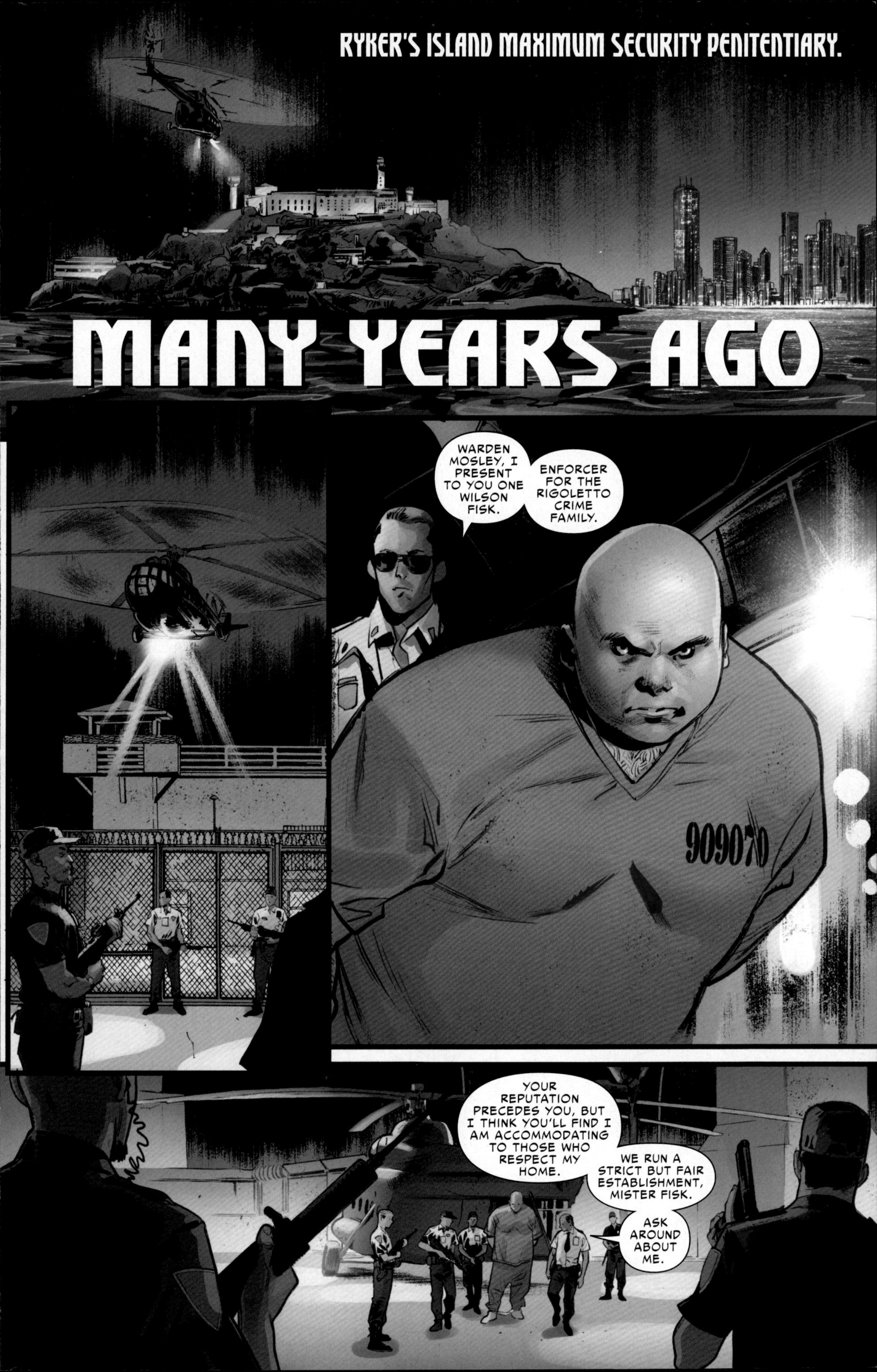
RYKER'S ISLAND MAXIMUM SECURITY PENITENTIARY.
MANY YEARS AGO
WARDEN MOSLEY, I PRESENT TO YOU ONE WILSON FISK.
ENFORCER FOR THE RIGOLETTO CRIME FAMILY.
909070
YOUR REPUTATION PRECEDES YOU, BUT I THINK YOU'LL FIND I AM ACCOMMODATING TO THOSE WHO RESPECT MY HOME.
WE RUN A STRICT BUT FAIR ESTABLISHMENT, MISTER FISK.
ASK AROUND ABOUT ME.

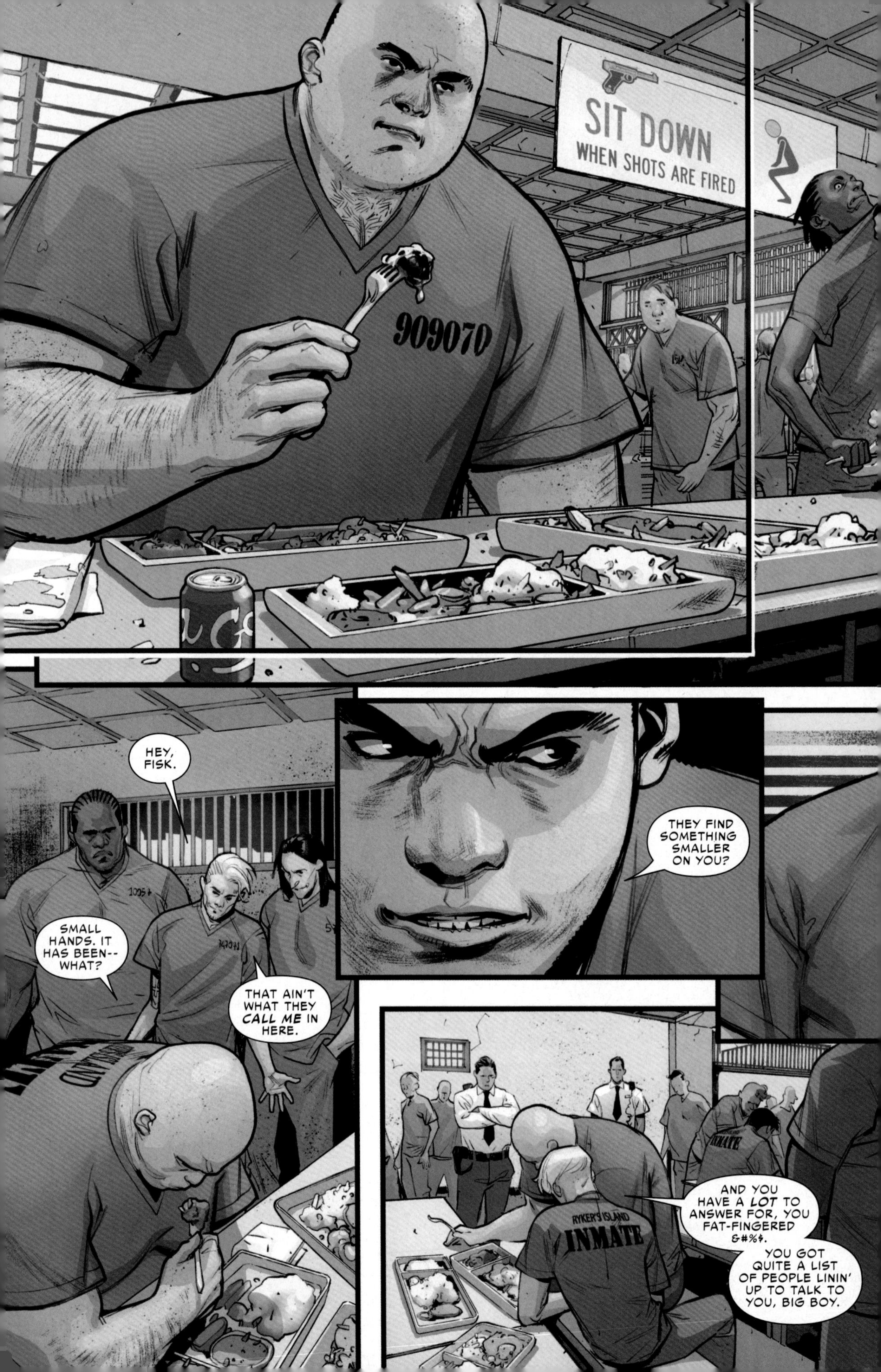

SIT DOWN
WHEN SHOTS ARE FIRED
909070
HEY, FISK.
THEY FIND SOMETHING SMALLER ON YOU?
SMALL HANDS. IT HAS BEEN-- WHAT?
THAT AIN'T WHAT THEY *CALL ME* IN HERE.
RYKER'S ISLAND
INMATE
AND YOU HAVE A *LOT* TO ANSWER FOR, YOU FAT-FINGERED &#%$.
YOU GOT QUITE A LIST OF PEOPLE LININ' UP TO TALK TO YOU, BIG BOY.

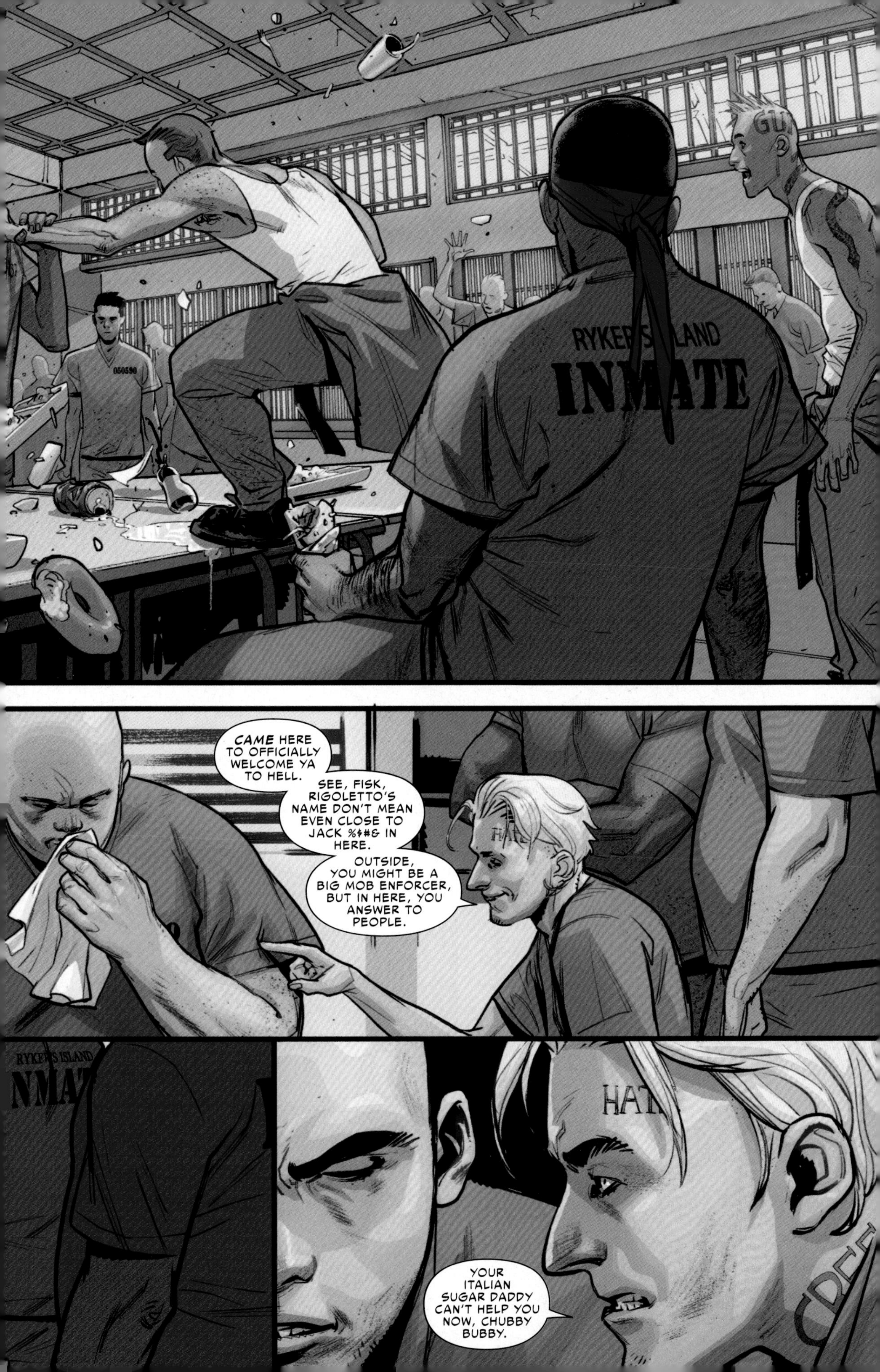
RYKERS ISLAND
INMATE
050590
CAME HERE TO OFFICIALLY WELCOME YA TO HELL.
SEE, FISK, RIGOLETTO'S NAME DON'T MEAN EVEN CLOSE TO JACK %$#& IN HERE.
OUTSIDE, YOU MIGHT BE A BIG MOB ENFORCER, BUT IN HERE, YOU ANSWER TO PEOPLE.
YOUR ITALIAN SUGAR DADDY CAN'T HELP YOU NOW, CHUBBY BUBBY.

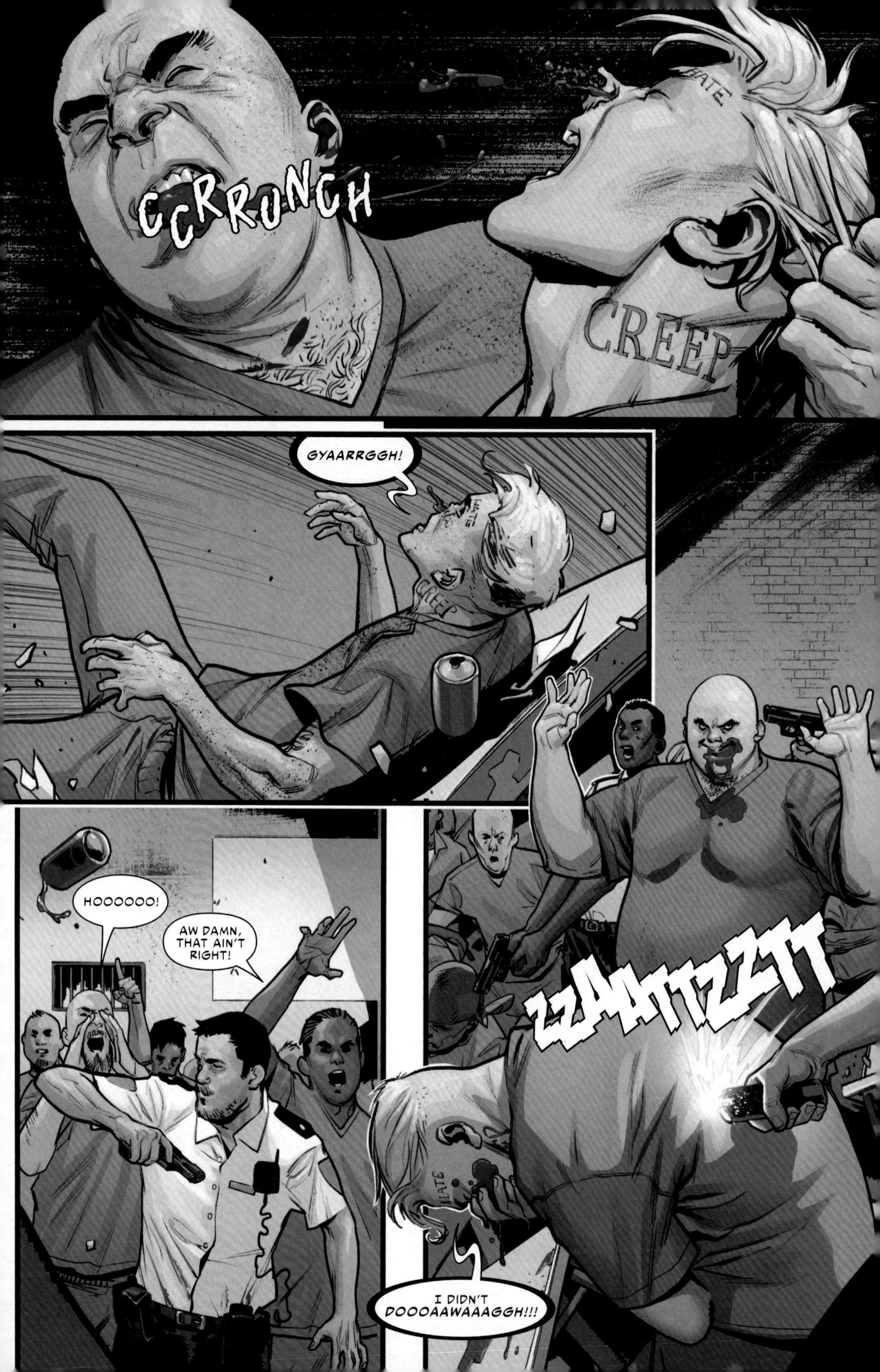
CCRRUNCH
HATE
CREEP
GYAARRGGH!
HOOOOOO!
AW DAMN, THAT AIN'T RIGHT!
ZZAAATTZZTT
I DIDN'T DOOOAAWAAAGGH!!!

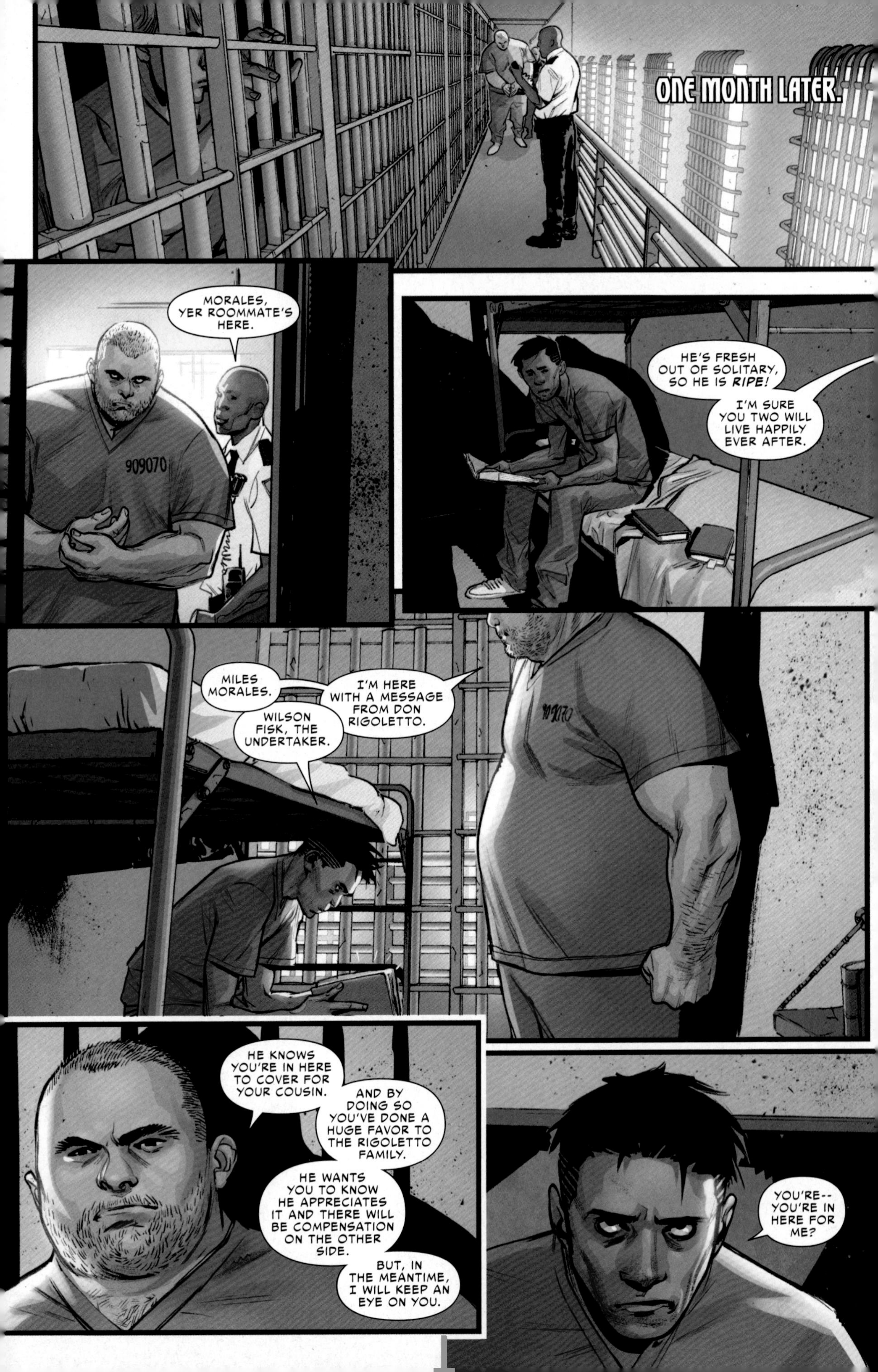
ONE MONTH LATER.
MORALES, YER ROOMMATE'S HERE.
909070
HE'S FRESH OUT OF SOLITARY, SO HE IS RIPE!
I'M SURE YOU TWO WILL LIVE HAPPILY EVER AFTER.
MILES MORALES.
WILSON FISK, THE UNDERTAKER.
I'M HERE WITH A MESSAGE FROM DON RIGOLETTO.
909070
HE KNOWS YOU'RE IN HERE TO COVER FOR YOUR COUSIN.
AND BY DOING SO YOU'VE DONE A HUGE FAVOR TO THE RIGOLETTO FAMILY.
HE WANTS YOU TO KNOW HE APPRECIATES IT AND THERE WILL BE COMPENSATION ON THE OTHER SIDE.
BUT, IN THE MEANTIME, I WILL KEEP AN EYE ON YOU.
YOU'RE-- YOU'RE IN HERE FOR ME?

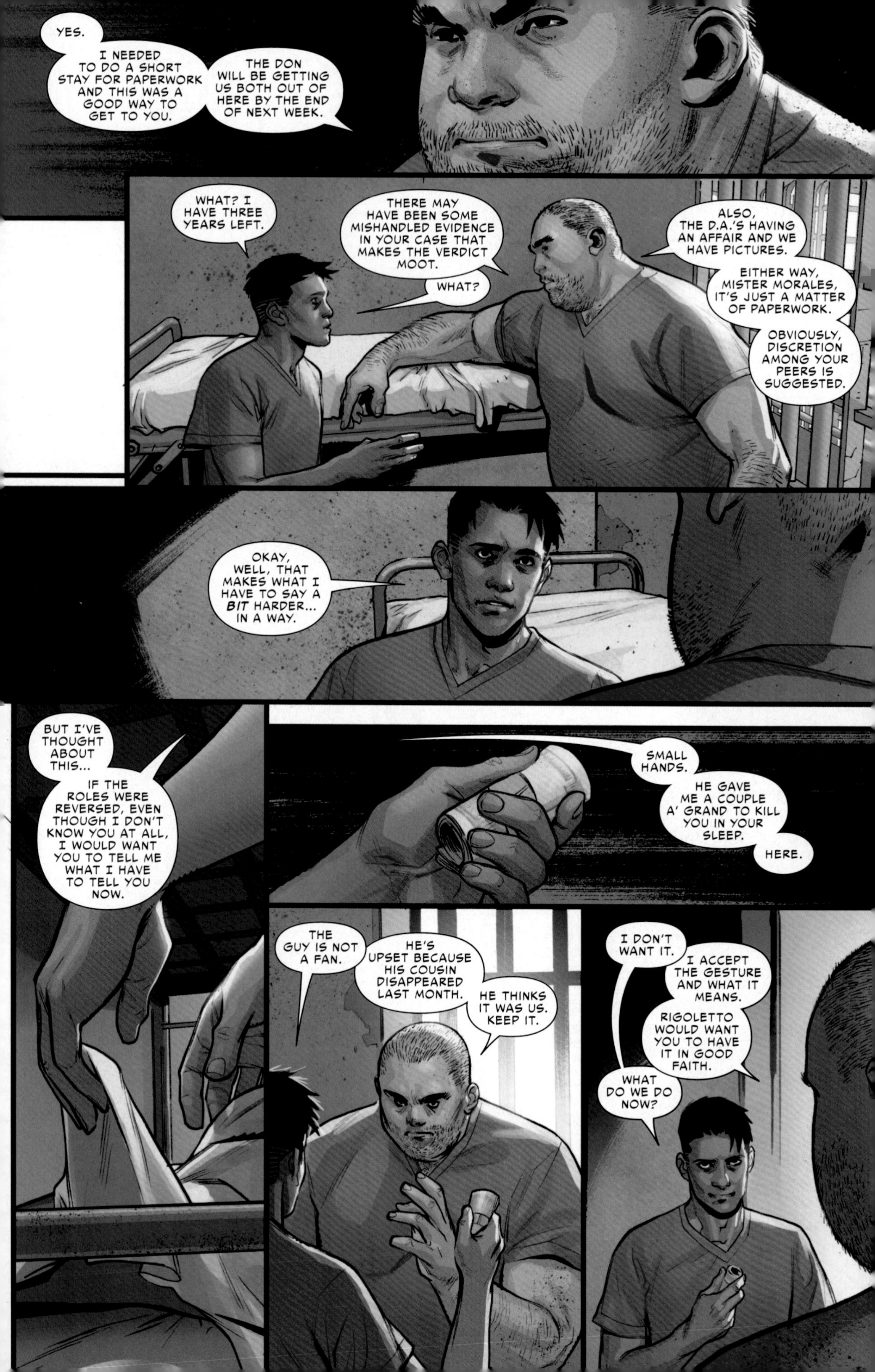
YES.
I NEEDED TO DO A SHORT STAY FOR PAPERWORK AND THIS WAS A GOOD WAY TO GET TO YOU.
THE DON WILL BE GETTING US BOTH OUT OF HERE BY THE END OF NEXT WEEK.
WHAT? I HAVE THREE YEARS LEFT.
THERE MAY HAVE BEEN SOME MISHANDLED EVIDENCE IN YOUR CASE THAT MAKES THE VERDICT MOOT.
WHAT?
ALSO, THE D.A.'S HAVING AN AFFAIR AND WE HAVE PICTURES.
EITHER WAY, MISTER MORALES, IT'S JUST A MATTER OF PAPERWORK.
OBVIOUSLY, DISCRETION AMONG YOUR PEERS IS SUGGESTED.
OKAY, WELL, THAT MAKES WHAT I HAVE TO SAY A BIT HARDER... IN A WAY.
BUT I'VE THOUGHT ABOUT THIS...
IF THE ROLES WERE REVERSED, EVEN THOUGH I DON'T KNOW YOU AT ALL, I WOULD WANT YOU TO TELL ME WHAT I HAVE TO TELL YOU NOW.
SMALL HANDS.
HE GAVE ME A COUPLE A' GRAND TO KILL YOU IN YOUR SLEEP.
HERE.
THE GUY IS NOT A FAN.
HE'S UPSET BECAUSE HIS COUSIN DISAPPEARED LAST MONTH.
HE THINKS IT WAS US. KEEP IT.
I DON'T WANT IT.
I ACCEPT THE GESTURE AND WHAT IT MEANS.
RIGOLETTO WOULD WANT YOU TO HAVE IT IN GOOD FAITH.
WHAT DO WE DO NOW?

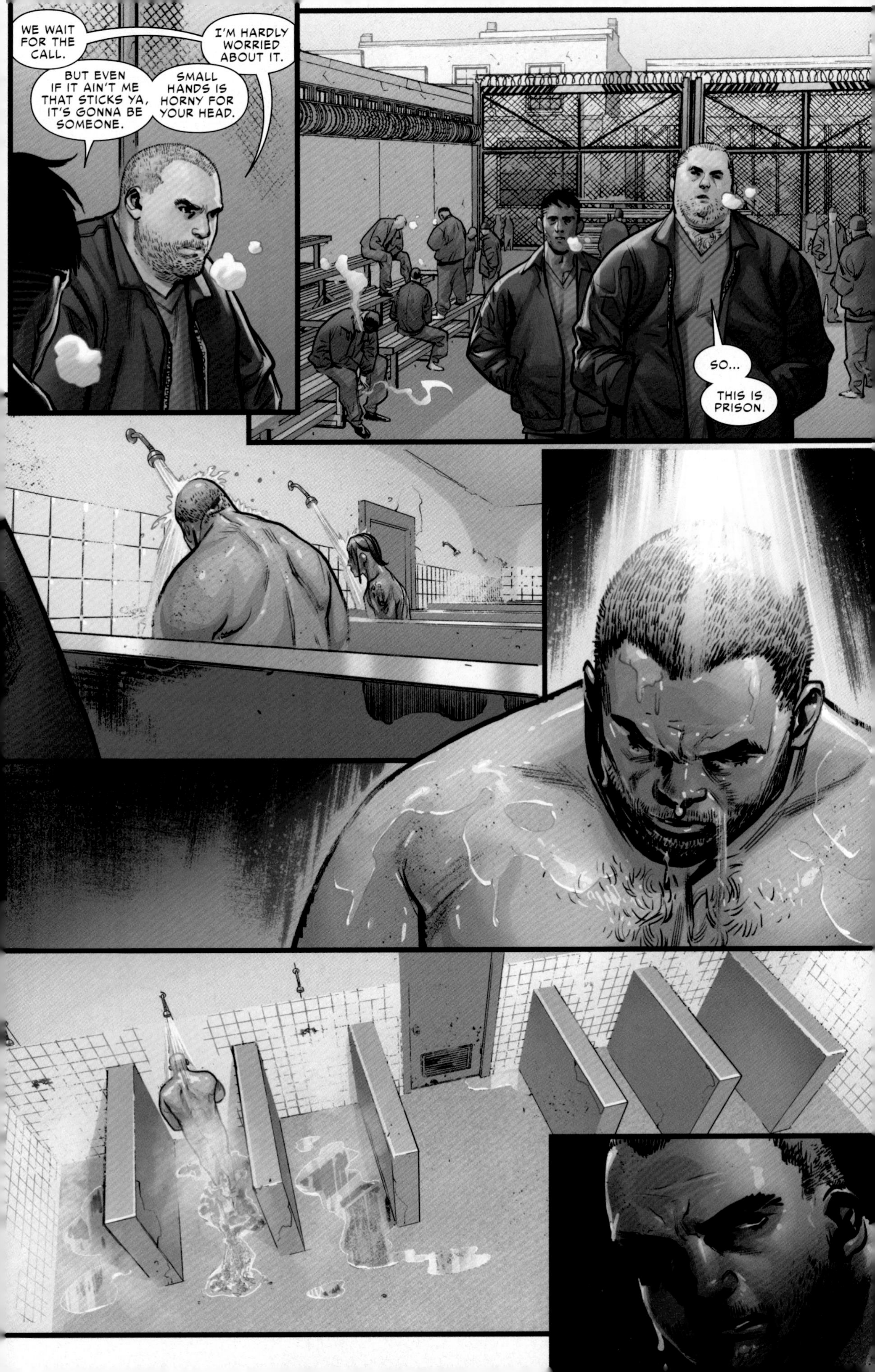
WE WAIT FOR THE CALL.
I'M HARDLY WORRIED ABOUT IT.
BUT EVEN IF IT AIN'T ME THAT STICKS YA, IT'S GONNA BE SOMEONE.
SMALL HANDS IS HORNY FOR YOUR HEAD.
SO...
THIS IS PRISON.

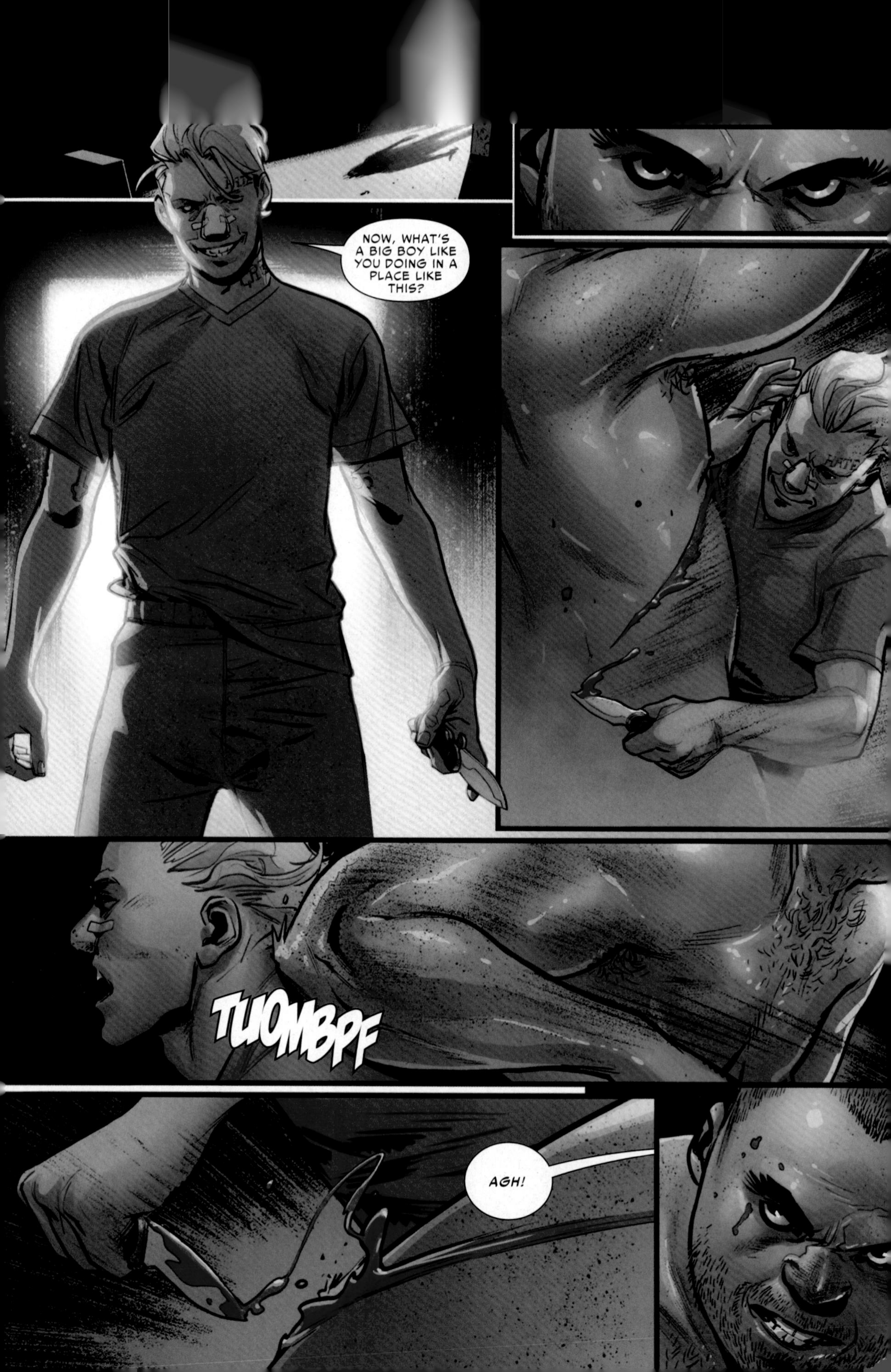
NOW, WHAT'S A BIG BOY LIKE YOU DOING IN A PLACE LIKE THIS?
TUOMBPF
AGH!

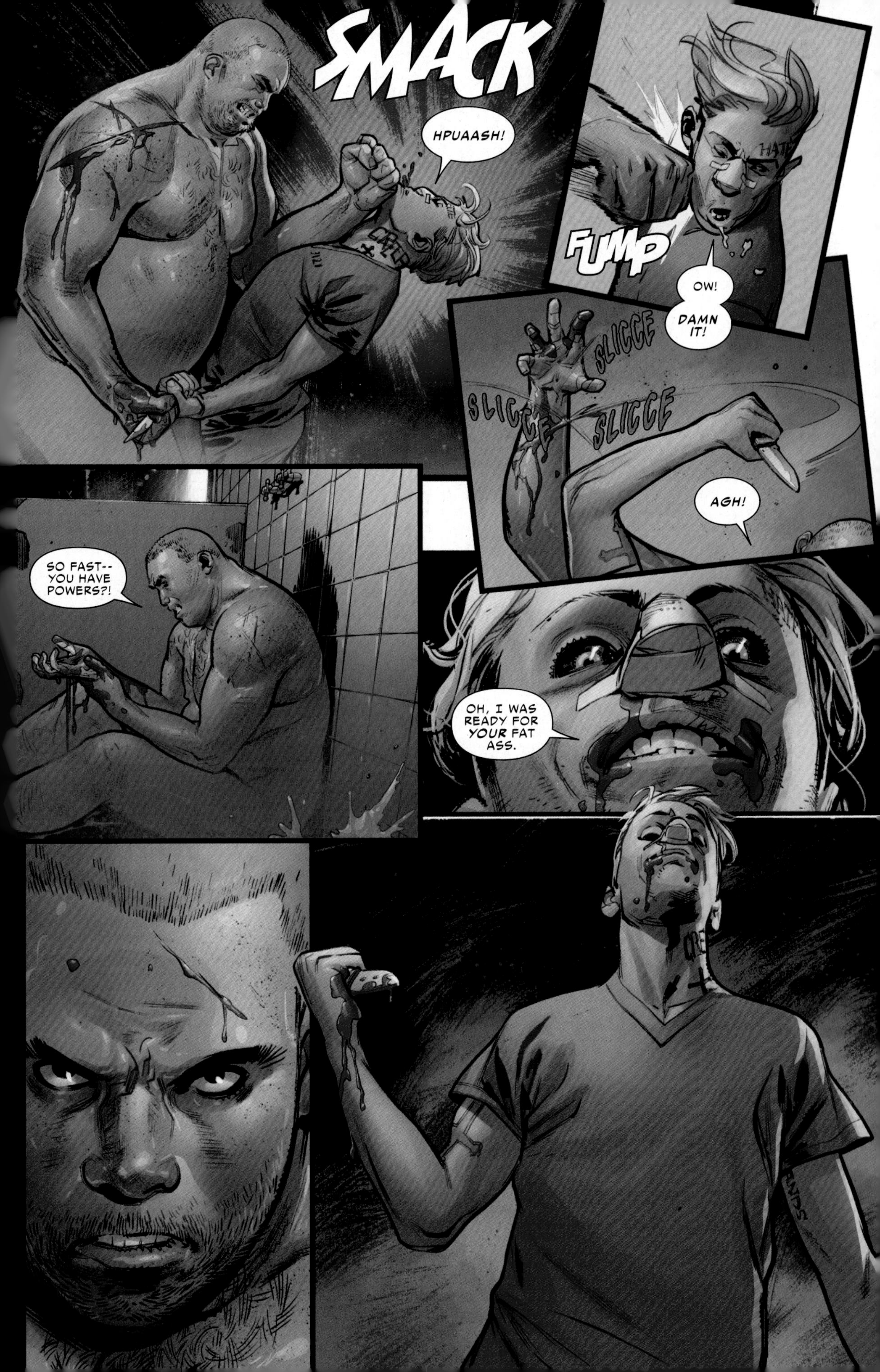
SMACK
HPUAASH!
FUMP
OW!
DAMN IT!
SLICCE
SLICCE
SLICCE
AGH!
SO FAST-- YOU HAVE POWERS?!
OH, I WAS READY FOR YOUR FAT ASS.

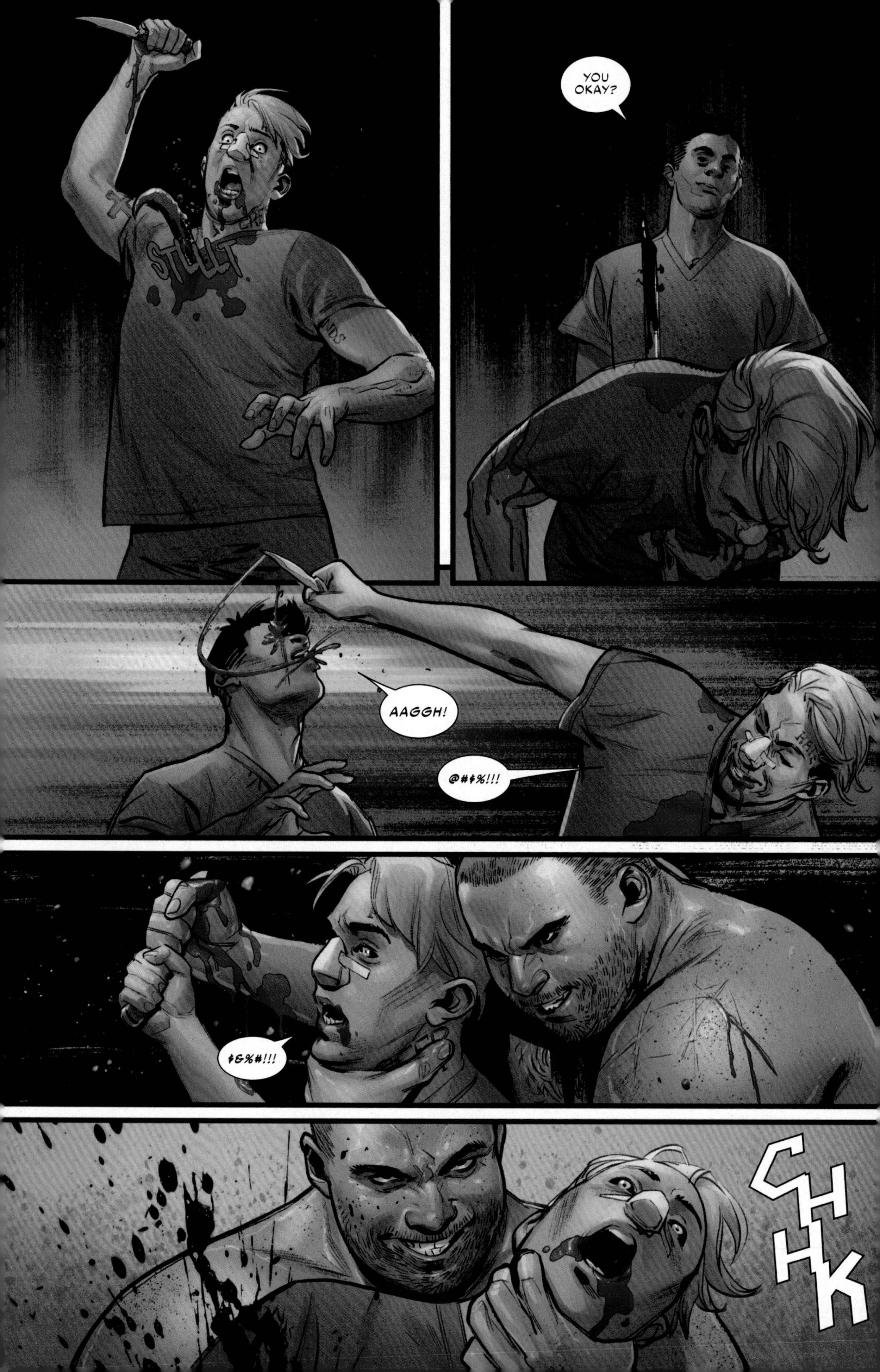

YOU OKAY?
AAGGH!
@#$%!!!
$&%#!!!
CHHK

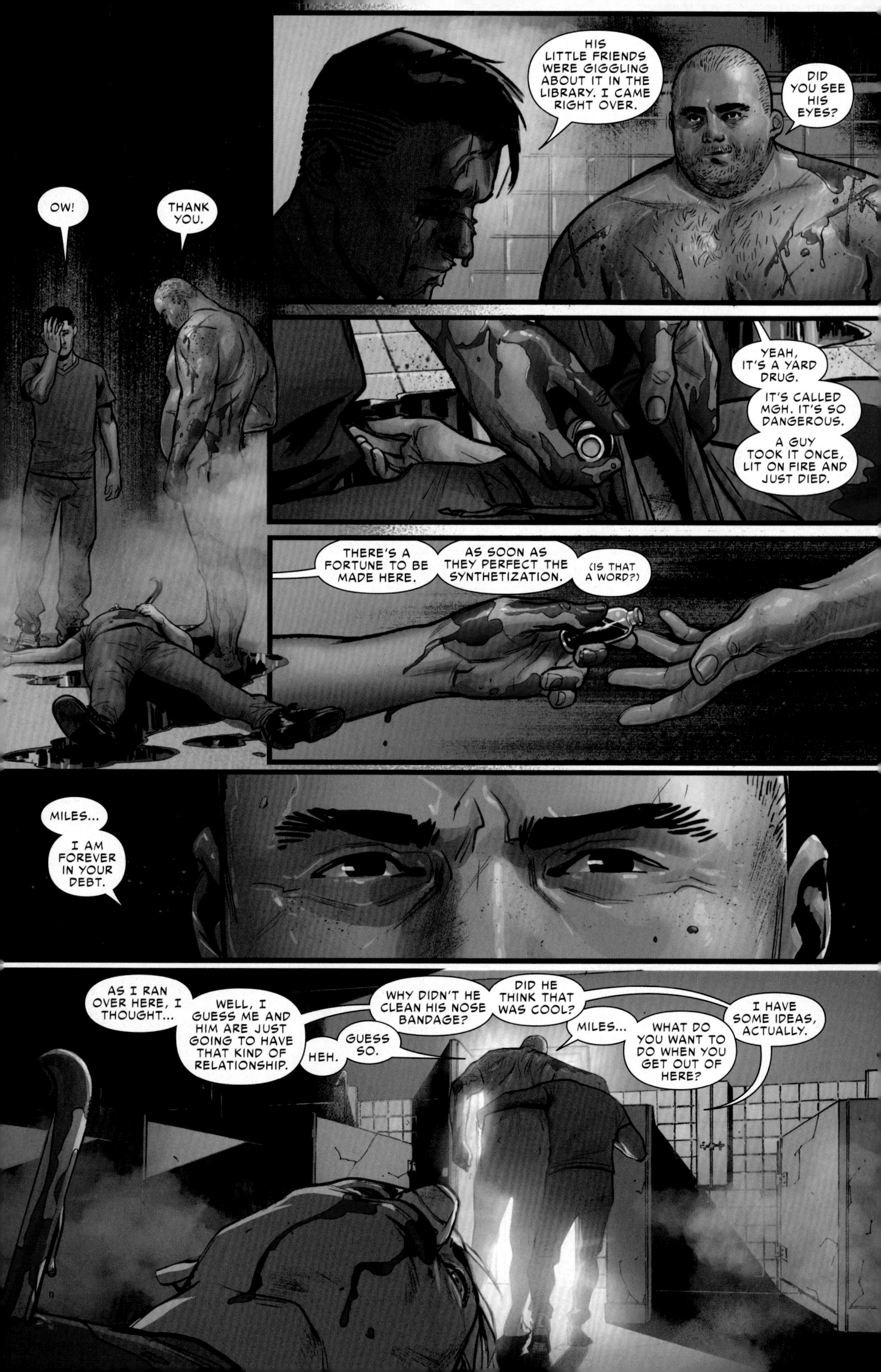
HIS LITTLE FRIENDS WERE GIGGLING ABOUT IT IN THE LIBRARY. I CAME RIGHT OVER.
DID YOU SEE HIS EYES?
OW!
THANK YOU.
YEAH, IT'S A YARD DRUG.
IT'S CALLED MGH. IT'S SO DANGEROUS.
A GUY TOOK IT ONCE, LIT ON FIRE AND JUST DIED.
THERE'S A FORTUNE TO BE MADE HERE.
AS SOON AS THEY PERFECT THE SYNTHETIZATION.
(IS THAT A WORD?)
MILES...
I AM FOREVER IN YOUR DEBT.
AS I RAN OVER HERE, I THOUGHT...
WELL, I GUESS ME AND HIM ARE JUST GOING TO HAVE THAT KIND OF RELATIONSHIP.
HEH.
GUESS SO.
WHY DIDN'T HE CLEAN HIS NOSE BANDAGE?
DID HE THINK THAT WAS COOL?
MILES...
WHAT DO YOU WANT TO DO WHEN YOU GET OUT OF HERE?
I HAVE SOME IDEAS, ACTUALLY.

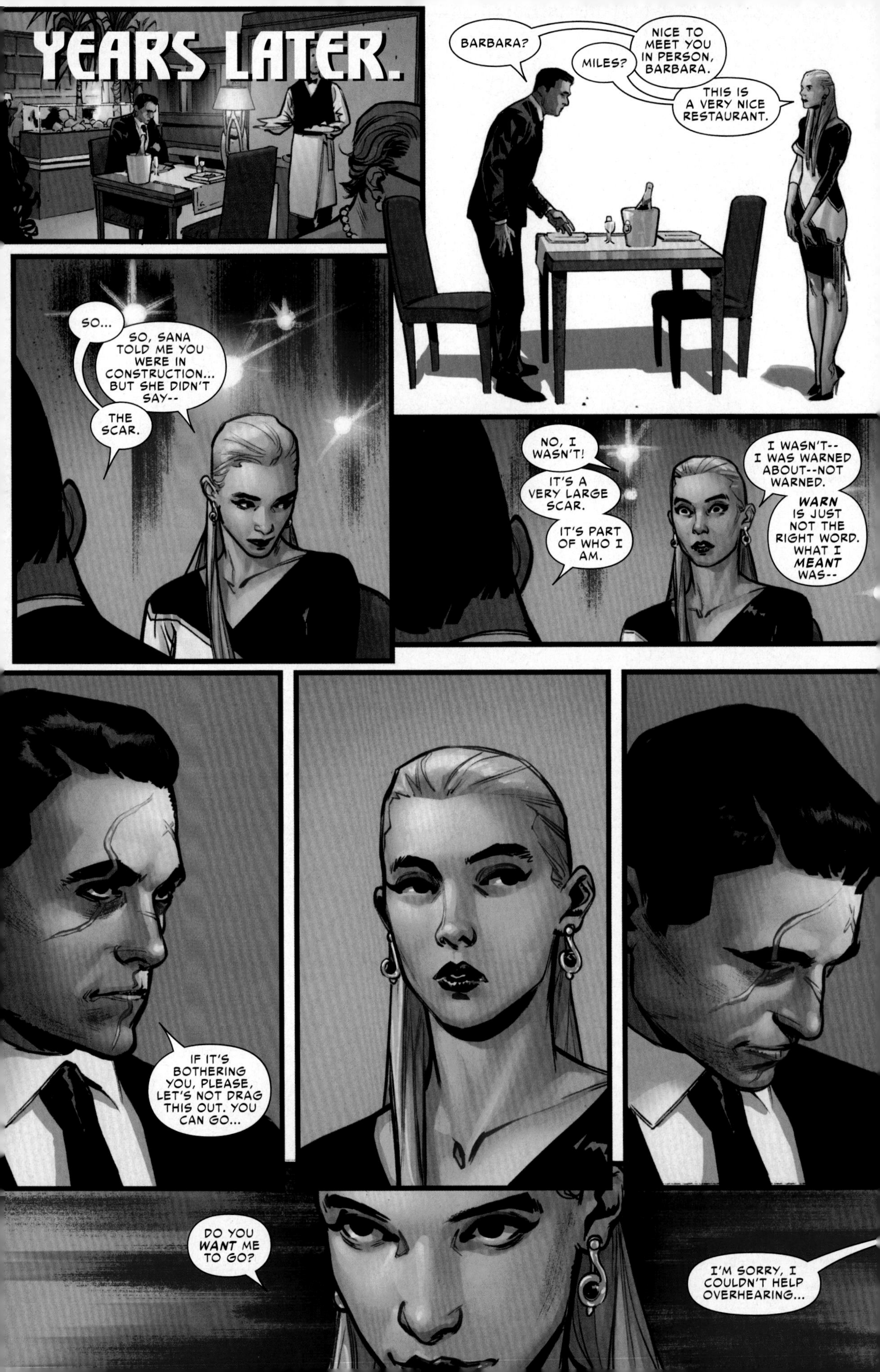
YEARS LATER.
BARBARA?
MILES?
NICE TO MEET YOU IN PERSON, BARBARA.
THIS IS A VERY NICE RESTAURANT.
SO...
SO, SANA TOLD ME YOU WERE IN CONSTRUCTION... BUT SHE DIDN'T SAY--
THE SCAR.
I WASN'T-- I WAS WARNED ABOUT--NOT WARNED.
WARN IS JUST NOT THE RIGHT WORD. WHAT I MEANT WAS--
NO, I WASN'T!
IT'S A VERY LARGE SCAR.
IT'S PART OF WHO I AM.
IF IT'S BOTHERING YOU, PLEASE, LET'S NOT DRAG THIS OUT. YOU CAN GO...
DO YOU WANT ME TO GO?
I'M SORRY, I COULDN'T HELP OVERHEARING...

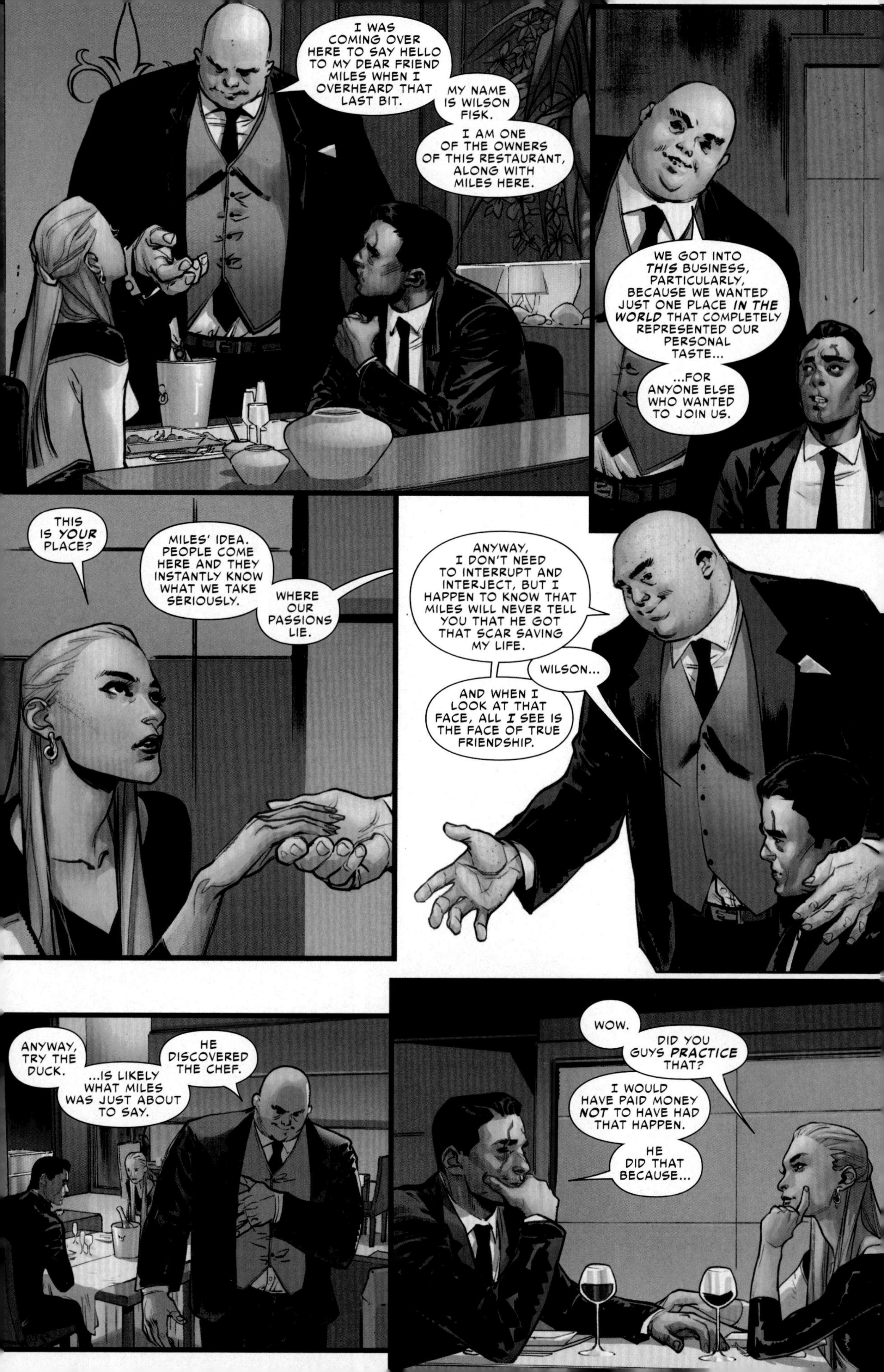
I WAS COMING OVER HERE TO SAY HELLO TO MY DEAR FRIEND MILES WHEN I OVERHEARD THAT LAST BIT.
MY NAME IS WILSON FISK.
I AM ONE OF THE OWNERS OF THIS RESTAURANT, ALONG WITH MILES HERE.
WE GOT INTO *THIS* BUSINESS, PARTICULARLY, BECAUSE WE WANTED JUST ONE PLACE *IN THE WORLD* THAT COMPLETELY REPRESENTED OUR PERSONAL TASTE...
...FOR ANYONE ELSE WHO WANTED TO JOIN US.
THIS IS *YOUR* PLACE?
MILES' IDEA. PEOPLE COME HERE AND THEY INSTANTLY KNOW WHAT WE TAKE SERIOUSLY.
WHERE OUR PASSIONS LIE.
ANYWAY, I DON'T NEED TO INTERRUPT AND INTERJECT, BUT I HAPPEN TO KNOW THAT MILES WILL NEVER TELL YOU THAT HE GOT THAT SCAR SAVING MY LIFE.
WILSON...
AND WHEN I LOOK AT THAT FACE, ALL *I* SEE IS THE FACE OF TRUE FRIENDSHIP.
ANYWAY, TRY THE DUCK.
HE DISCOVERED THE CHEF.
...IS LIKELY WHAT MILES WAS JUST ABOUT TO SAY.
WOW.
DID YOU GUYS *PRACTICE* THAT?
I WOULD HAVE PAID MONEY *NOT* TO HAVE HAD THAT HAPPEN.
HE DID THAT BECAUSE...

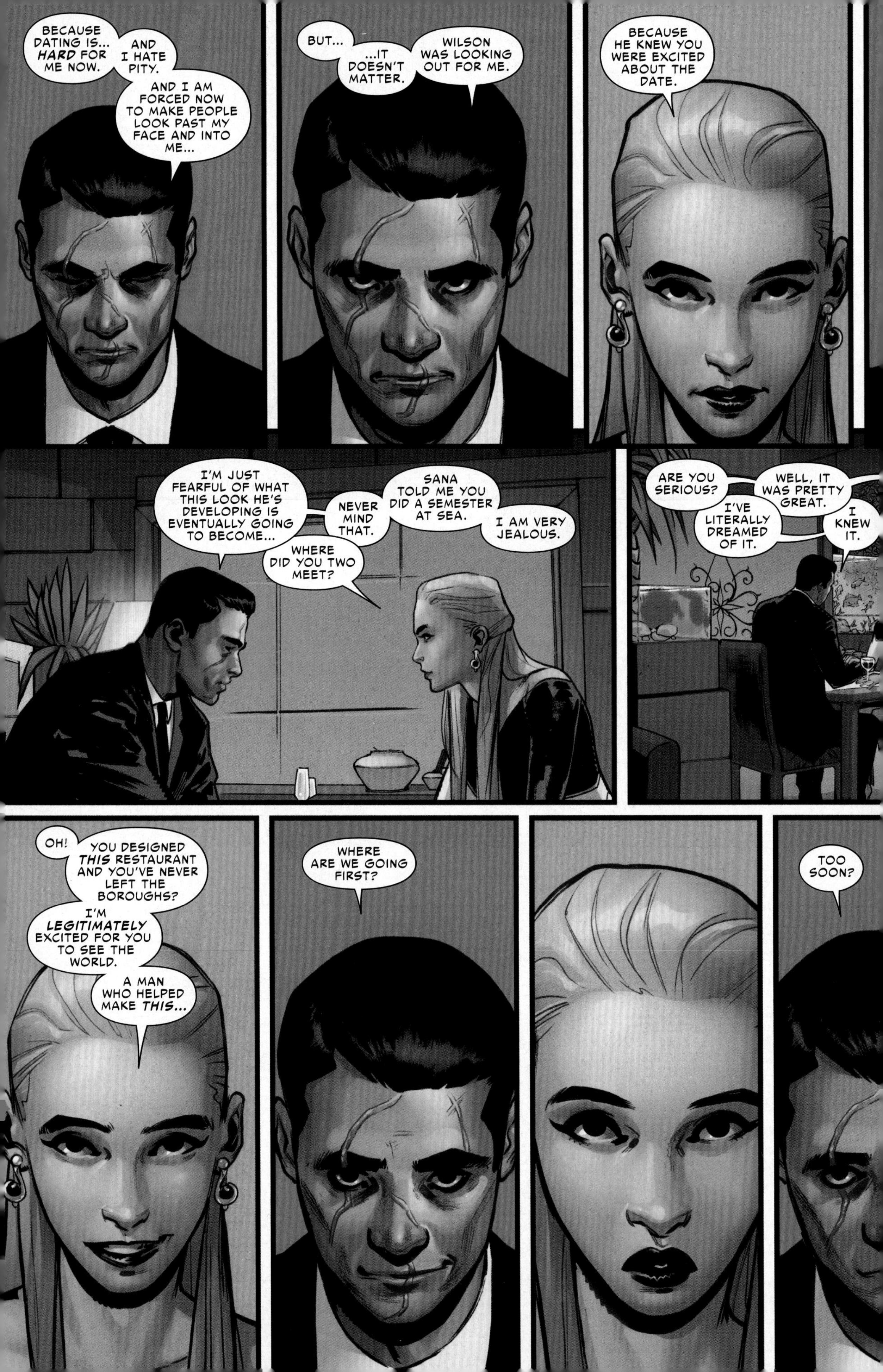

BECAUSE DATING IS... *HARD* FOR ME NOW.
AND I HATE PITY.
AND I AM FORCED NOW TO MAKE PEOPLE LOOK PAST MY FACE AND INTO ME...
BUT...
...IT DOESN'T MATTER.
WILSON WAS LOOKING OUT FOR ME.
BECAUSE HE KNEW YOU WERE EXCITED ABOUT THE DATE.
I'M JUST FEARFUL OF WHAT THIS LOOK HE'S DEVELOPING IS EVENTUALLY GOING TO BECOME...
NEVER MIND THAT.
WHERE DID YOU TWO MEET?
SANA TOLD ME YOU DID A SEMESTER AT SEA.
I AM VERY JEALOUS.
ARE YOU SERIOUS?
I'VE LITERALLY DREAMED OF IT.
WELL, IT WAS PRETTY GREAT.
I KNEW IT.
OH!
YOU DESIGNED *THIS* RESTAURANT AND YOU'VE NEVER LEFT THE BOROUGHS?
I'M *LEGITIMATELY* EXCITED FOR YOU TO SEE THE WORLD.
A MAN WHO HELPED MAKE *THIS*...
WHERE ARE WE GOING FIRST?
TOO SOON?

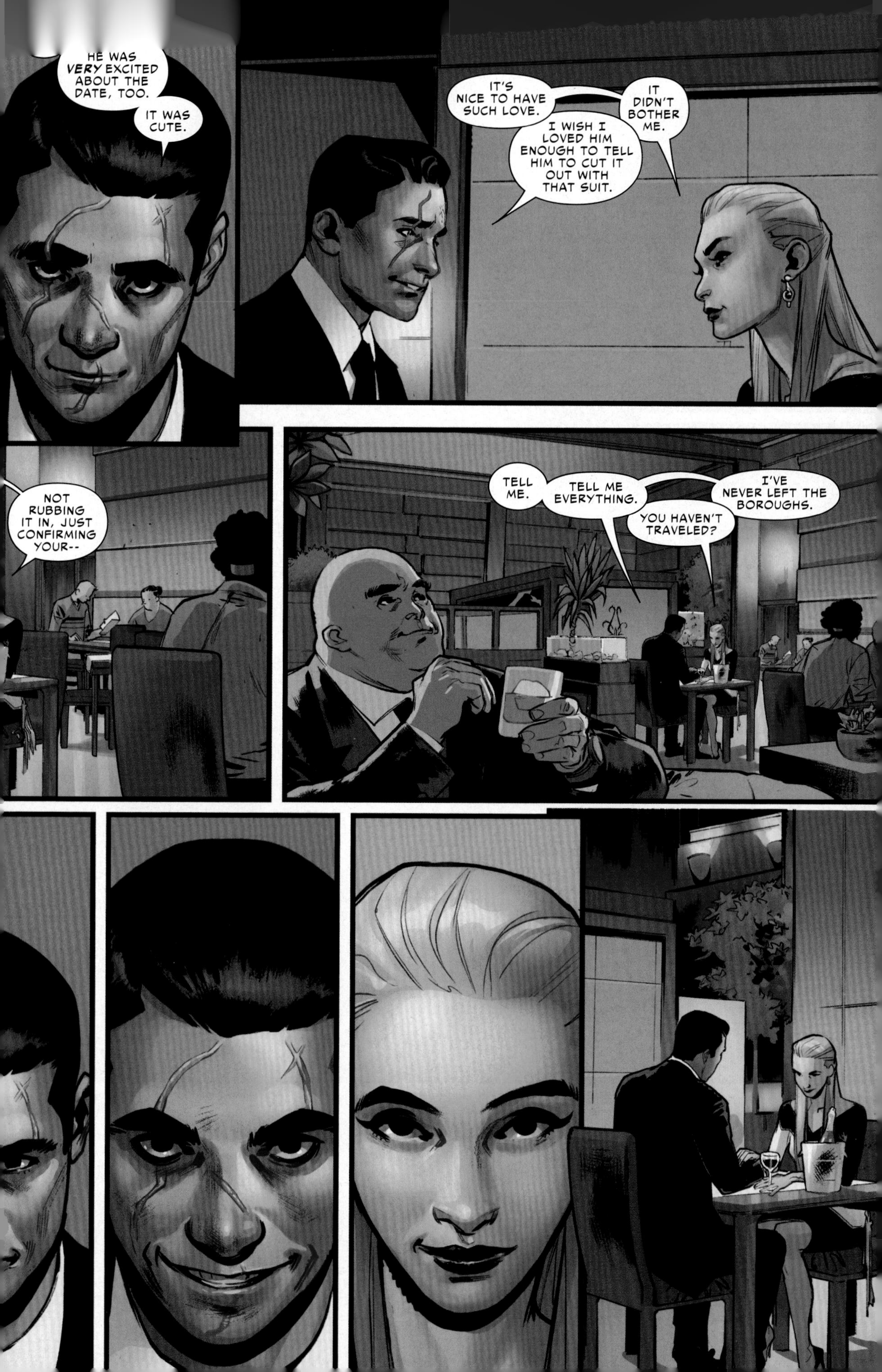
HE WAS VERY EXCITED ABOUT THE DATE, TOO.
IT WAS CUTE.
IT'S NICE TO HAVE SUCH LOVE.
IT DIDN'T BOTHER ME.
I WISH I LOVED HIM ENOUGH TO TELL HIM TO CUT IT OUT WITH THAT SUIT.
NOT RUBBING IT IN, JUST CONFIRMING YOUR--
TELL ME.
TELL ME EVERYTHING.
I'VE NEVER LEFT THE BOROUGHS.
YOU HAVEN'T TRAVELED?

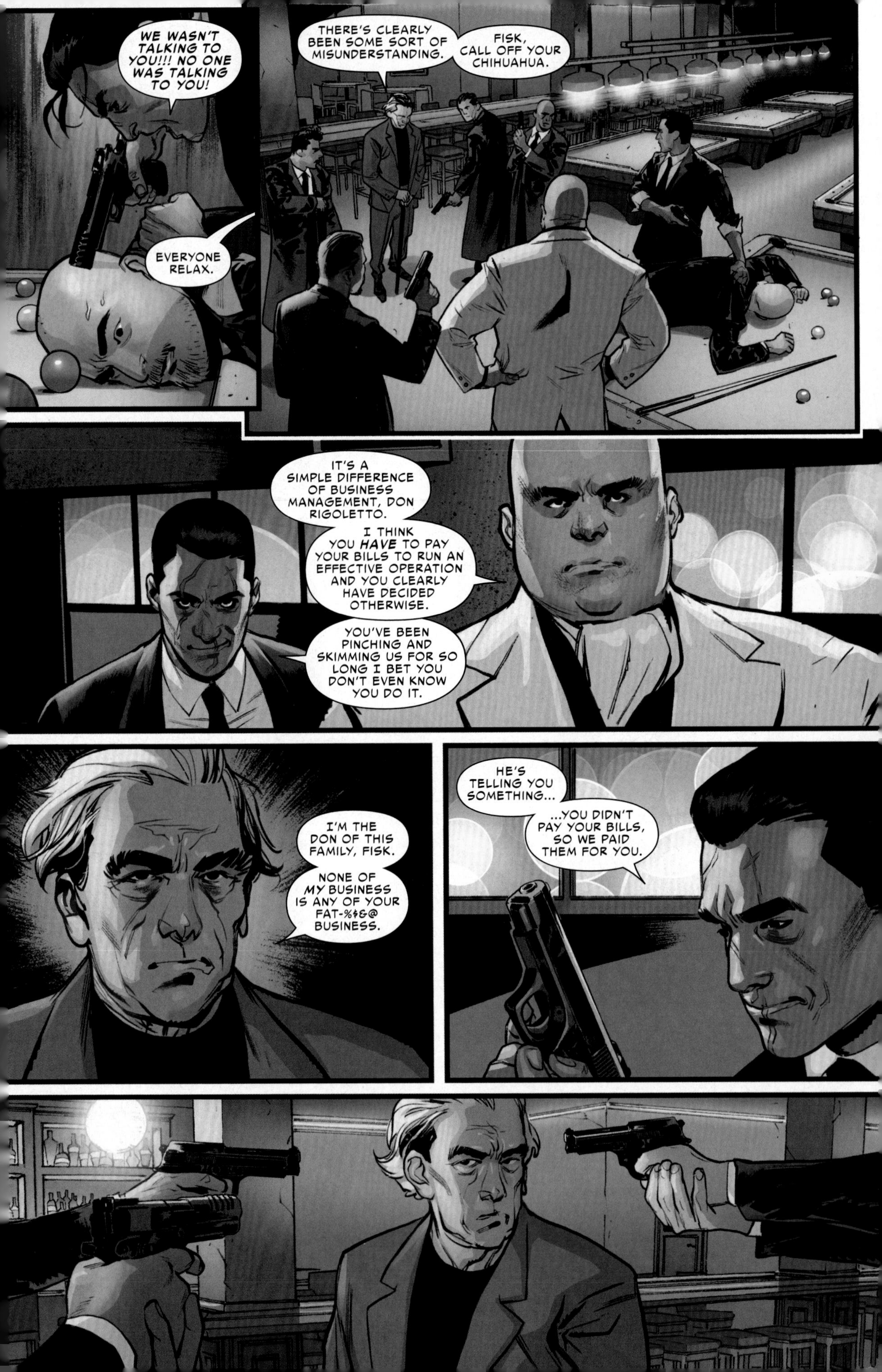
WE WASN'T TALKING TO YOU!!! NO ONE WAS TALKING TO YOU!
EVERYONE RELAX.
THERE'S CLEARLY BEEN SOME SORT OF MISUNDERSTANDING.
FISK, CALL OFF YOUR CHIHUAHUA.
IT'S A SIMPLE DIFFERENCE OF BUSINESS MANAGEMENT, DON RIGOLETTO.
I THINK YOU HAVE TO PAY YOUR BILLS TO RUN AN EFFECTIVE OPERATION AND YOU CLEARLY HAVE DECIDED OTHERWISE.
YOU'VE BEEN PINCHING AND SKIMMING US FOR SO LONG I BET YOU DON'T EVEN KNOW YOU DO IT.
I'M THE DON OF THIS FAMILY, FISK.
NONE OF MY BUSINESS IS ANY OF YOUR FAT-%$&@ BUSINESS.
HE'S TELLING YOU SOMETHING...
...YOU DIDN'T PAY YOUR BILLS, SO WE PAID THEM FOR YOU.

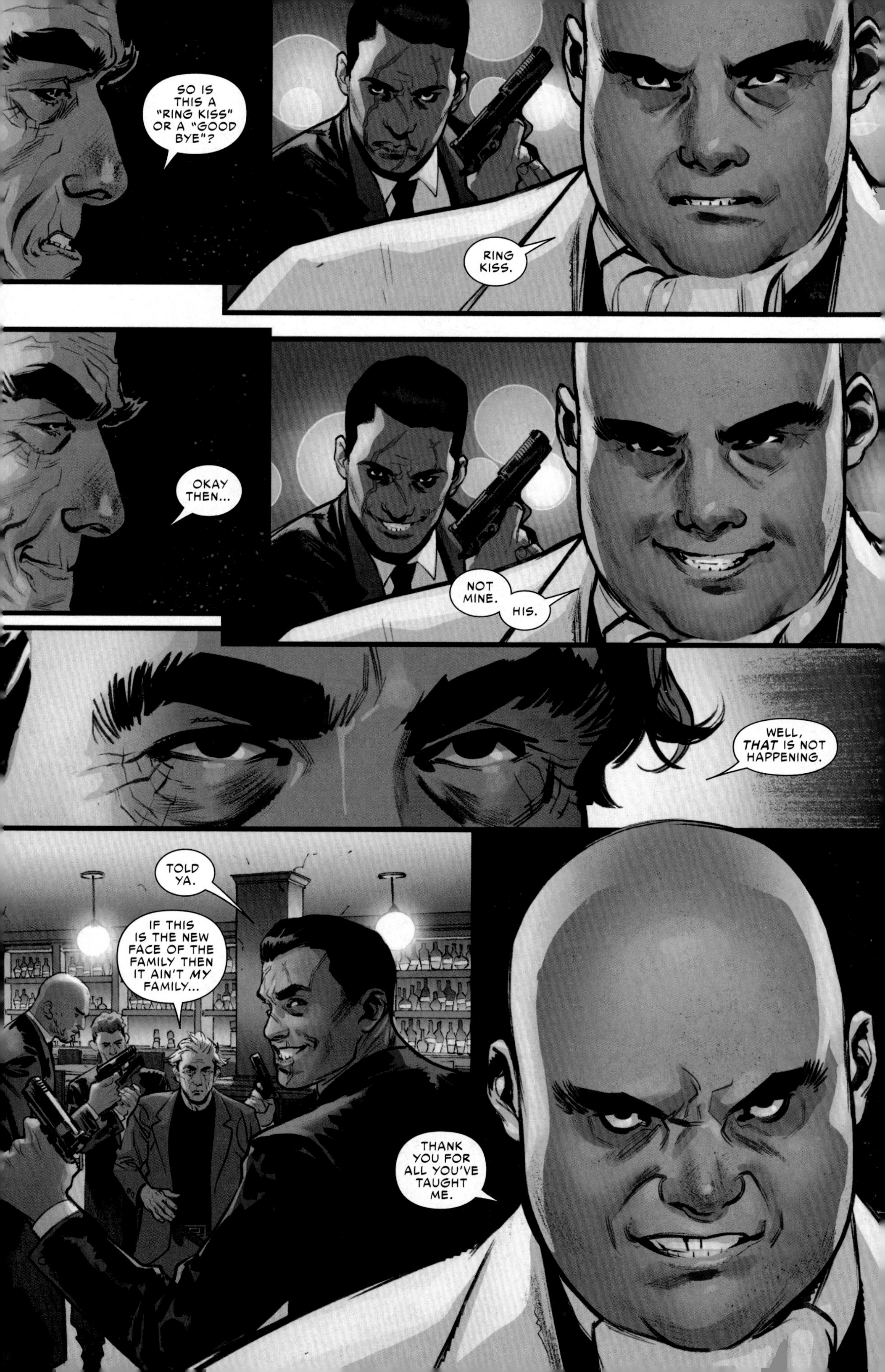
SO IS THIS A "RING KISS" OR A "GOOD BYE"?
RING KISS.
OKAY THEN...
NOT MINE.
HIS.
WELL, *THAT* IS NOT HAPPENING.
TOLD YA.
IF THIS IS THE NEW FACE OF THE FAMILY THEN IT AIN'T *MY* FAMILY...
THANK YOU FOR ALL YOU'VE TAUGHT ME.

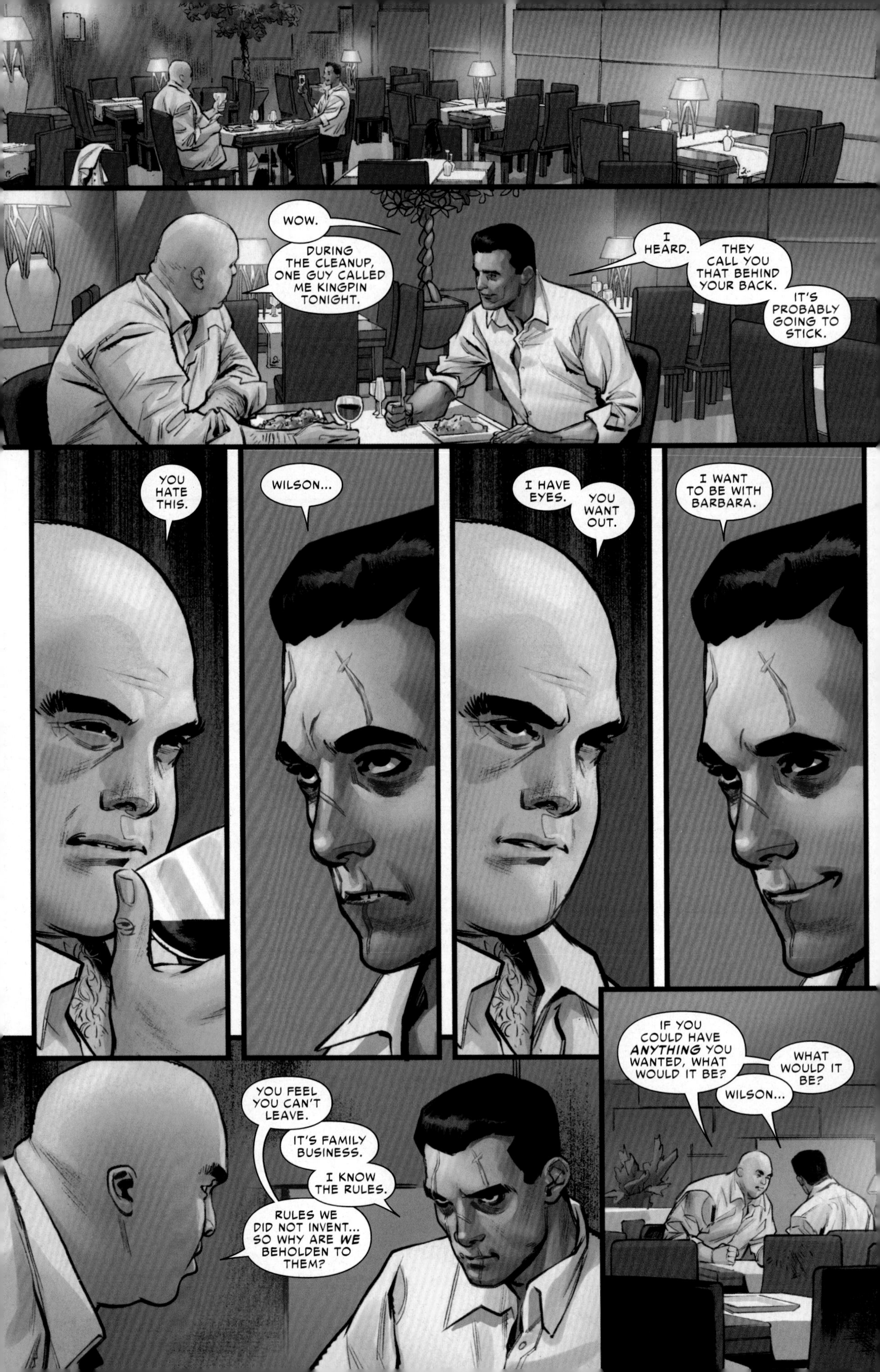
WOW.
DURING THE CLEANUP, ONE GUY CALLED ME KINGPIN TONIGHT.
I HEARD.
THEY CALL YOU THAT BEHIND YOUR BACK.
IT'S PROBABLY GOING TO STICK.
YOU HATE THIS.
WILSON...
I HAVE EYES.
YOU WANT OUT.
I WANT TO BE WITH BARBARA.
YOU FEEL YOU CAN'T LEAVE.
IT'S FAMILY BUSINESS.
I KNOW THE RULES.
RULES WE DID NOT INVENT... SO WHY ARE *WE* BEHOLDEN TO THEM?
IF YOU COULD HAVE *ANYTHING* YOU WANTED, WHAT WOULD IT BE?
WILSON...
WHAT WOULD IT BE?

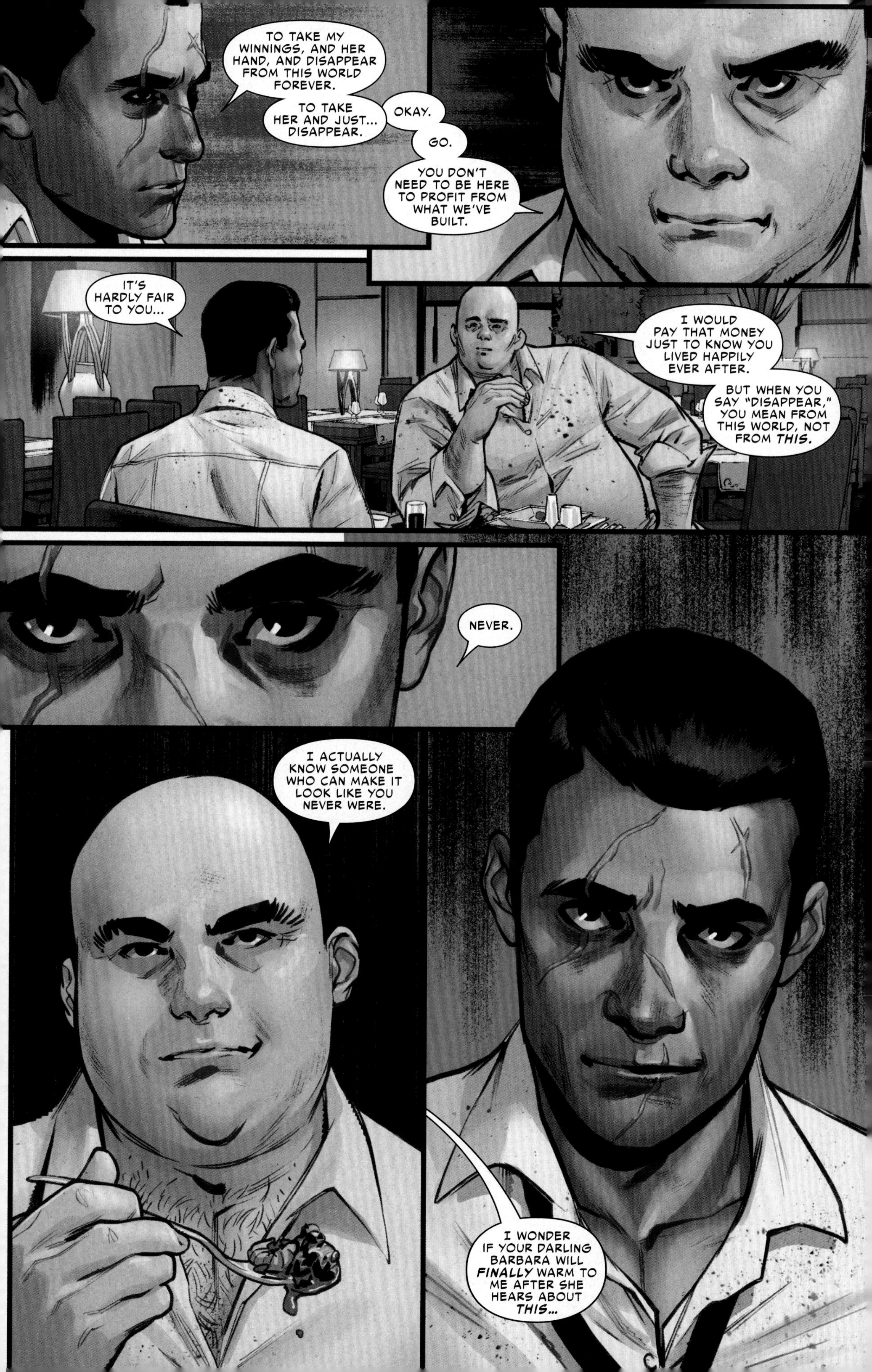
TO TAKE MY WINNINGS, AND HER HAND, AND DISAPPEAR FROM THIS WORLD FOREVER.
TO TAKE HER AND JUST... DISAPPEAR.
OKAY.
GO.
YOU DON'T NEED TO BE HERE TO PROFIT FROM WHAT WE'VE BUILT.
IT'S HARDLY FAIR TO YOU...
I WOULD PAY THAT MONEY JUST TO KNOW YOU LIVED HAPPILY EVER AFTER.
BUT WHEN YOU SAY "DISAPPEAR," YOU MEAN FROM THIS WORLD, NOT FROM *THIS.*
NEVER.
I ACTUALLY KNOW SOMEONE WHO CAN MAKE IT LOOK LIKE YOU NEVER WERE.
I WONDER IF YOUR DARLING BARBARA WILL *FINALLY* WARM TO ME AFTER SHE HEARS ABOUT *THIS...*

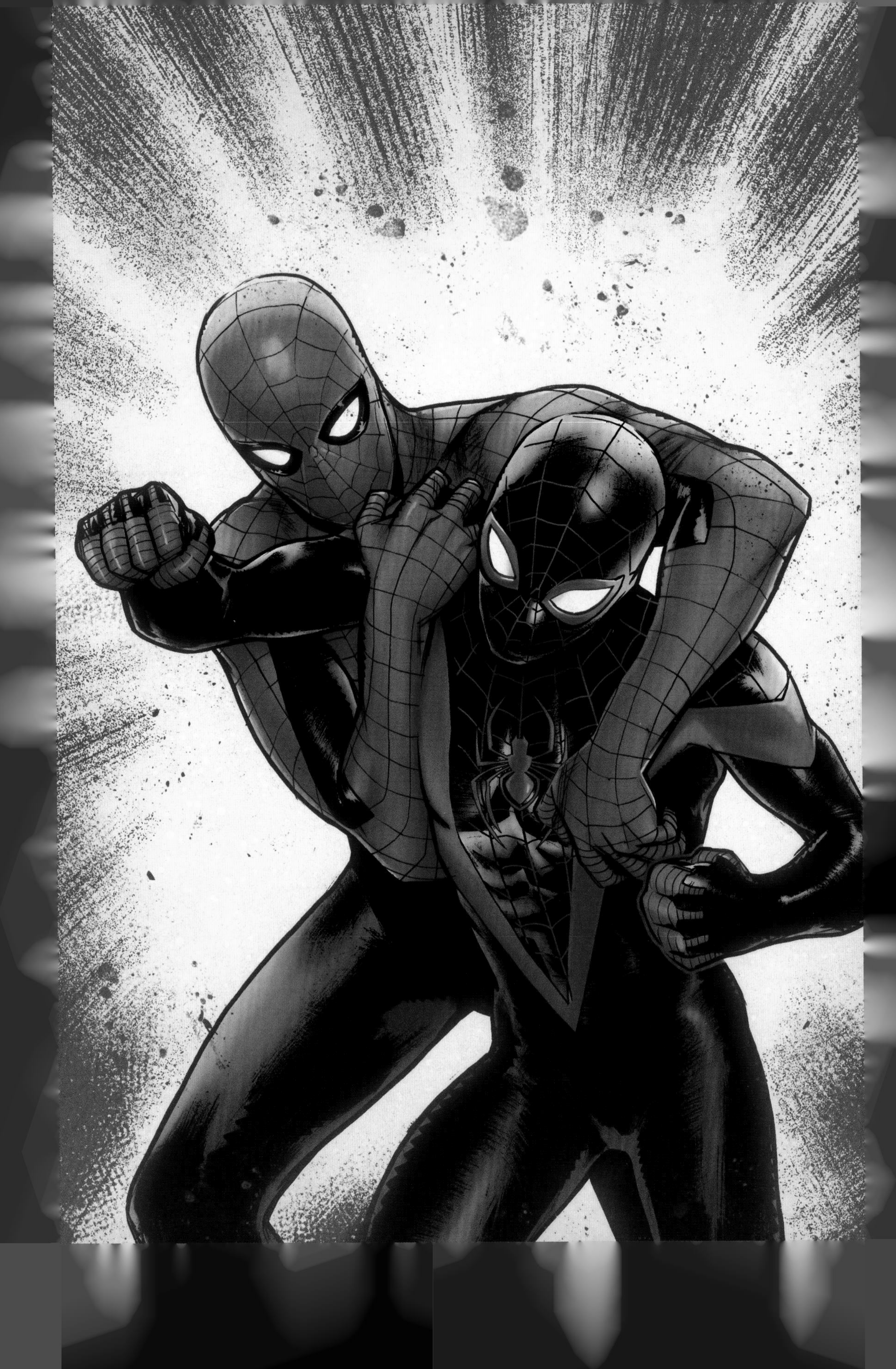

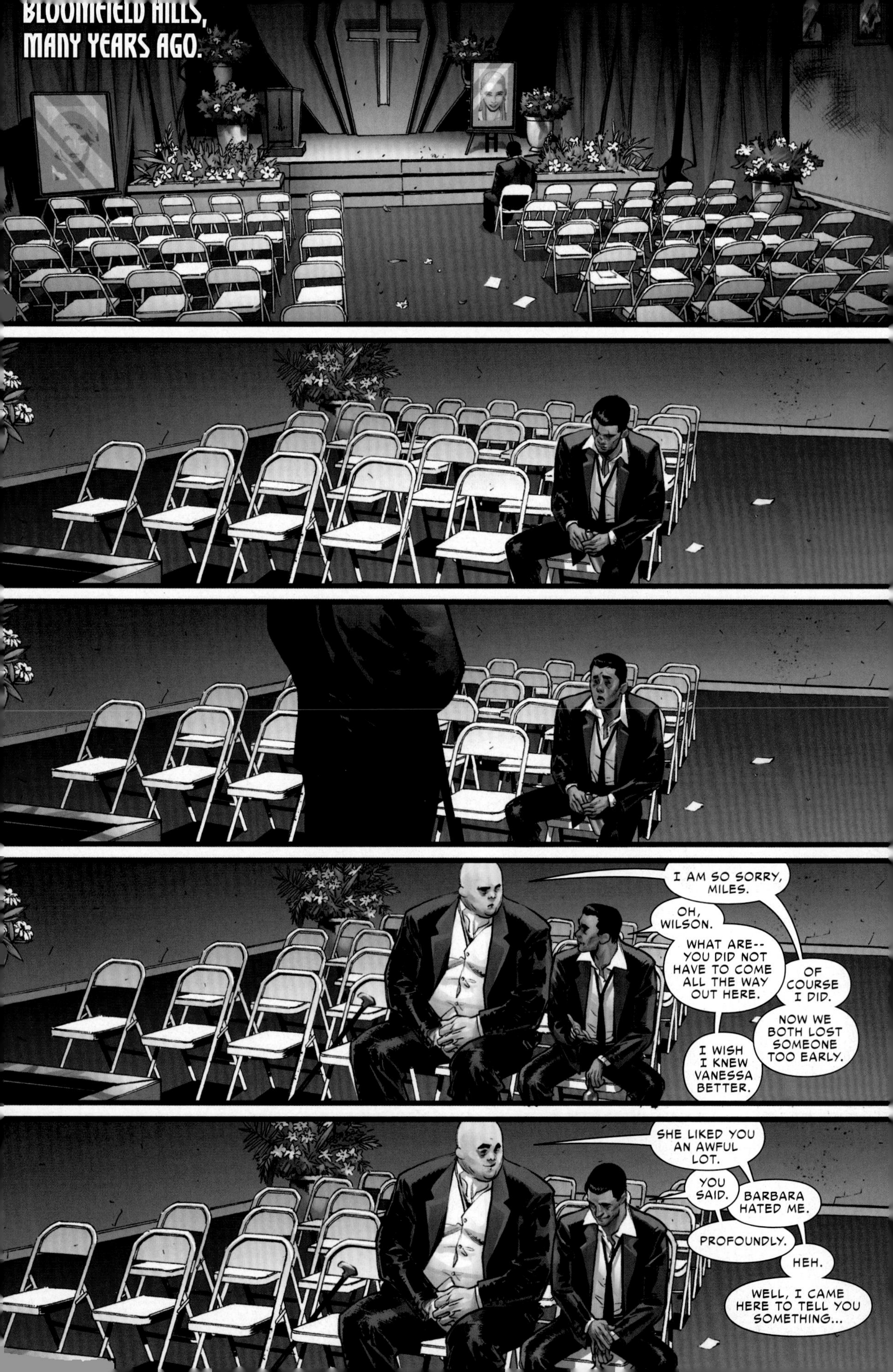
BLOOMFIELD HILLS, MANY YEARS AGO.
I AM SO SORRY, MILES.
OH, WILSON.
WHAT ARE-- YOU DID NOT HAVE TO COME ALL THE WAY OUT HERE.
OF COURSE I DID.
NOW WE BOTH LOST SOMEONE TOO EARLY.
I WISH I KNEW VANESSA BETTER.
SHE LIKED YOU AN AWFUL LOT.
YOU SAID.
BARBARA HATED ME.
PROFOUNDLY.
HEH.
WELL, I CAME HERE TO TELL YOU SOMETHING...

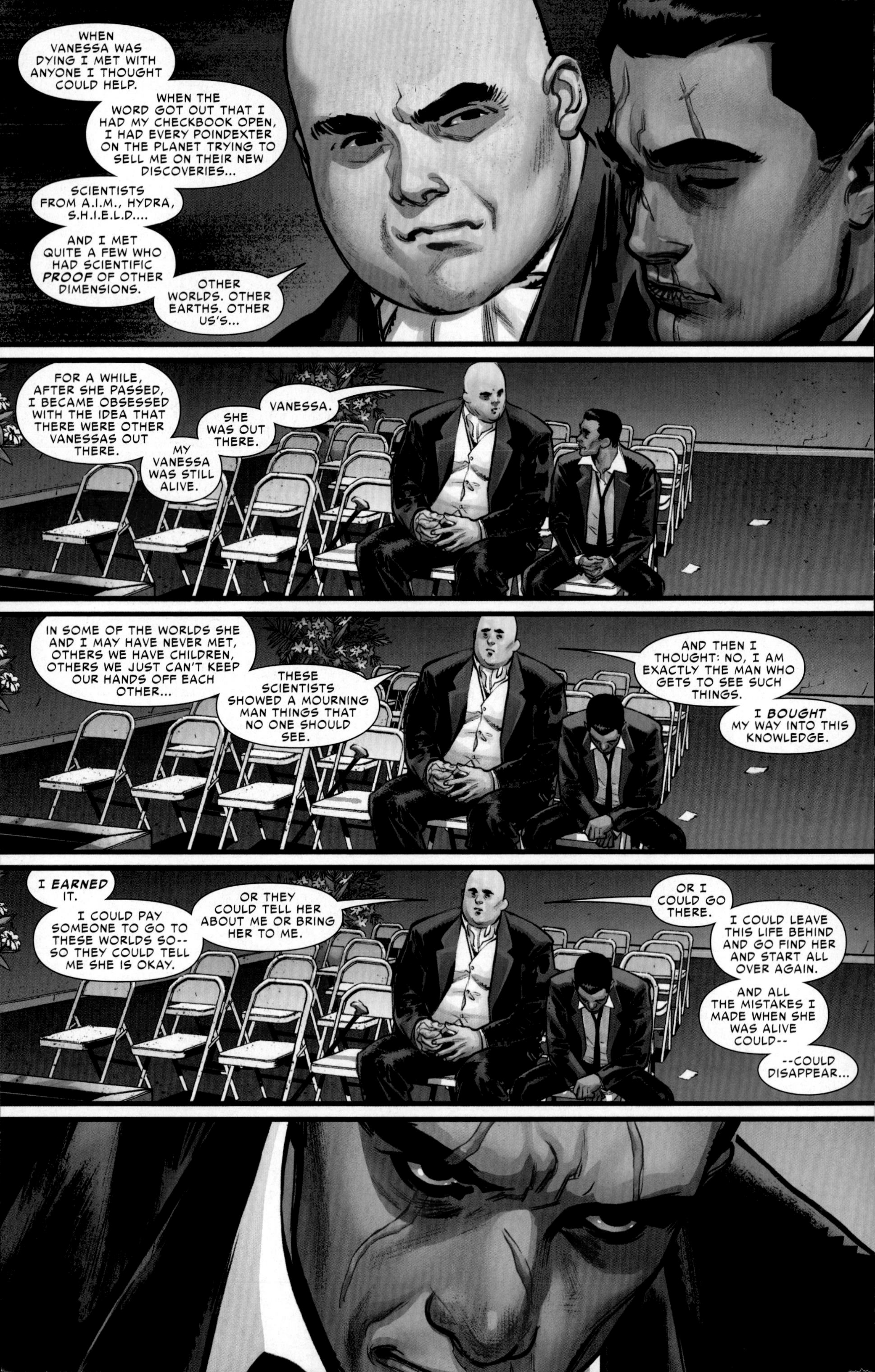

WHEN VANESSA WAS DYING I MET WITH ANYONE I THOUGHT COULD HELP.
WHEN THE WORD GOT OUT THAT I HAD MY CHECKBOOK OPEN, I HAD EVERY POINDEXTER ON THE PLANET TRYING TO SELL ME ON THEIR NEW DISCOVERIES...
SCIENTISTS FROM A.I.M., HYDRA, S.H.I.E.L.D....
AND I MET QUITE A FEW WHO HAD SCIENTIFIC *PROOF* OF OTHER DIMENSIONS.
OTHER WORLDS. OTHER EARTHS. OTHER US'S...
FOR A WHILE, AFTER SHE PASSED, I BECAME OBSESSED WITH THE IDEA THAT THERE WERE OTHER VANESSAS OUT THERE.
MY VANESSA WAS STILL ALIVE.
SHE WAS OUT THERE.
VANESSA.
IN SOME OF THE WORLDS SHE AND I MAY HAVE NEVER MET, OTHERS WE HAVE CHILDREN, OTHERS WE JUST CAN'T KEEP OUR HANDS OFF EACH OTHER...
THESE SCIENTISTS SHOWED A MOURNING MAN THINGS THAT NO ONE SHOULD SEE.
AND THEN I THOUGHT: NO, I AM EXACTLY THE MAN WHO GETS TO SEE SUCH THINGS.
I *BOUGHT* MY WAY INTO THIS KNOWLEDGE.
I *EARNED* IT.
I COULD PAY SOMEONE TO GO TO THESE WORLDS SO-- SO THEY COULD TELL ME SHE IS OKAY.
OR THEY COULD TELL HER ABOUT ME OR BRING HER TO ME.
OR I COULD GO THERE.
I COULD LEAVE THIS LIFE BEHIND AND GO FIND HER AND START ALL OVER AGAIN.
AND ALL THE MISTAKES I MADE WHEN SHE WAS ALIVE COULD--
--COULD DISAPPEAR...

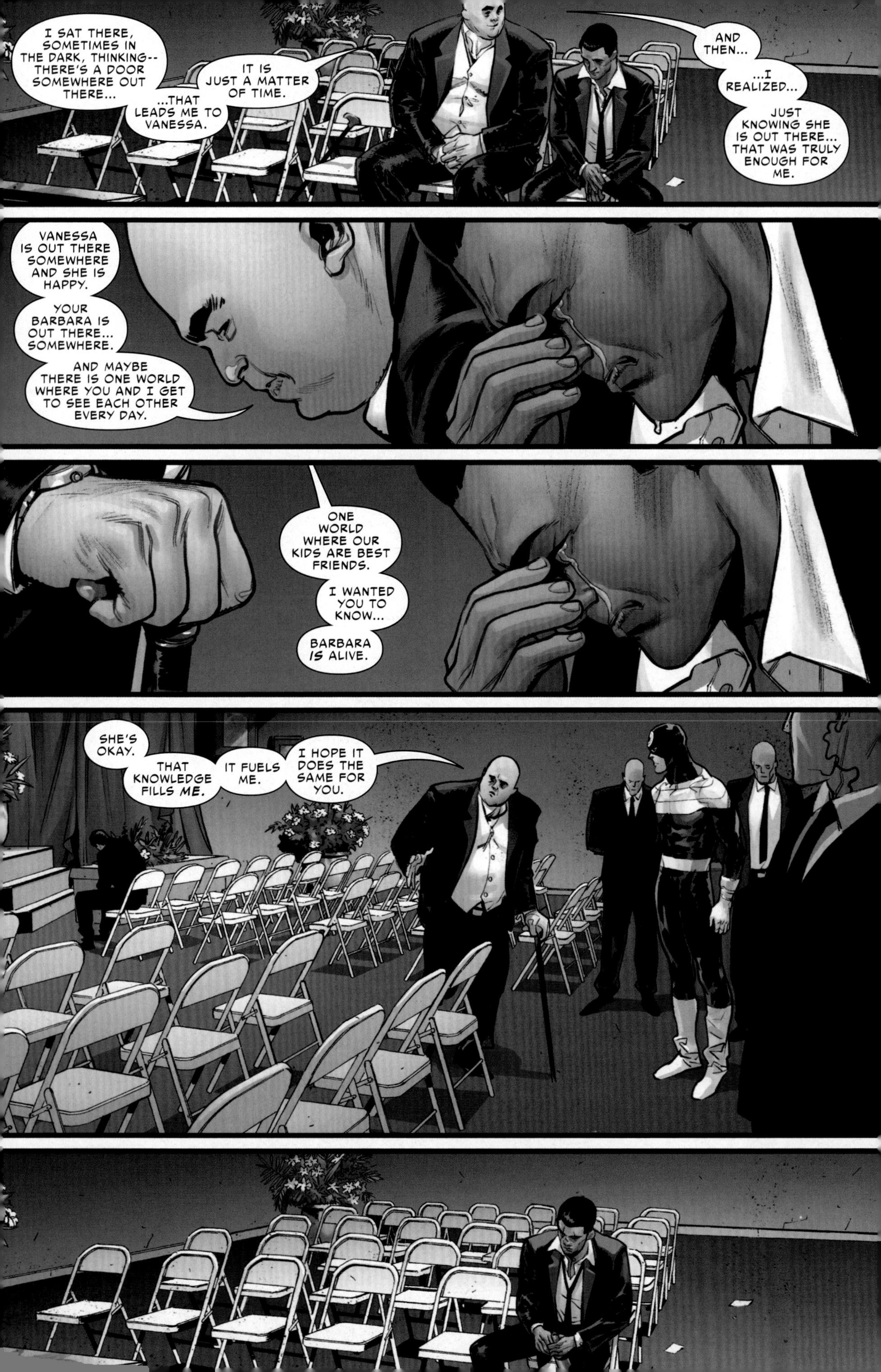
I SAT THERE, SOMETIMES IN THE DARK, THINKING-- THERE'S A DOOR SOMEWHERE OUT THERE...
...THAT LEADS ME TO VANESSA.
IT IS JUST A MATTER OF TIME.
AND THEN...
...I REALIZED...
JUST KNOWING SHE IS OUT THERE... THAT WAS TRULY ENOUGH FOR ME.
VANESSA IS OUT THERE SOMEWHERE AND SHE IS HAPPY.
YOUR BARBARA IS OUT THERE... SOMEWHERE.
AND MAYBE THERE IS ONE WORLD WHERE YOU AND I GET TO SEE EACH OTHER EVERY DAY.
ONE WORLD WHERE OUR KIDS ARE BEST FRIENDS.
I WANTED YOU TO KNOW...
BARBARA *IS* ALIVE.
SHE'S OKAY.
THAT KNOWLEDGE FILLS *ME.*
IT FUELS ME.
I HOPE IT DOES THE SAME FOR YOU.

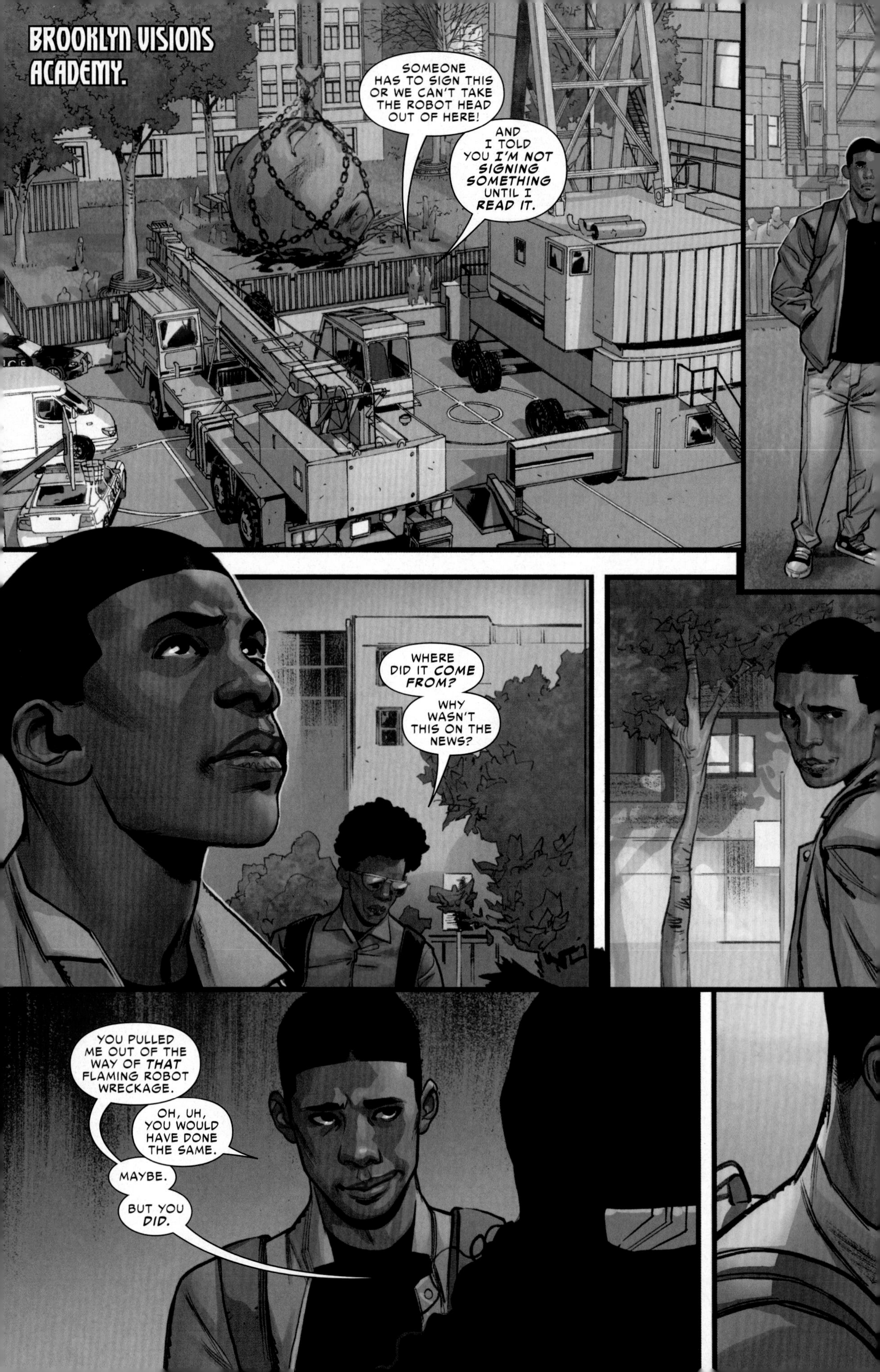
BROOKLYN VISIONS ACADEMY.
SOMEONE HAS TO SIGN THIS OR WE CAN'T TAKE THE ROBOT HEAD OUT OF HERE!
AND I TOLD YOU I'M NOT SIGNING SOMETHING UNTIL I READ IT.
WHERE DID IT COME FROM?
WHY WASN'T THIS ON THE NEWS?
YOU PULLED ME OUT OF THE WAY OF THAT FLAMING ROBOT WRECKAGE.
OH, UH, YOU WOULD HAVE DONE THE SAME.
MAYBE.
BUT YOU DID.

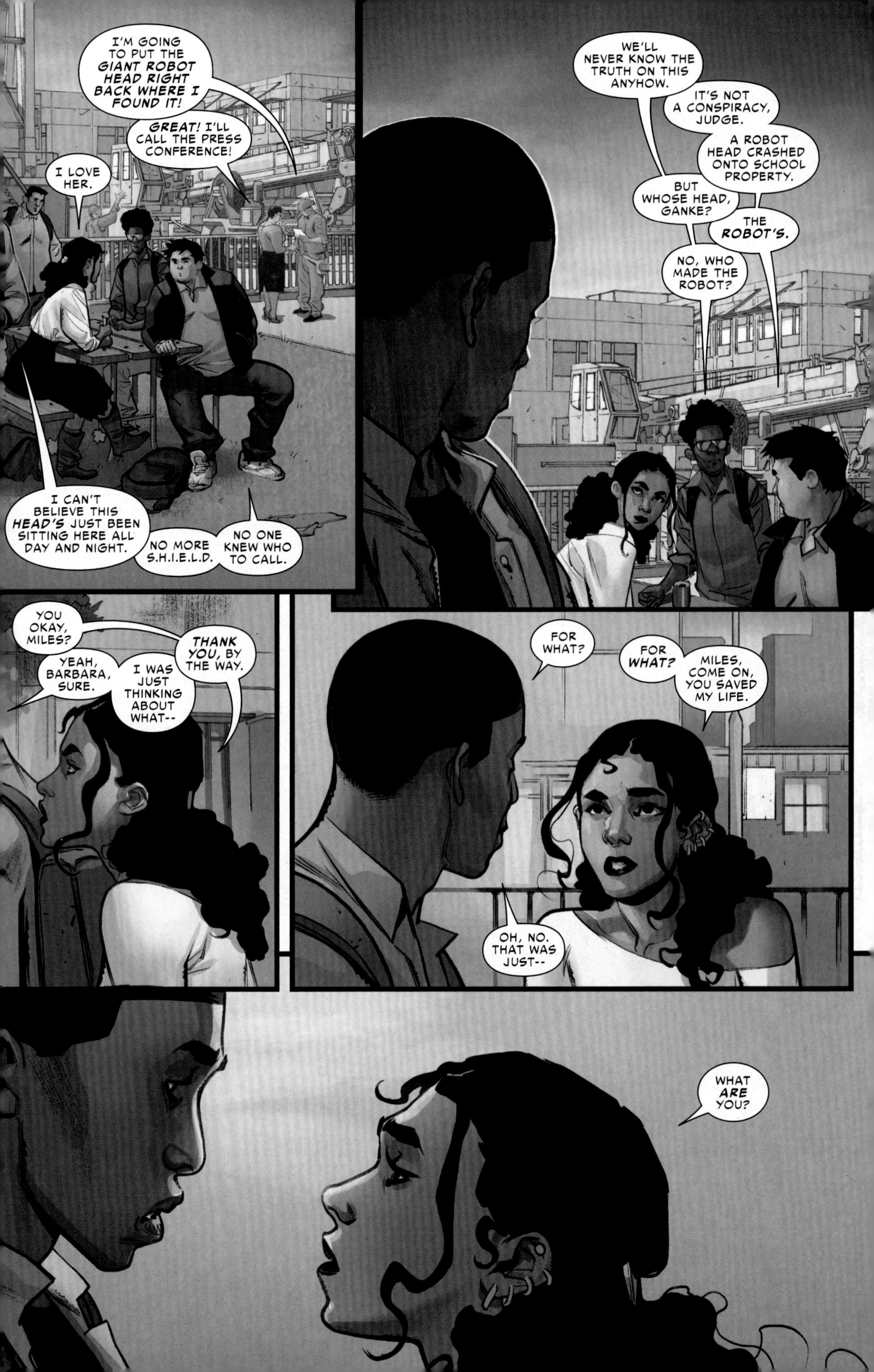
I'M GOING TO PUT THE GIANT ROBOT HEAD RIGHT BACK WHERE I FOUND IT!
GREAT! I'LL CALL THE PRESS CONFERENCE!
I LOVE HER.
I CAN'T BELIEVE THIS HEAD'S JUST BEEN SITTING HERE ALL DAY AND NIGHT.
NO MORE S.H.I.E.L.D.
NO ONE KNEW WHO TO CALL.
WE'LL NEVER KNOW THE TRUTH ON THIS ANYHOW.
IT'S NOT A CONSPIRACY, JUDGE.
A ROBOT HEAD CRASHED ONTO SCHOOL PROPERTY.
BUT WHOSE HEAD, GANKE?
THE ROBOT'S.
NO, WHO MADE THE ROBOT?
YOU OKAY, MILES?
YEAH, BARBARA, SURE.
I WAS JUST THINKING ABOUT WHAT--
THANK YOU, BY THE WAY.
FOR WHAT?
FOR WHAT? MILES, COME ON, YOU SAVED MY LIFE.
OH, NO. THAT WAS JUST--
WHAT ARE YOU?

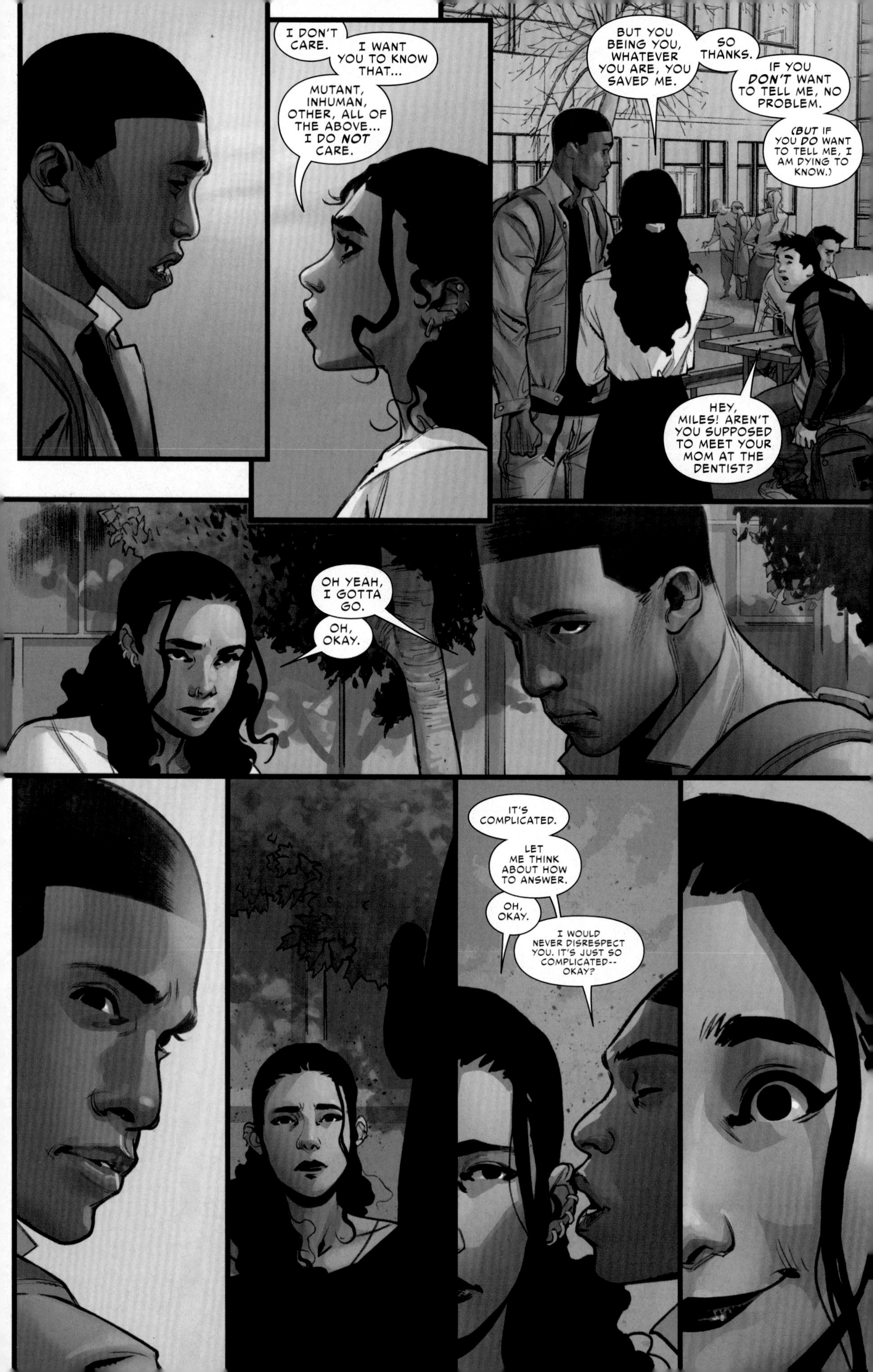
I DON'T CARE.
I WANT YOU TO KNOW THAT...
MUTANT, INHUMAN, OTHER, ALL OF THE ABOVE... I DO *NOT* CARE.
BUT YOU BEING YOU, WHATEVER YOU ARE, YOU SAVED ME.
SO THANKS.
IF YOU *DON'T* WANT TO TELL ME, NO PROBLEM.
(*BUT* IF YOU *DO* WANT TO TELL ME, I AM DYING TO KNOW.)
HEY, MILES! AREN'T YOU SUPPOSED TO MEET YOUR MOM AT THE DENTIST?
OH YEAH, I GOTTA GO.
OH, OKAY.
IT'S COMPLICATED.
LET ME THINK ABOUT HOW TO ANSWER.
OH, OKAY.
I WOULD NEVER DISRESPECT YOU. IT'S JUST SO COMPLICATED-- OKAY?

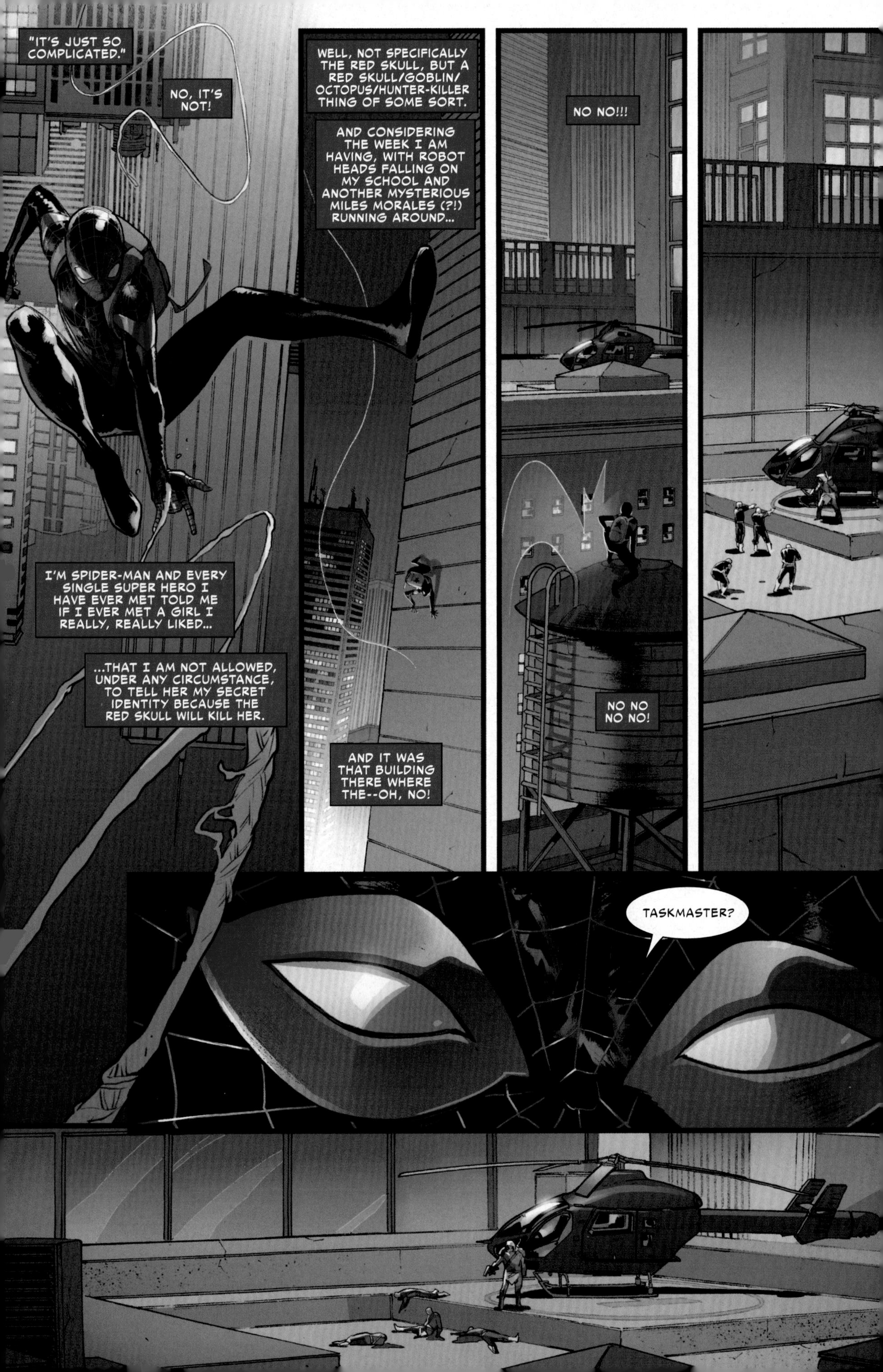
"IT'S JUST SO COMPLICATED."
NO, IT'S NOT!
I'M SPIDER-MAN AND EVERY SINGLE SUPER HERO I HAVE EVER MET TOLD ME IF I EVER MET A GIRL I REALLY, REALLY LIKED...
...THAT I AM NOT ALLOWED, UNDER ANY CIRCUMSTANCE, TO TELL HER MY SECRET IDENTITY BECAUSE THE RED SKULL WILL KILL HER.
WELL, NOT SPECIFICALLY THE RED SKULL, BUT A RED SKULL/GOBLIN/ OCTOPUS/HUNTER-KILLER THING OF SOME SORT.
AND CONSIDERING THE WEEK I AM HAVING, WITH ROBOT HEADS FALLING ON MY SCHOOL AND ANOTHER MYSTERIOUS MILES MORALES (?!) RUNNING AROUND...
AND IT WAS THAT BUILDING THERE WHERE THE--OH, NO!
NO NO!!!
NO NO NO NO!
TASKMASTER?

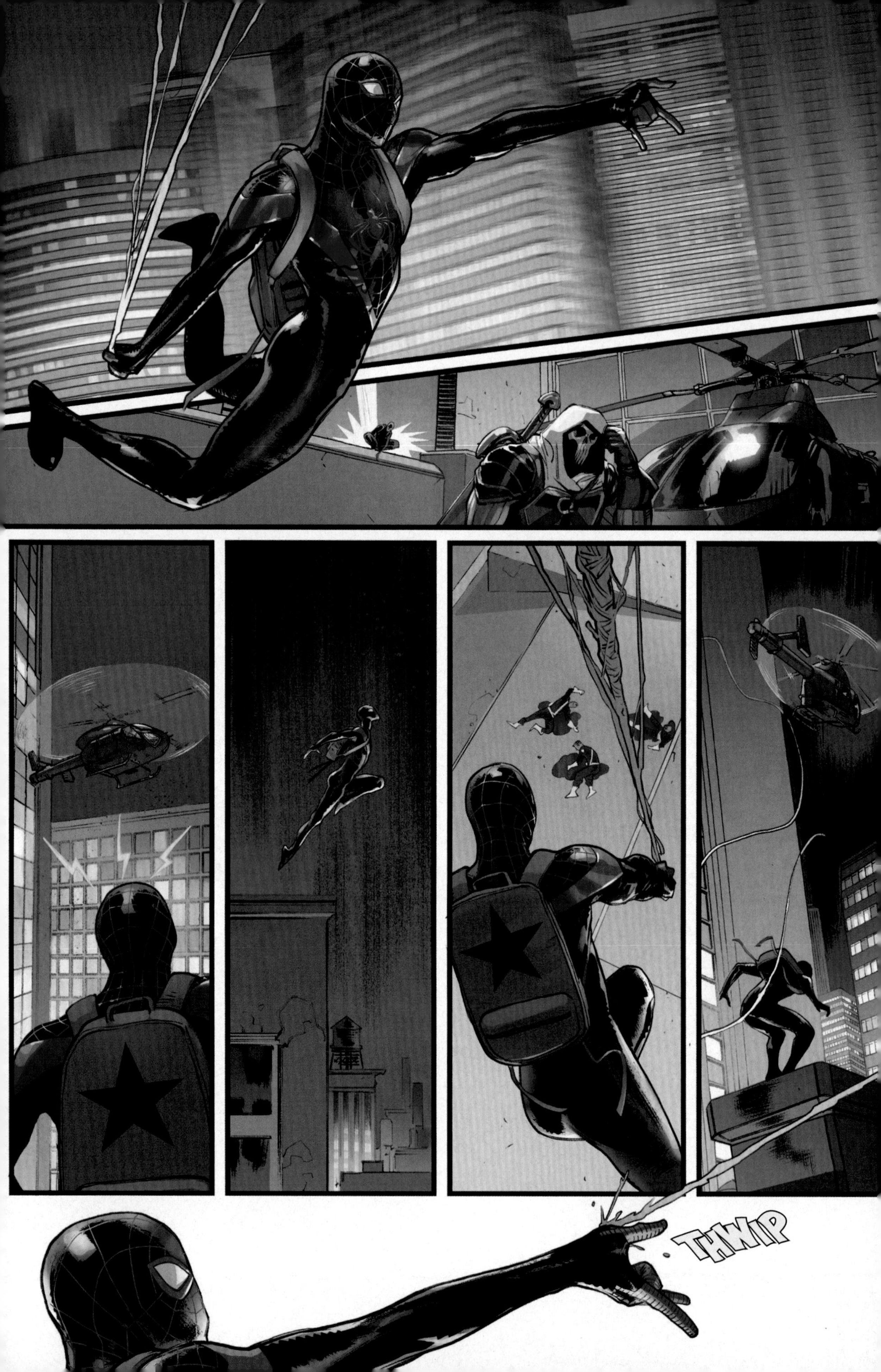
THWIP

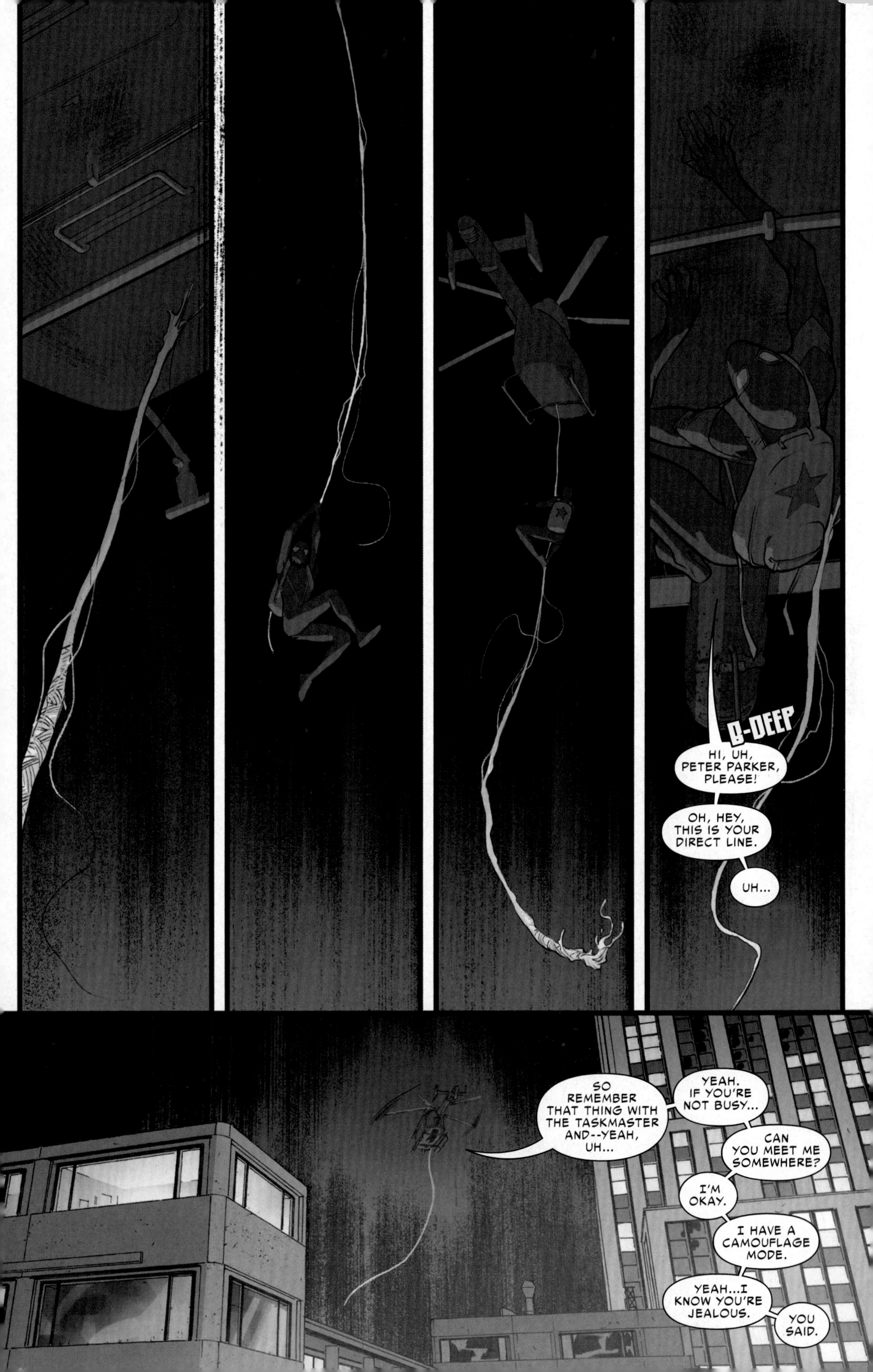
B-DEEP
HI, UH, PETER PARKER, PLEASE!
OH, HEY, THIS IS YOUR DIRECT LINE.
UH...
SO REMEMBER THAT THING WITH THE TASKMASTER AND--YEAH, UH...
YEAH. IF YOU'RE NOT BUSY...
CAN YOU MEET ME SOMEWHERE?
I'M OKAY.
I HAVE A CAMOUFLAGE MODE.
YEAH...I KNOW YOU'RE JEALOUS.
YOU SAID.

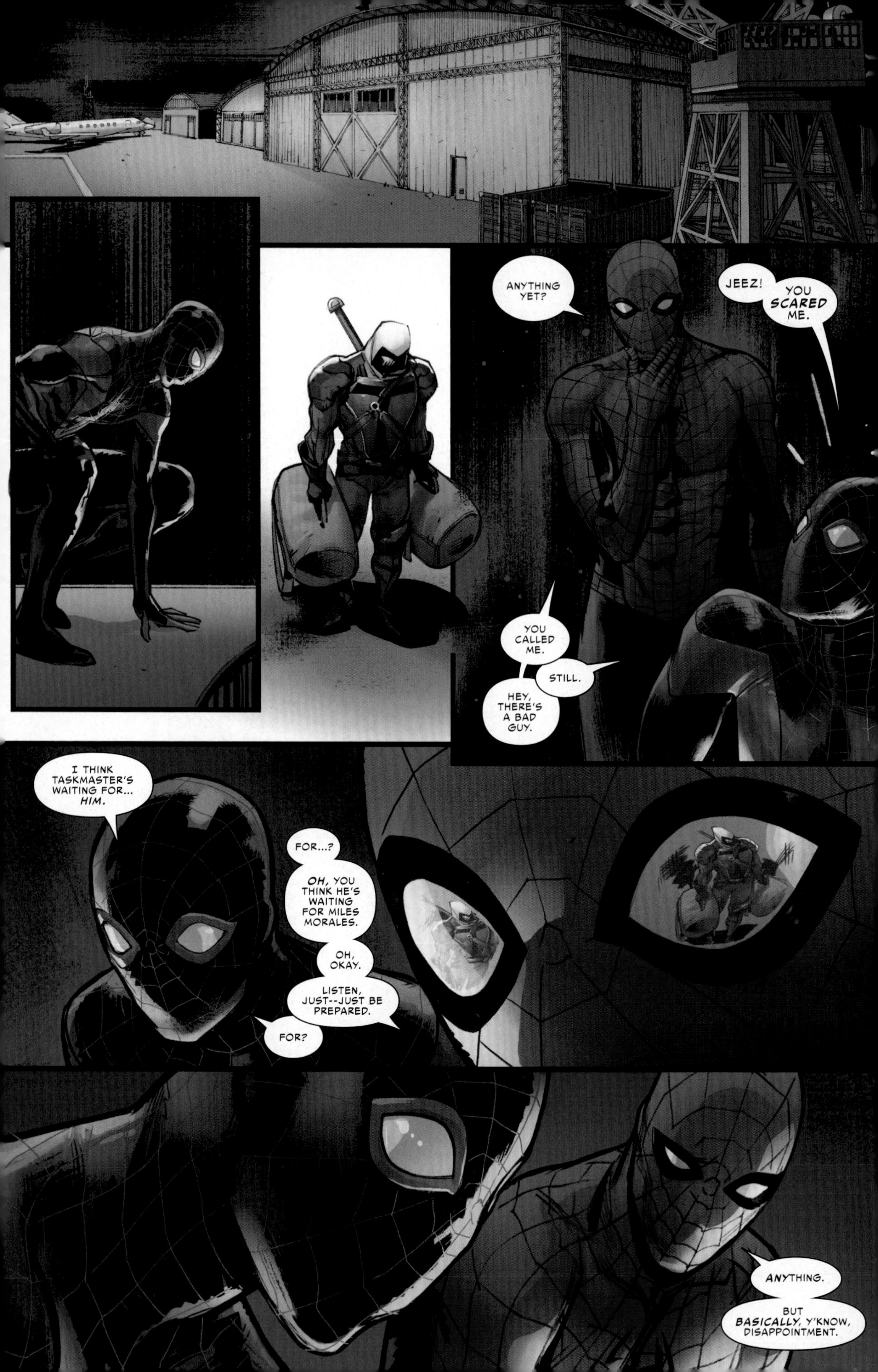
ANYTHING YET?
JEEZ!
YOU SCARED ME.
YOU CALLED ME.
STILL.
HEY, THERE'S A BAD GUY.
I THINK TASKMASTER'S WAITING FOR... HIM.
FOR...?
OH, YOU THINK HE'S WAITING FOR MILES MORALES.
OH, OKAY.
LISTEN, JUST--JUST BE PREPARED.
FOR?
ANYTHING.
BUT BASICALLY, Y'KNOW, DISAPPOINTMENT.

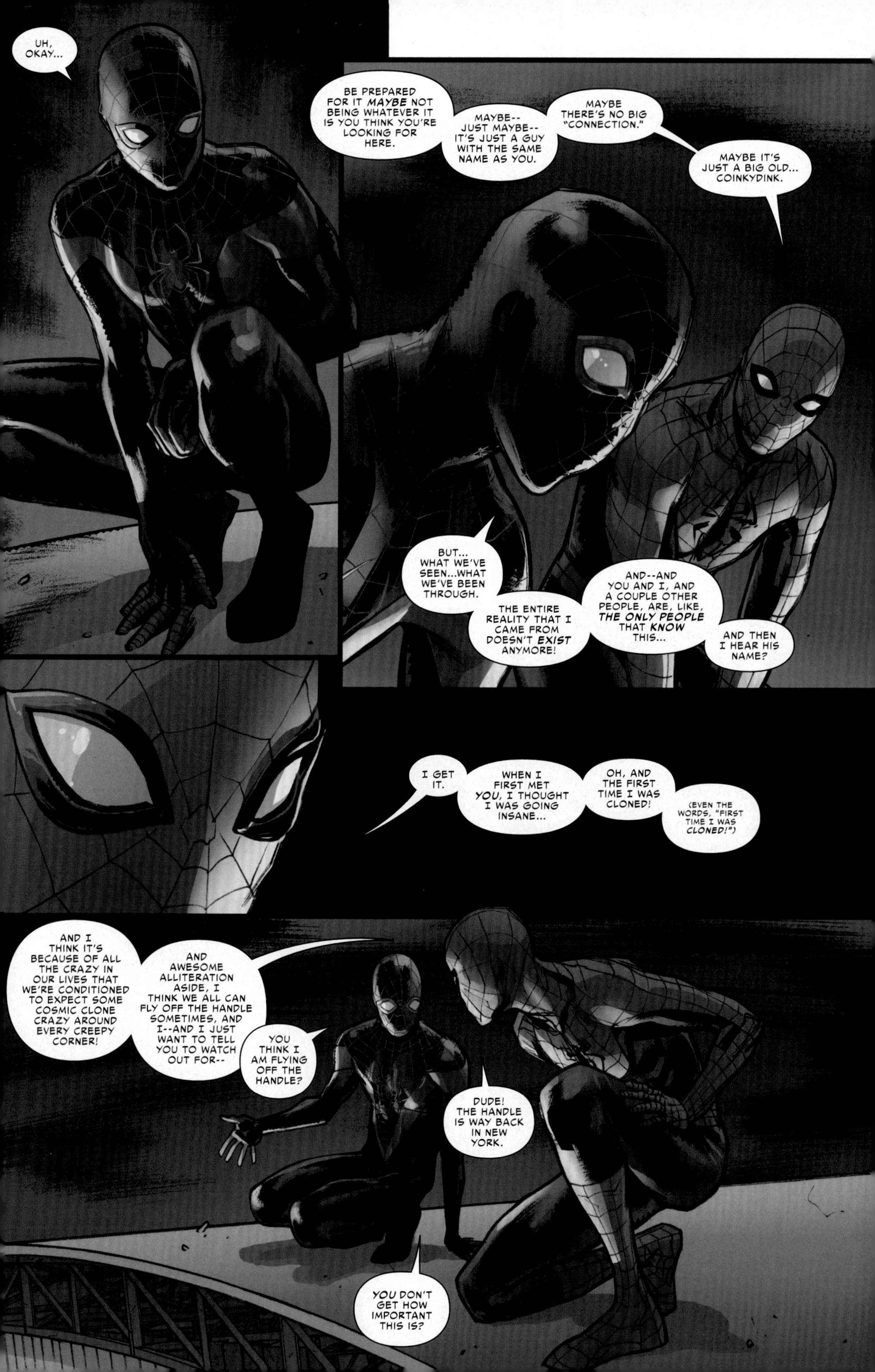
UH, OKAY...
BE PREPARED FOR IT MAYBE NOT BEING WHATEVER IT IS YOU THINK YOU'RE LOOKING FOR HERE.
MAYBE-- JUST MAYBE-- IT'S JUST A GUY WITH THE SAME NAME AS YOU.
MAYBE THERE'S NO BIG "CONNECTION."
MAYBE IT'S JUST A BIG OLD... COINKYDINK.
BUT... WHAT WE'VE SEEN...WHAT WE'VE BEEN THROUGH.
THE ENTIRE REALITY THAT I CAME FROM DOESN'T EXIST ANYMORE!
AND--AND YOU AND I, AND A COUPLE OTHER PEOPLE, ARE, LIKE, THE ONLY PEOPLE THAT KNOW THIS...
AND THEN I HEAR HIS NAME?
I GET IT.
WHEN I FIRST MET YOU, I THOUGHT I WAS GOING INSANE...
OH, AND THE FIRST TIME I WAS CLONED!
(EVEN THE WORDS, "FIRST TIME I WAS CLONED!")
AND I THINK IT'S BECAUSE OF ALL THE CRAZY IN OUR LIVES THAT WE'RE CONDITIONED TO EXPECT SOME COSMIC CLONE CRAZY AROUND EVERY CREEPY CORNER!
AND AWESOME ALLITERATION ASIDE, I THINK WE ALL CAN FLY OFF THE HANDLE SOMETIMES, AND I--AND I JUST WANT TO TELL YOU TO WATCH OUT FOR--
YOU THINK I AM FLYING OFF THE HANDLE?
DUDE! THE HANDLE IS WAY BACK IN NEW YORK.
YOU DON'T GET HOW IMPORTANT THIS IS?

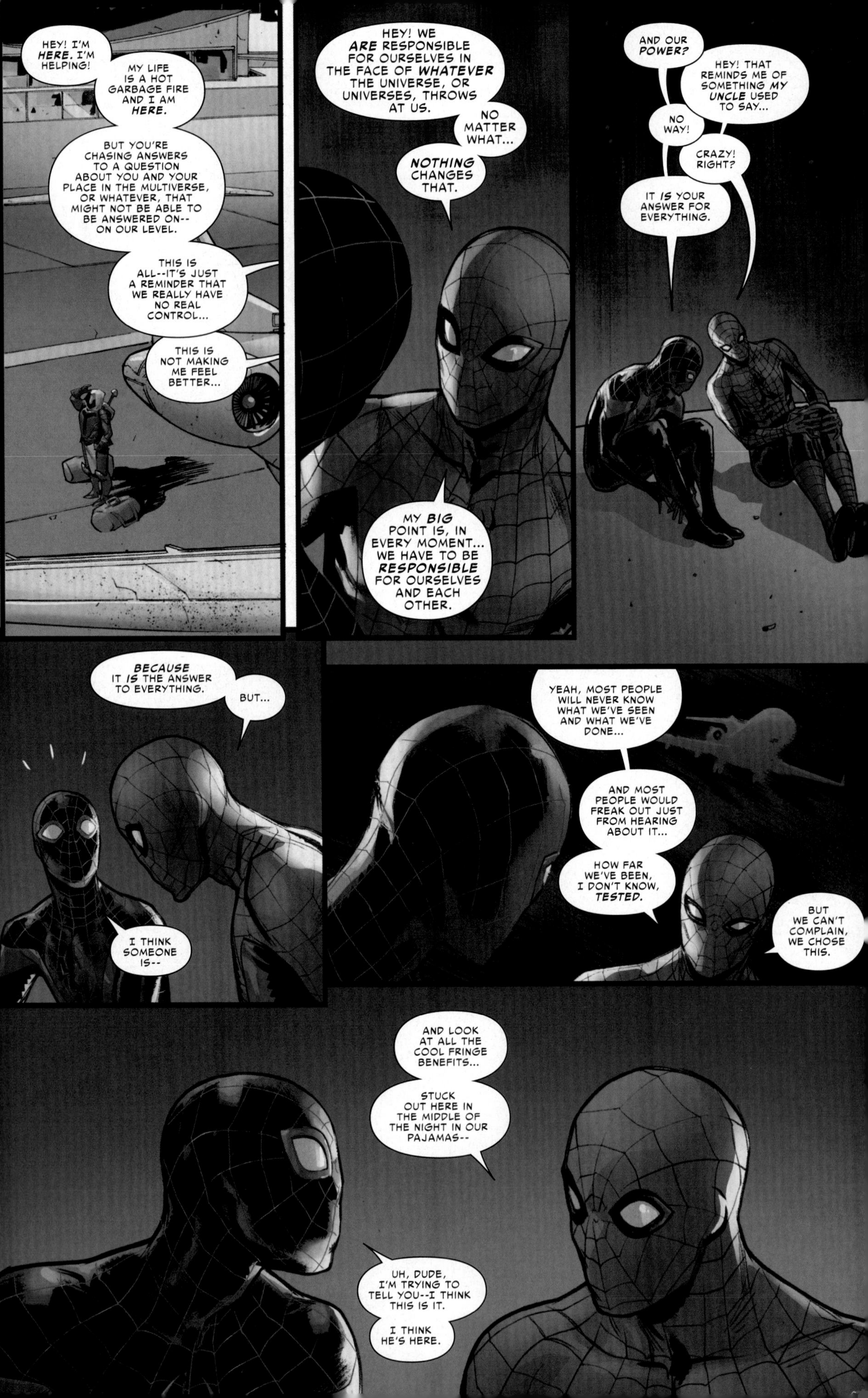

HEY! I'M *HERE.* I'M HELPING!
MY LIFE IS A HOT GARBAGE FIRE AND I AM *HERE.*
BUT YOU'RE CHASING ANSWERS TO A QUESTION ABOUT YOU AND YOUR PLACE IN THE MULTIVERSE, OR WHATEVER, THAT MIGHT NOT BE ABLE TO BE ANSWERED ON-- ON OUR LEVEL.
THIS IS ALL--IT'S JUST A REMINDER THAT WE REALLY HAVE NO REAL CONTROL...
THIS IS NOT MAKING ME FEEL BETTER...
HEY! WE *ARE* RESPONSIBLE FOR OURSELVES IN THE FACE OF *WHATEVER* THE UNIVERSE, OR UNIVERSES, THROWS AT US.
NO MATTER WHAT...
NOTHING CHANGES THAT.
MY *BIG* POINT IS, IN EVERY MOMENT... WE HAVE TO BE *RESPONSIBLE* FOR OURSELVES AND EACH OTHER.
AND OUR *POWER?*
HEY! THAT REMINDS ME OF SOMETHING *MY UNCLE* USED TO SAY...
NO WAY!
CRAZY! RIGHT?
IT *IS* YOUR ANSWER FOR EVERYTHING.
BECAUSE IT *IS* THE ANSWER TO EVERYTHING.
BUT...
I THINK SOMEONE IS--
YEAH, MOST PEOPLE WILL NEVER KNOW WHAT WE'VE SEEN AND WHAT WE'VE DONE...
AND MOST PEOPLE WOULD FREAK OUT JUST FROM HEARING ABOUT IT...
HOW FAR WE'VE BEEN, I DON'T KNOW, *TESTED.*
BUT WE CAN'T COMPLAIN, WE CHOSE THIS.
AND LOOK AT ALL THE COOL FRINGE BENEFITS...
STUCK OUT HERE IN THE MIDDLE OF THE NIGHT IN OUR PAJAMAS--
UH, DUDE, I'M TRYING TO TELL YOU--I THINK THIS IS IT.
I THINK HE'S HERE.

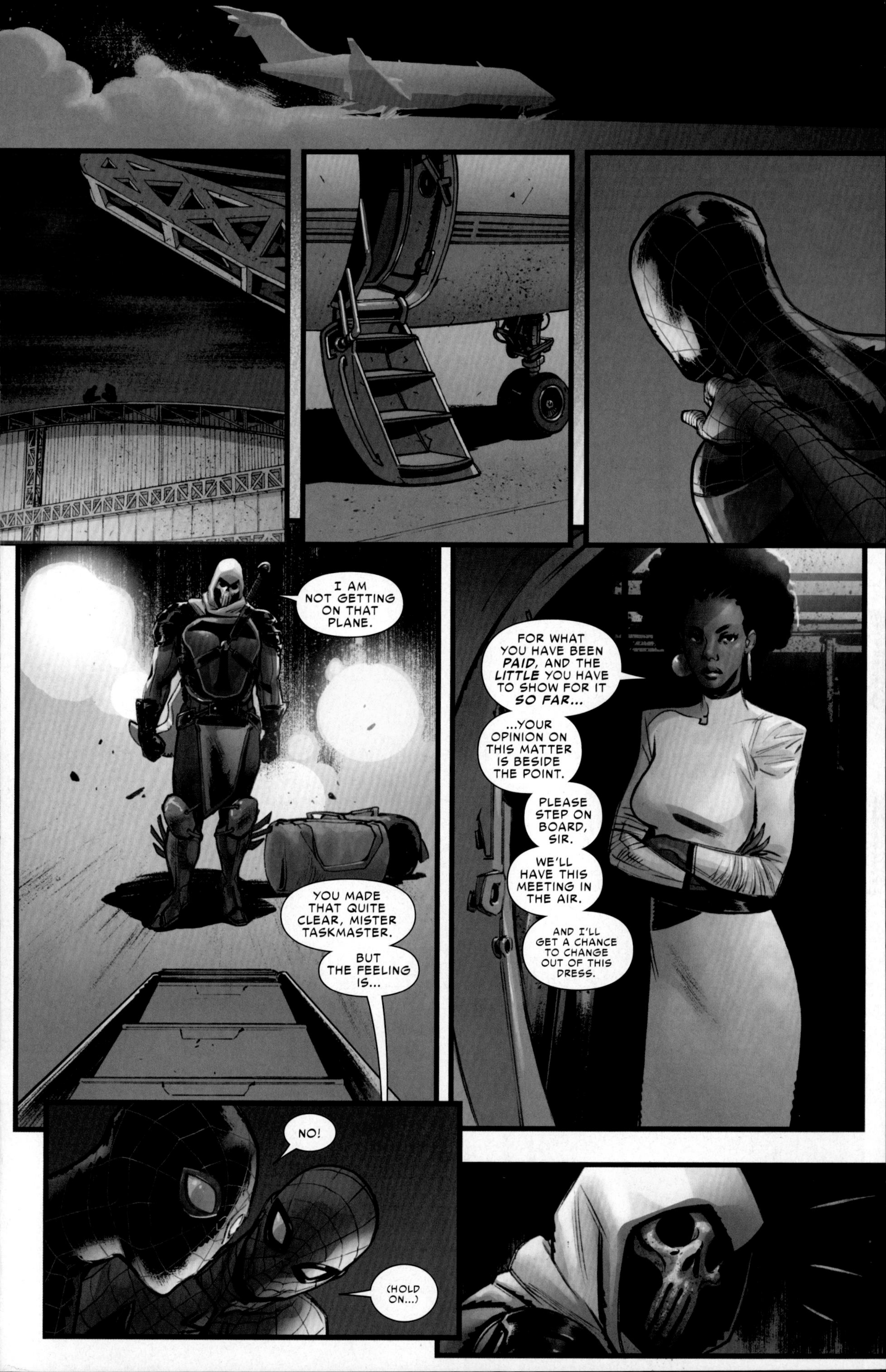
I AM NOT GETTING ON THAT PLANE.
YOU MADE THAT QUITE CLEAR, MISTER TASKMASTER.
BUT THE FEELING IS...
FOR WHAT YOU HAVE BEEN PAID, AND THE LITTLE YOU HAVE TO SHOW FOR IT SO FAR...
...YOUR OPINION ON THIS MATTER IS BESIDE THE POINT.
PLEASE STEP ON BOARD, SIR.
WE'LL HAVE THIS MEETING IN THE AIR.
AND I'LL GET A CHANCE TO CHANGE OUT OF THIS DRESS.
NO!
(HOLD ON...)

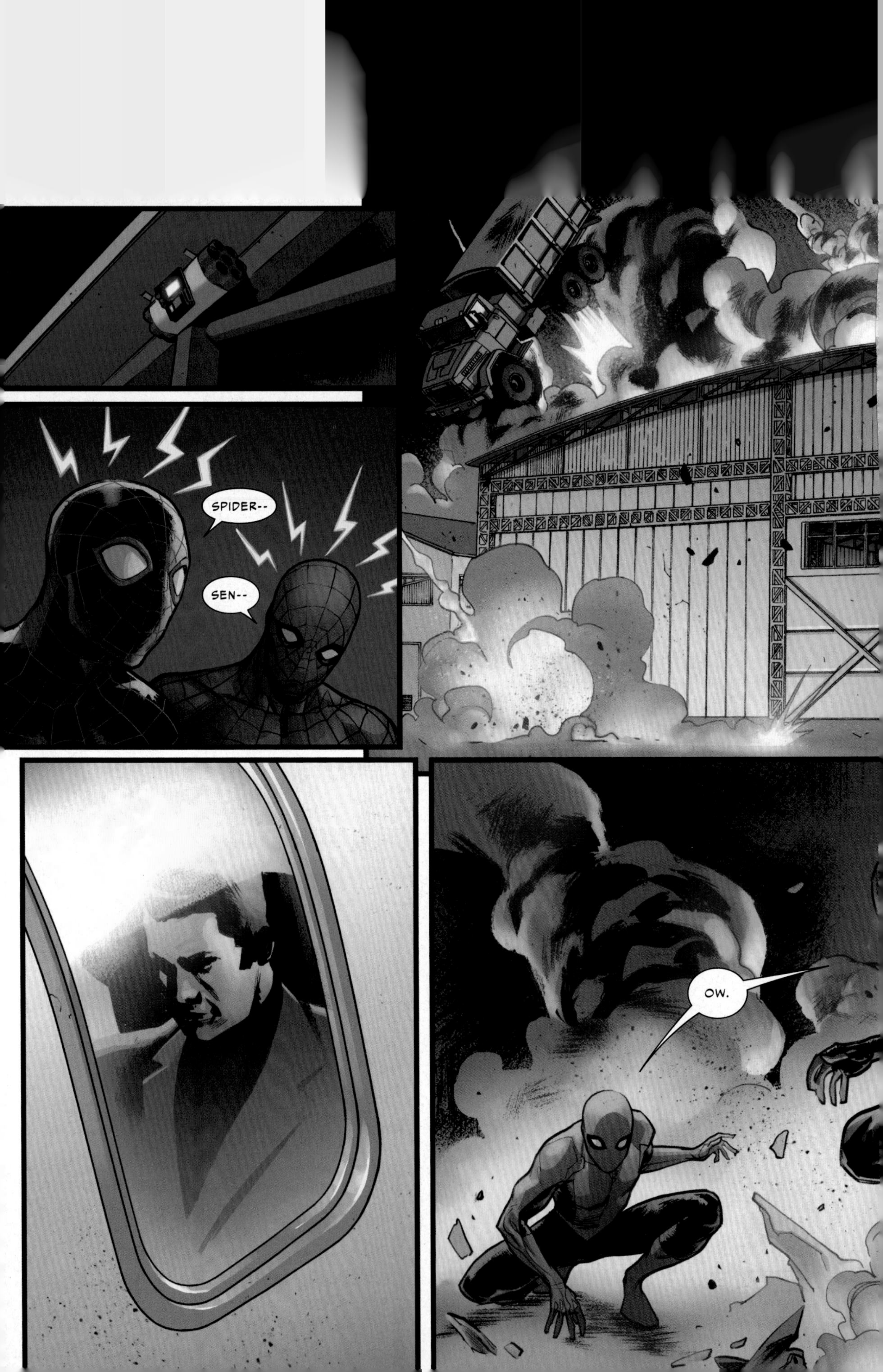
SPIDER--
SEN--
OW.

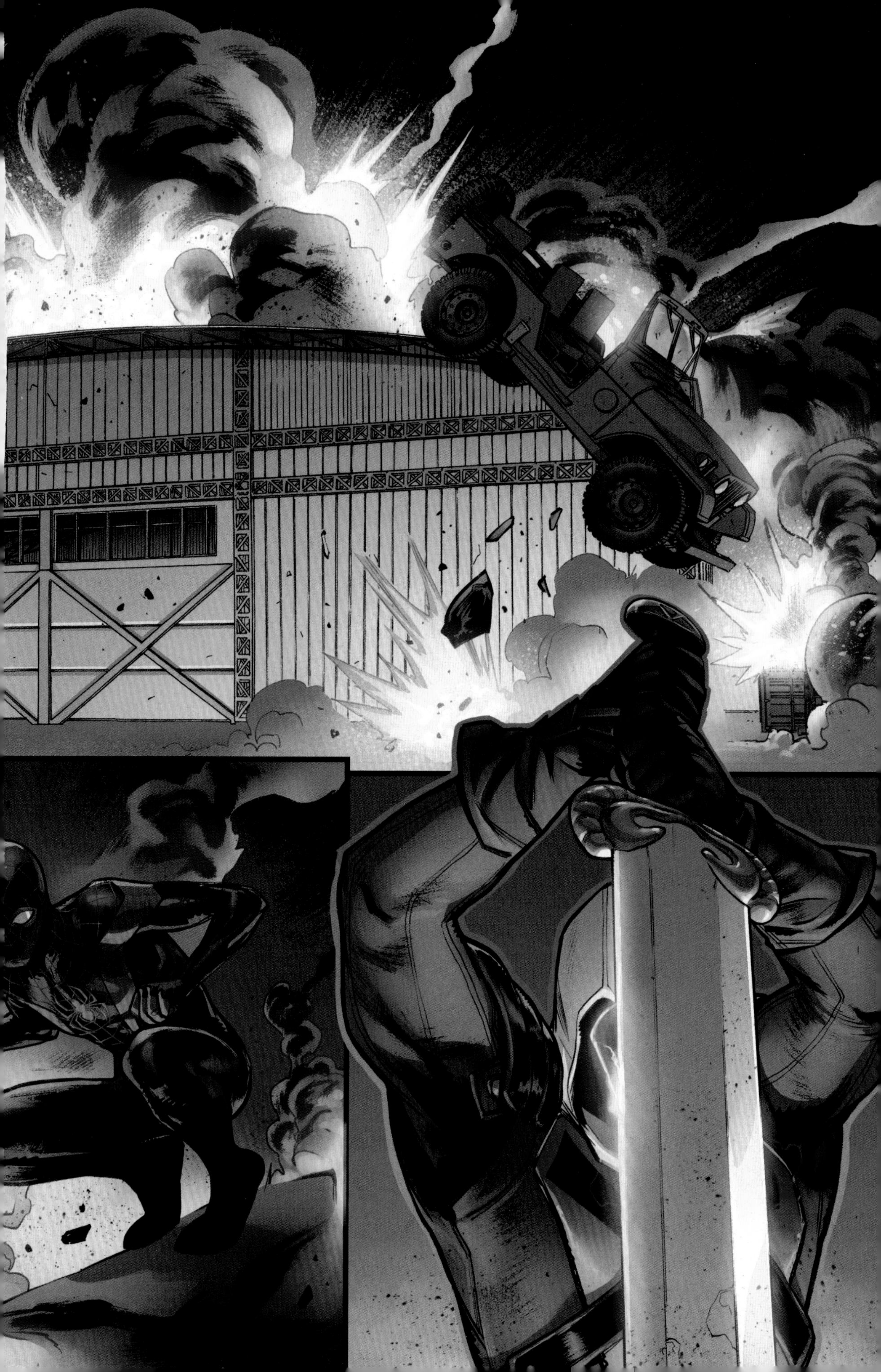

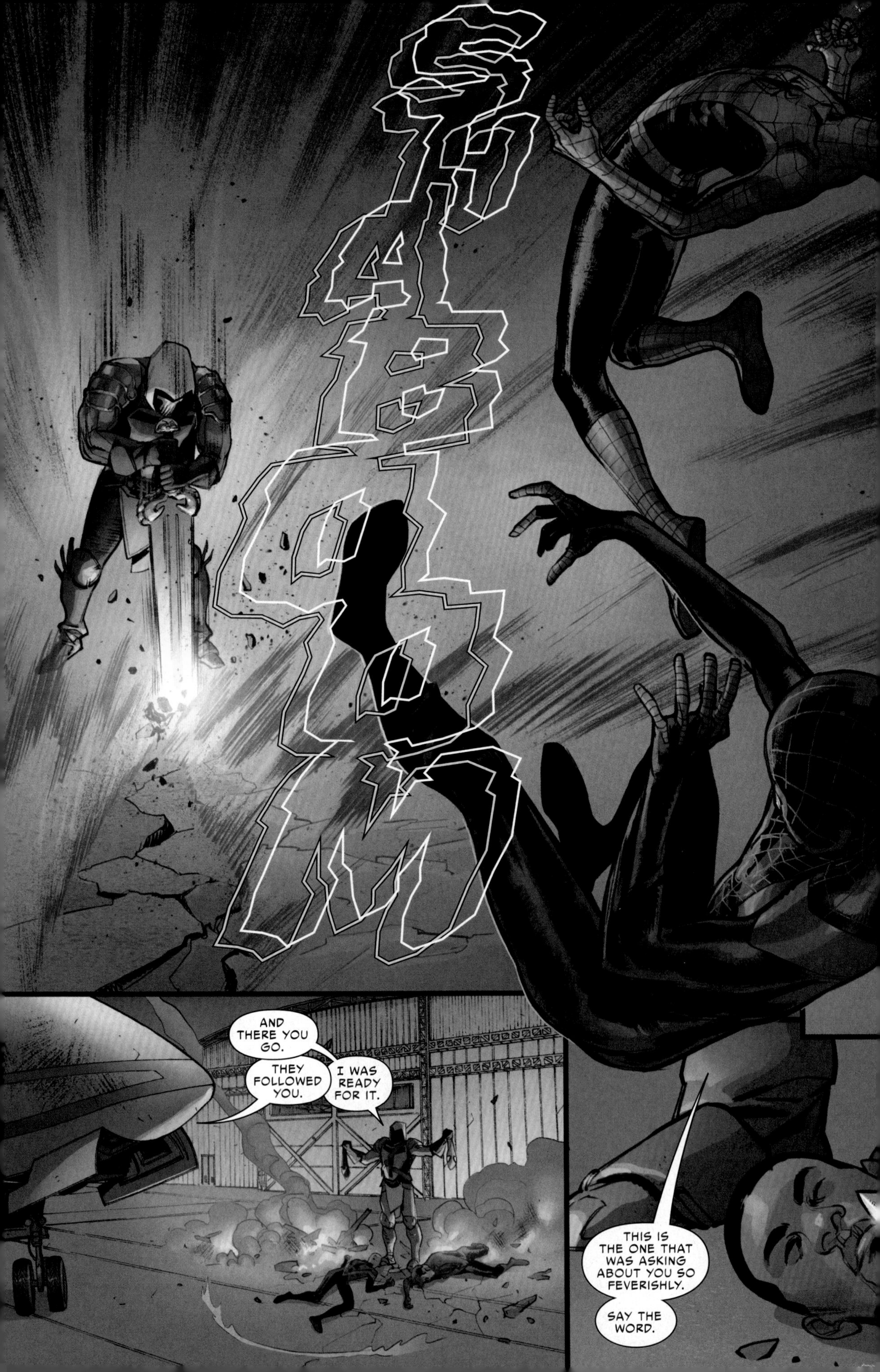
SHABOOM
AND THERE YOU GO.
THEY FOLLOWED YOU.
I WAS READY FOR IT.
THIS IS THE ONE THAT WAS ASKING ABOUT YOU SO FEVERISHLY.
SAY THE WORD.

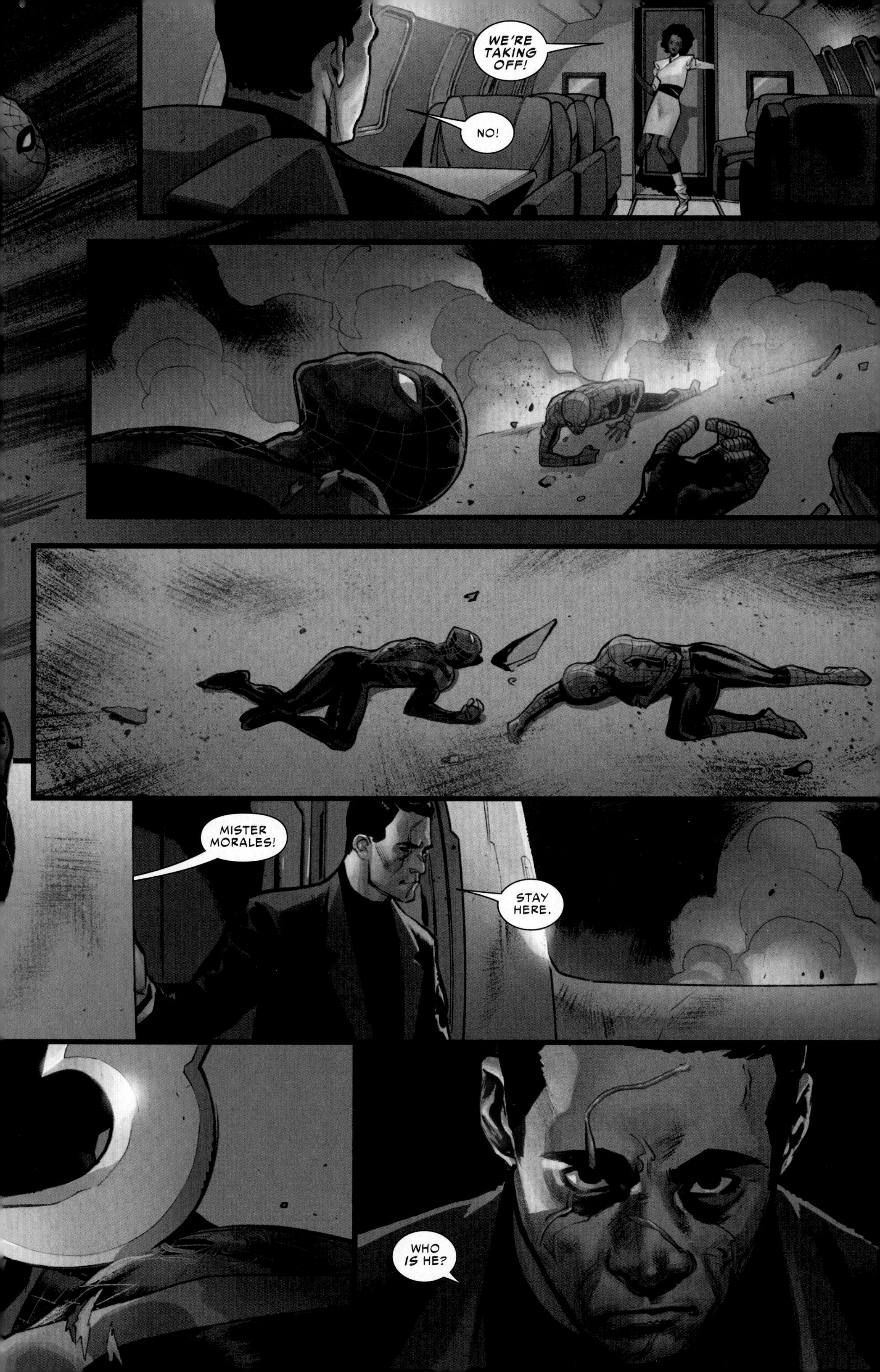
WE'RE TAKING OFF!
NO!
MISTER MORALES!
STAY HERE.
WHO IS HE?

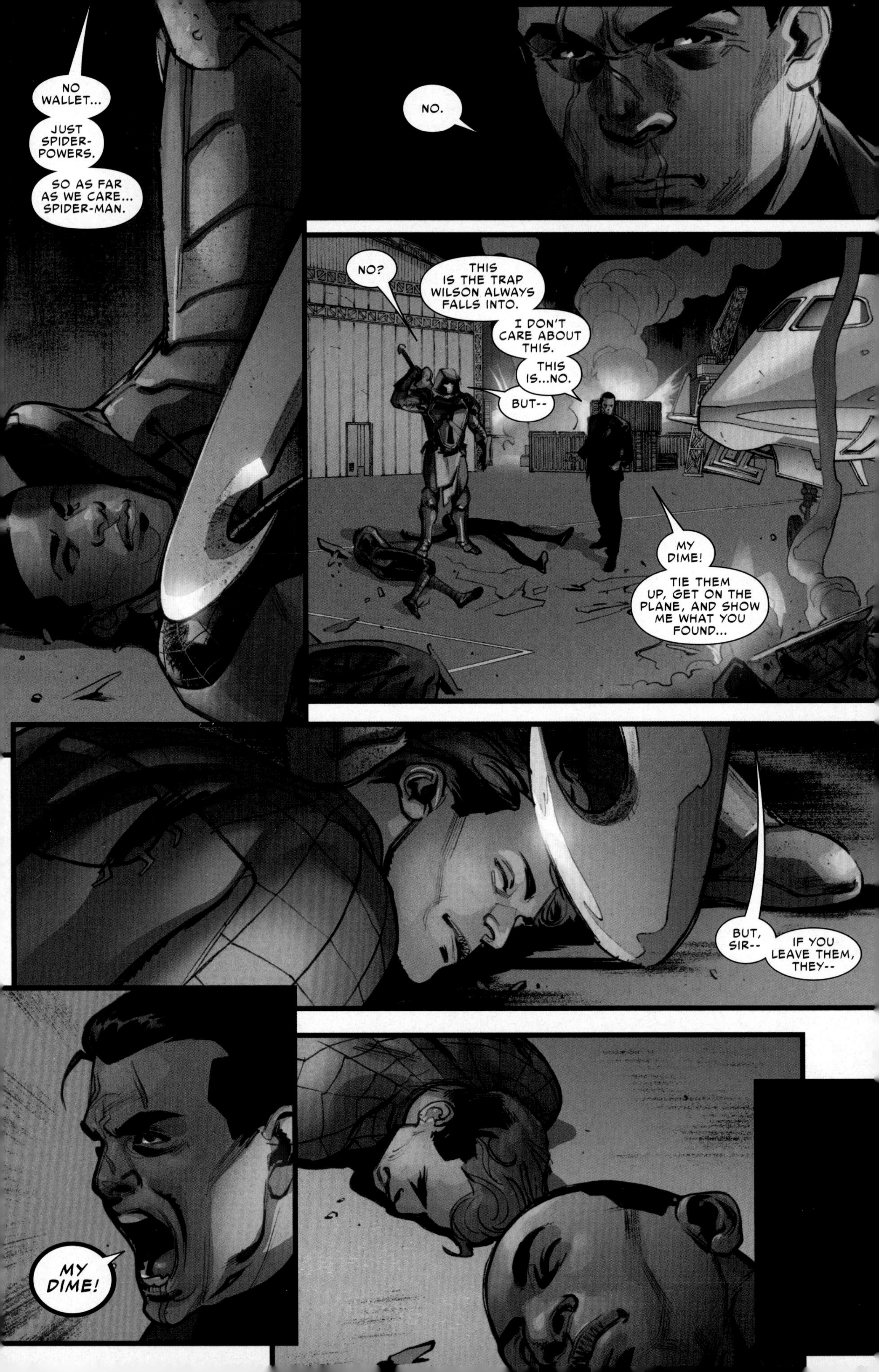
NO WALLET...
JUST SPIDER-POWERS.
SO AS FAR AS WE CARE... SPIDER-MAN.
NO.
NO?
THIS IS THE TRAP WILSON ALWAYS FALLS INTO.
I DON'T CARE ABOUT THIS.
THIS IS...NO.
BUT--
MY DIME!
TIE THEM UP, GET ON THE PLANE, AND SHOW ME WHAT YOU FOUND...
BUT, SIR--
IF YOU LEAVE THEM, THEY--
MY DIME!

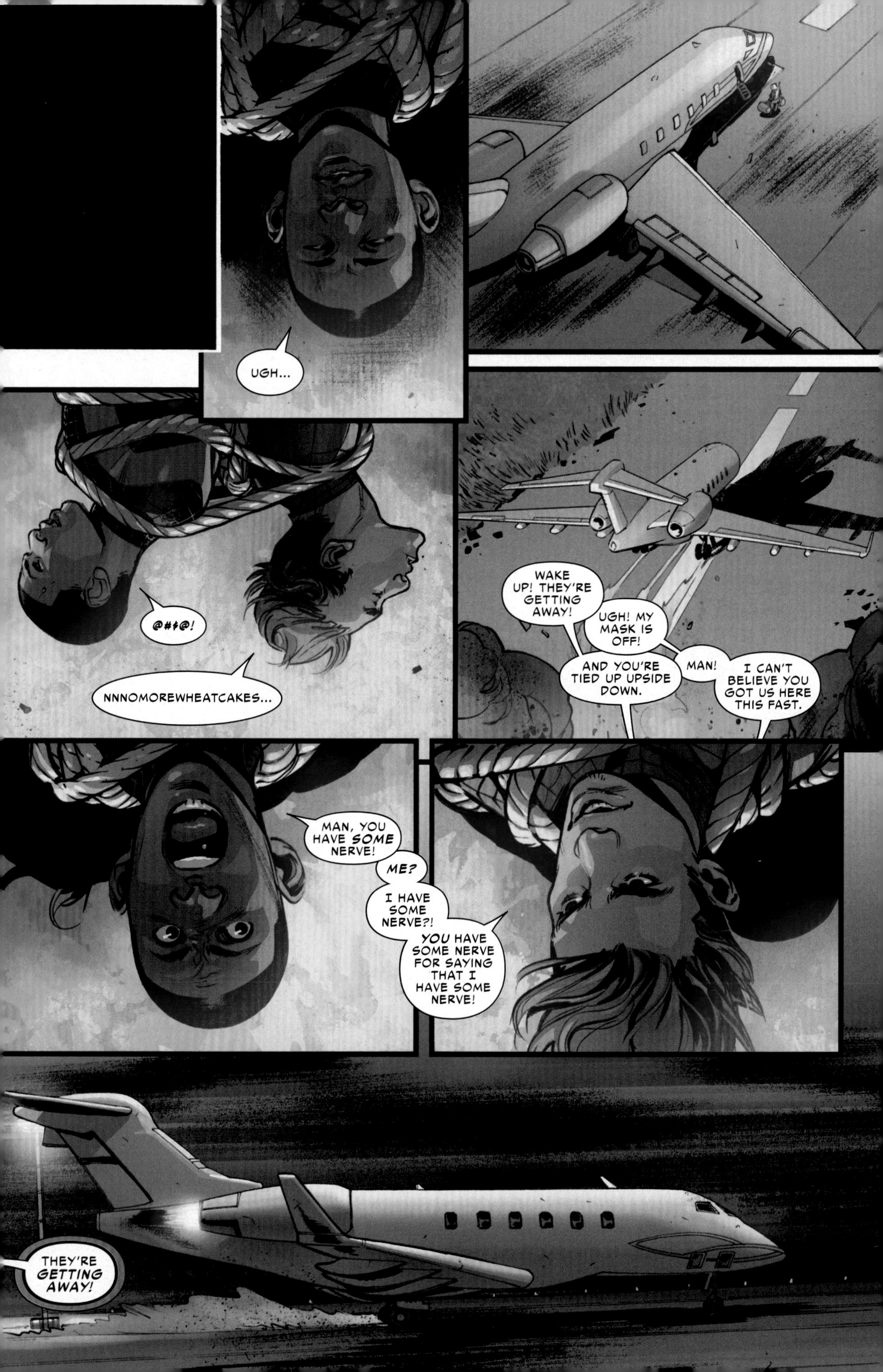
UGH...
@#$@!
NNNOMOREWHEATCAKES...
WAKE UP! THEY'RE GETTING AWAY!
UGH! MY MASK IS OFF!
AND YOU'RE TIED UP UPSIDE DOWN.
MAN!
I CAN'T BELIEVE YOU GOT US HERE THIS FAST.
MAN, YOU HAVE *SOME* NERVE!
ME?
I HAVE SOME NERVE?!
YOU HAVE SOME NERVE FOR SAYING THAT I HAVE SOME NERVE!
THEY'RE *GETTING* AWAY!

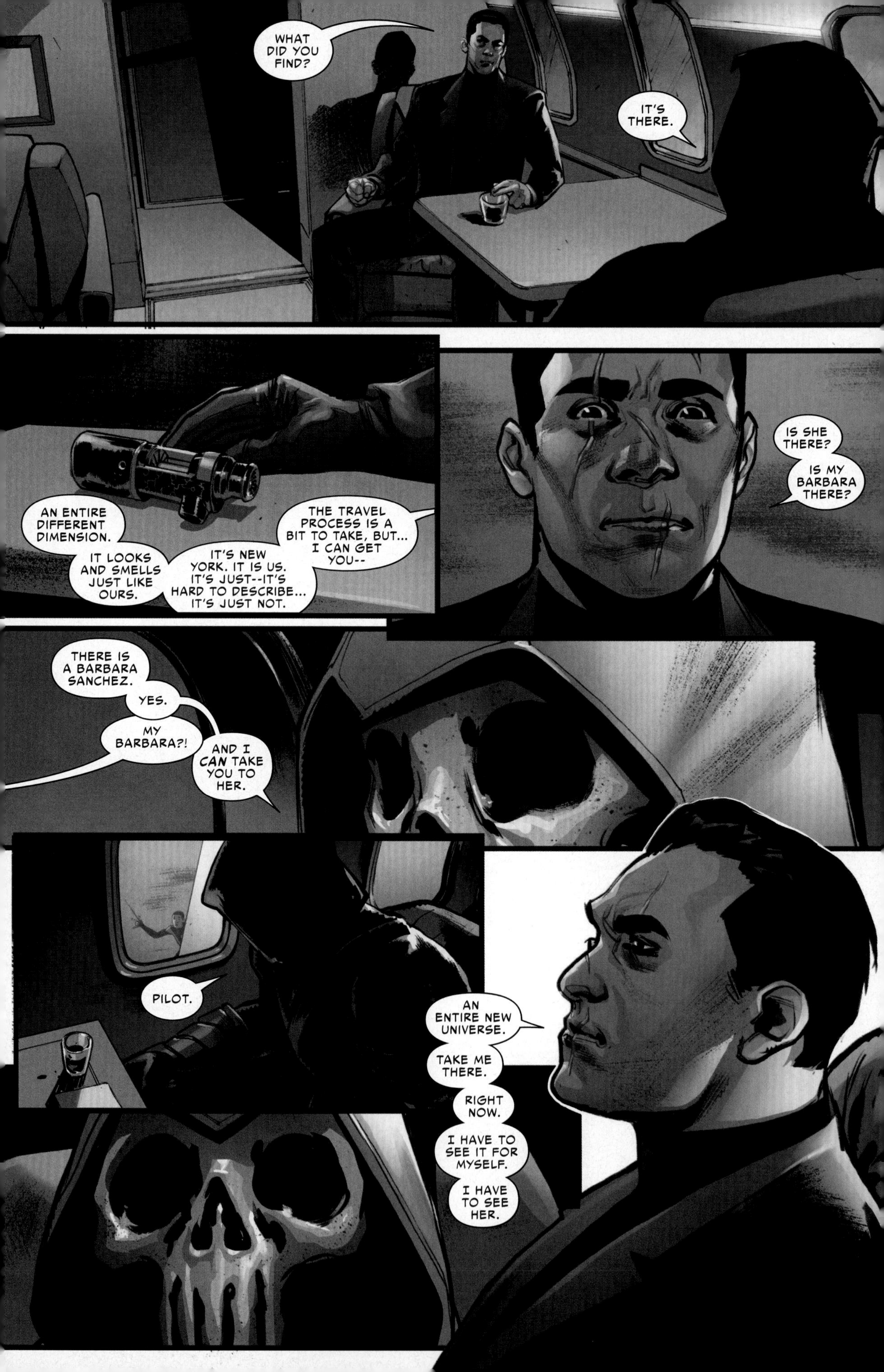
WHAT DID YOU FIND?
IT'S THERE.
AN ENTIRE DIFFERENT DIMENSION.
IT LOOKS AND SMELLS JUST LIKE OURS.
IT'S NEW YORK. IT IS US. IT'S JUST--IT'S HARD TO DESCRIBE... IT'S JUST NOT.
THE TRAVEL PROCESS IS A BIT TO TAKE, BUT... I CAN GET YOU--
IS SHE THERE?
IS MY BARBARA THERE?
THERE IS A BARBARA SANCHEZ.
YES.
MY BARBARA?!
AND I CAN TAKE YOU TO HER.
PILOT.
AN ENTIRE NEW UNIVERSE.
TAKE ME THERE.
RIGHT NOW.
I HAVE TO SEE IT FOR MYSELF.
I HAVE TO SEE HER.

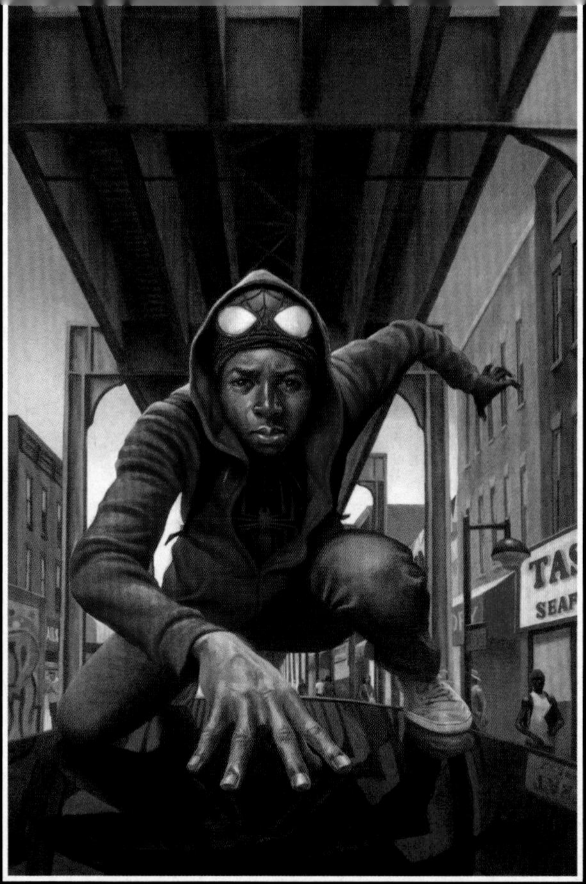
TAS
SEAF

#1 VARIANT BY **KADIR NELSON**

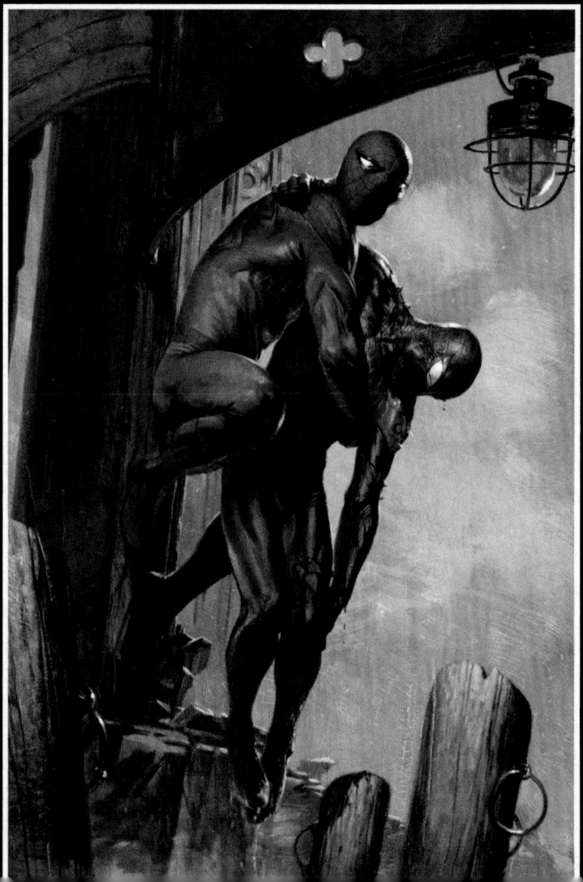

#2 VARIANT BY **GABRIELE DELL'OTTO**

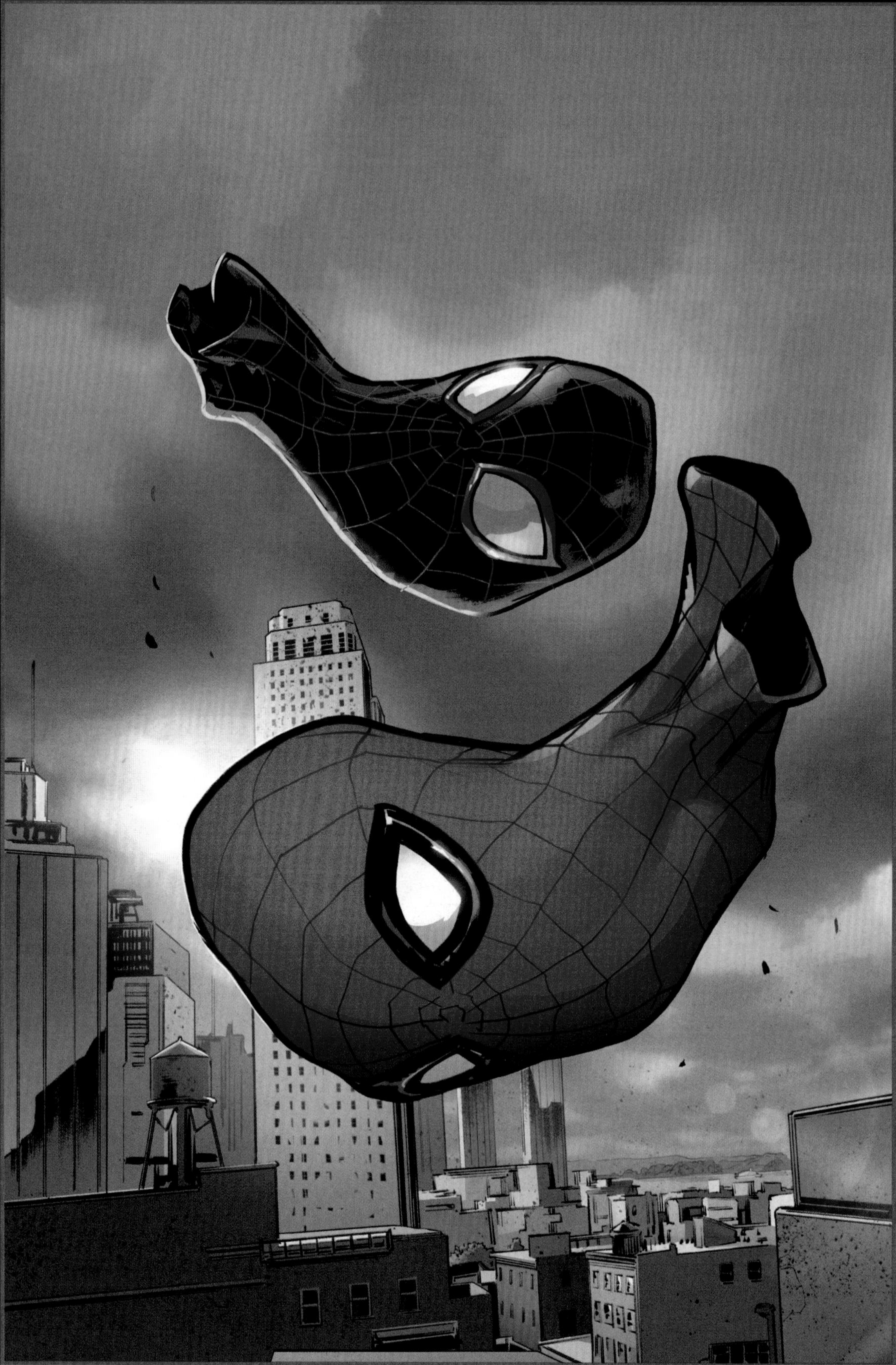

V

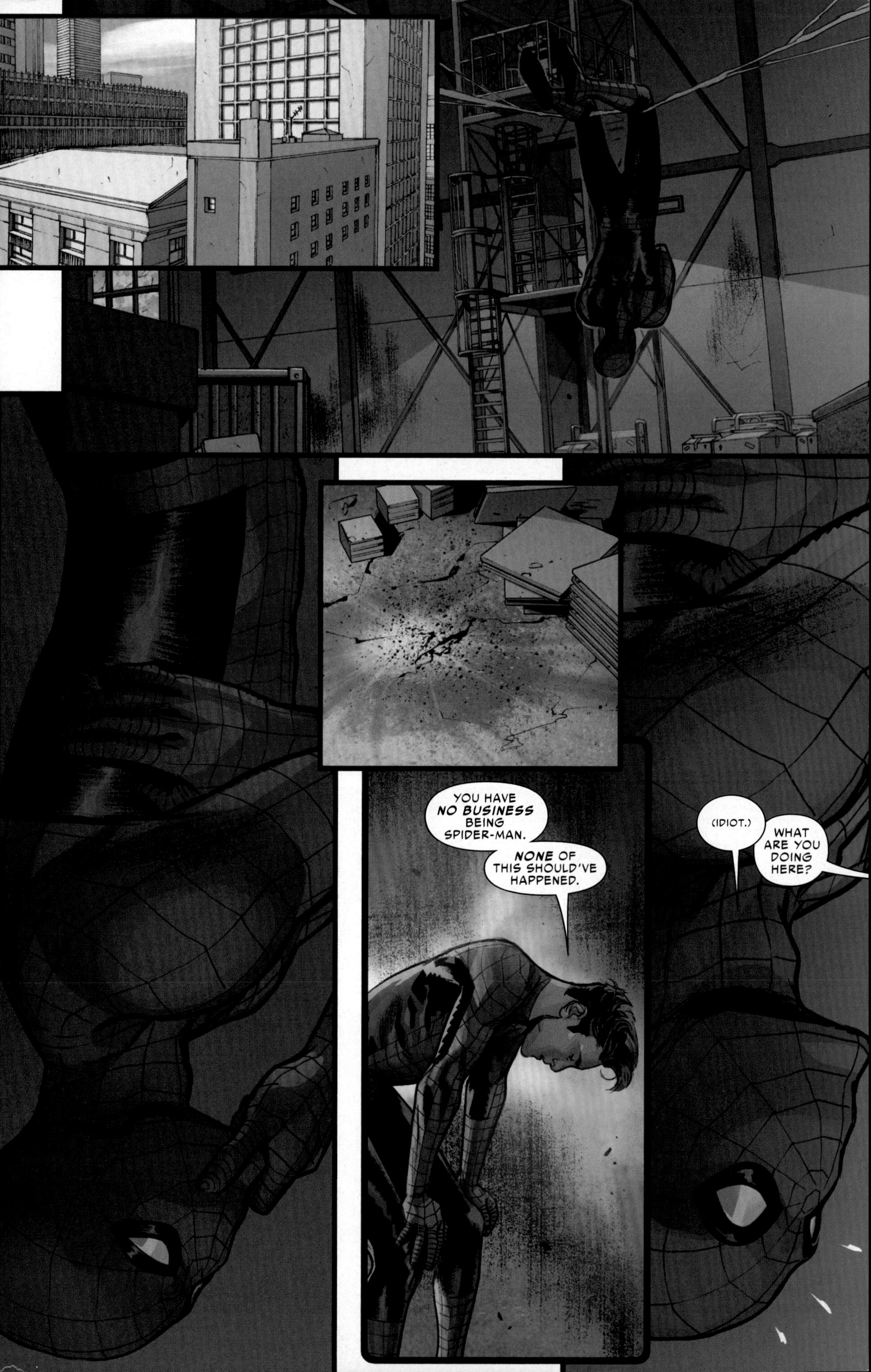

YOU HAVE NO BUSINESS BEING SPIDER-MAN.
NONE OF THIS SHOULD'VE HAPPENED.
(IDIOT.)
WHAT ARE YOU DOING HERE?

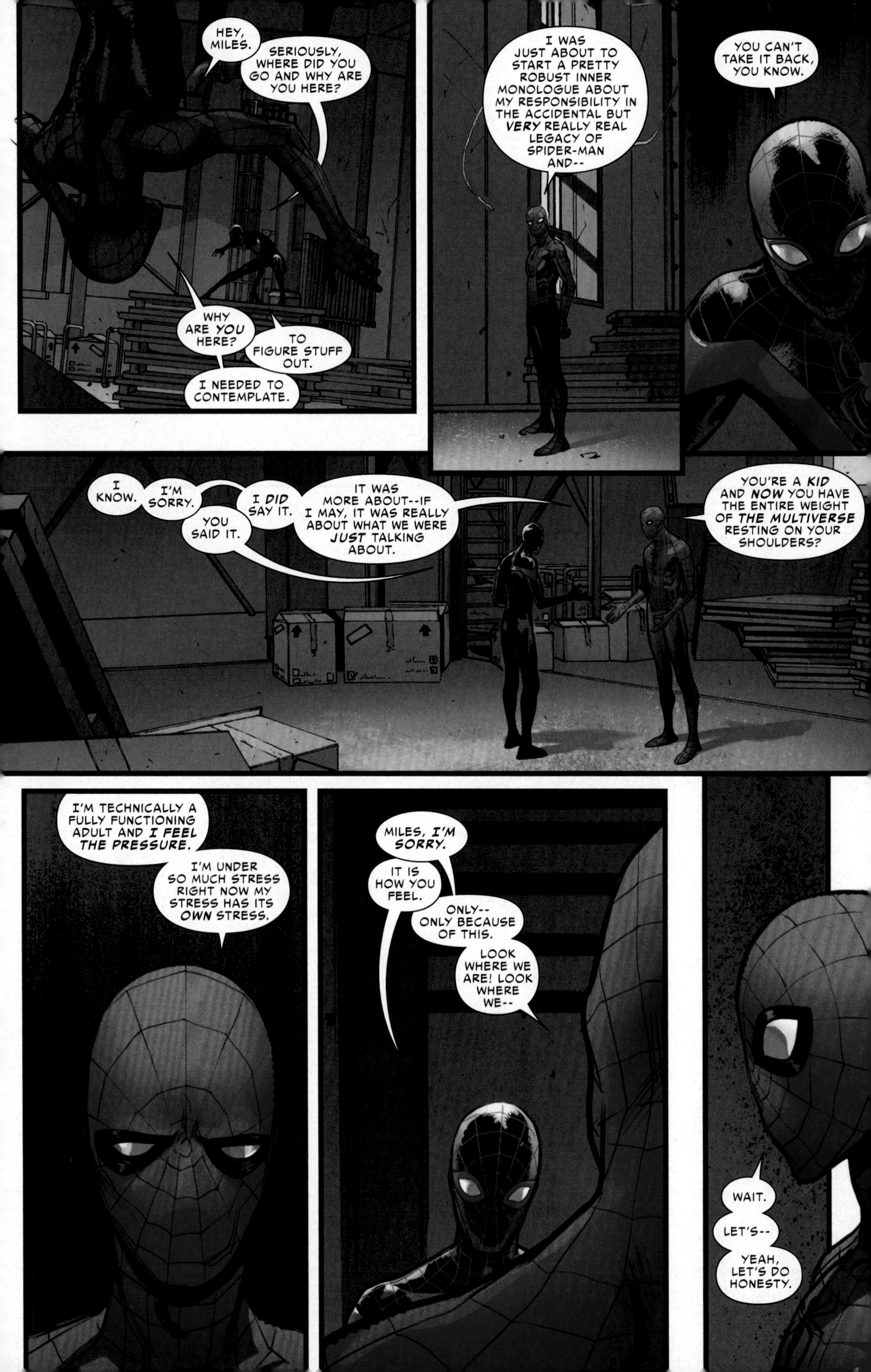
HEY, MILES.
SERIOUSLY, WHERE DID YOU GO AND WHY ARE YOU HERE?
WHY ARE *YOU* HERE?
TO FIGURE STUFF OUT.
I NEEDED TO CONTEMPLATE.
I WAS JUST ABOUT TO START A PRETTY ROBUST INNER MONOLOGUE ABOUT MY RESPONSIBILITY IN THE ACCIDENTAL BUT ***VERY*** REALLY REAL LEGACY OF SPIDER-MAN AND--
YOU CAN'T TAKE IT BACK, YOU KNOW.
I KNOW.
I'M SORRY.
YOU SAID IT.
I *DID* SAY IT.
IT WAS MORE ABOUT--IF I MAY, IT WAS REALLY ABOUT WHAT WE WERE *JUST* TALKING ABOUT.
YOU'RE A ***KID*** AND ***NOW*** YOU HAVE THE ENTIRE WEIGHT OF ***THE MULTIVERSE*** RESTING ON YOUR SHOULDERS?
I'M TECHNICALLY A FULLY FUNCTIONING ADULT AND ***I FEEL THE PRESSURE.***
I'M UNDER SO MUCH STRESS RIGHT NOW MY STRESS HAS ITS ***OWN*** STRESS.
MILES, ***I'M SORRY.***
IT IS HOW YOU FEEL.
ONLY-- ONLY BECAUSE OF THIS.
LOOK WHERE WE ARE! LOOK WHERE WE--
WAIT.
LET'S--
YEAH, LET'S DO HONESTY.

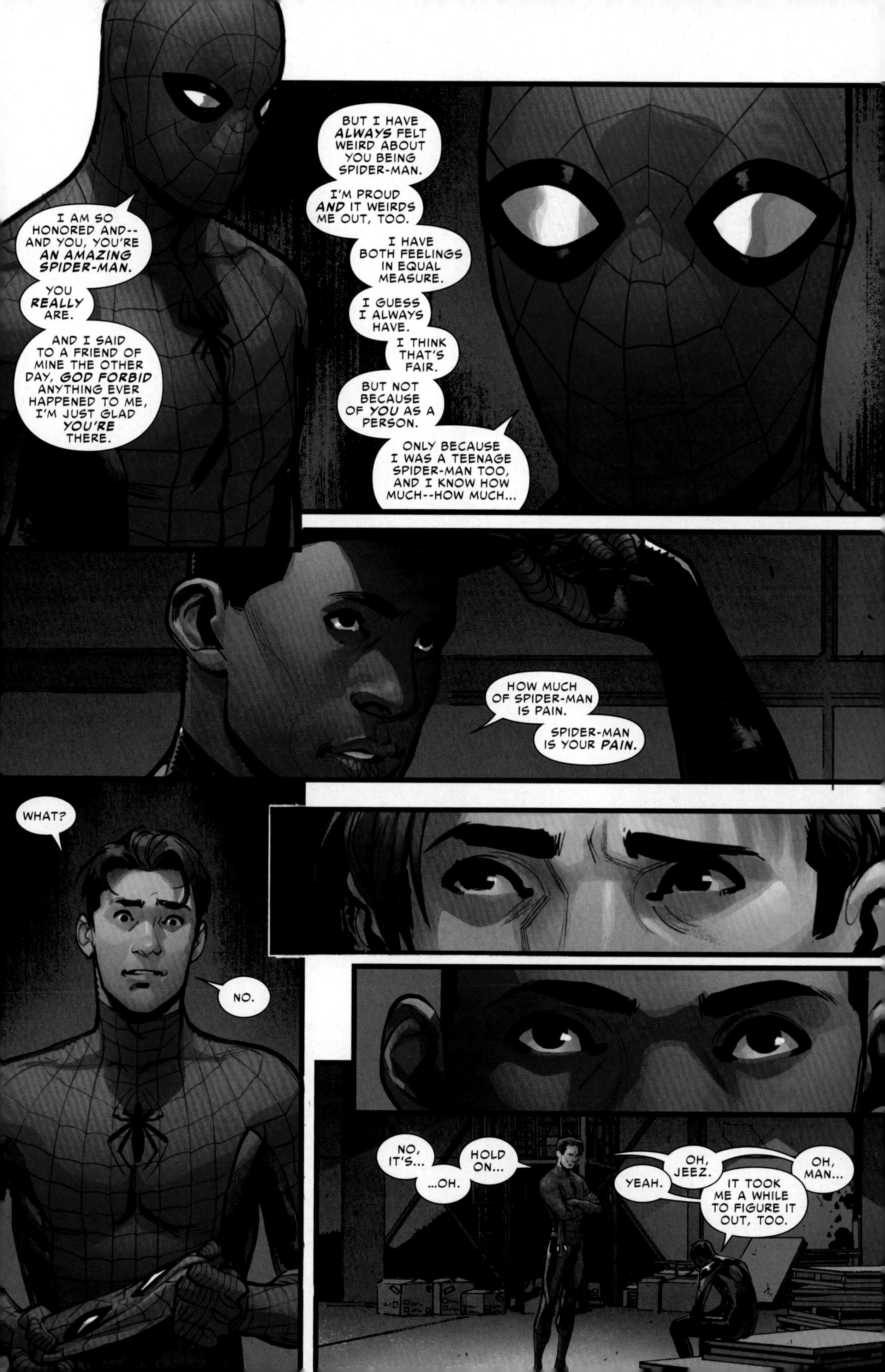

I AM SO HONORED AND-- AND YOU, YOU'RE *AN AMAZING SPIDER-MAN.*
YOU *REALLY* ARE.
AND I SAID TO A FRIEND OF MINE THE OTHER DAY, *GOD FORBID* ANYTHING EVER HAPPENED TO ME, I'M JUST GLAD *YOU'RE* THERE.
BUT I HAVE *ALWAYS* FELT WEIRD ABOUT YOU BEING SPIDER-MAN.
I'M PROUD *AND* IT WEIRDS ME OUT, TOO.
I HAVE BOTH FEELINGS IN EQUAL MEASURE.
I GUESS I ALWAYS HAVE.
I THINK THAT'S FAIR.
BUT NOT BECAUSE OF *YOU* AS A PERSON.
ONLY BECAUSE I WAS A TEENAGE SPIDER-MAN TOO, AND I KNOW HOW MUCH--HOW MUCH...
HOW MUCH OF SPIDER-MAN IS PAIN.
SPIDER-MAN IS YOUR *PAIN.*
WHAT?
NO.
NO, IT'S...
...OH.
HOLD ON...
OH, JEEZ.
OH, MAN...
YEAH.
IT TOOK ME A WHILE TO FIGURE IT OUT, TOO.

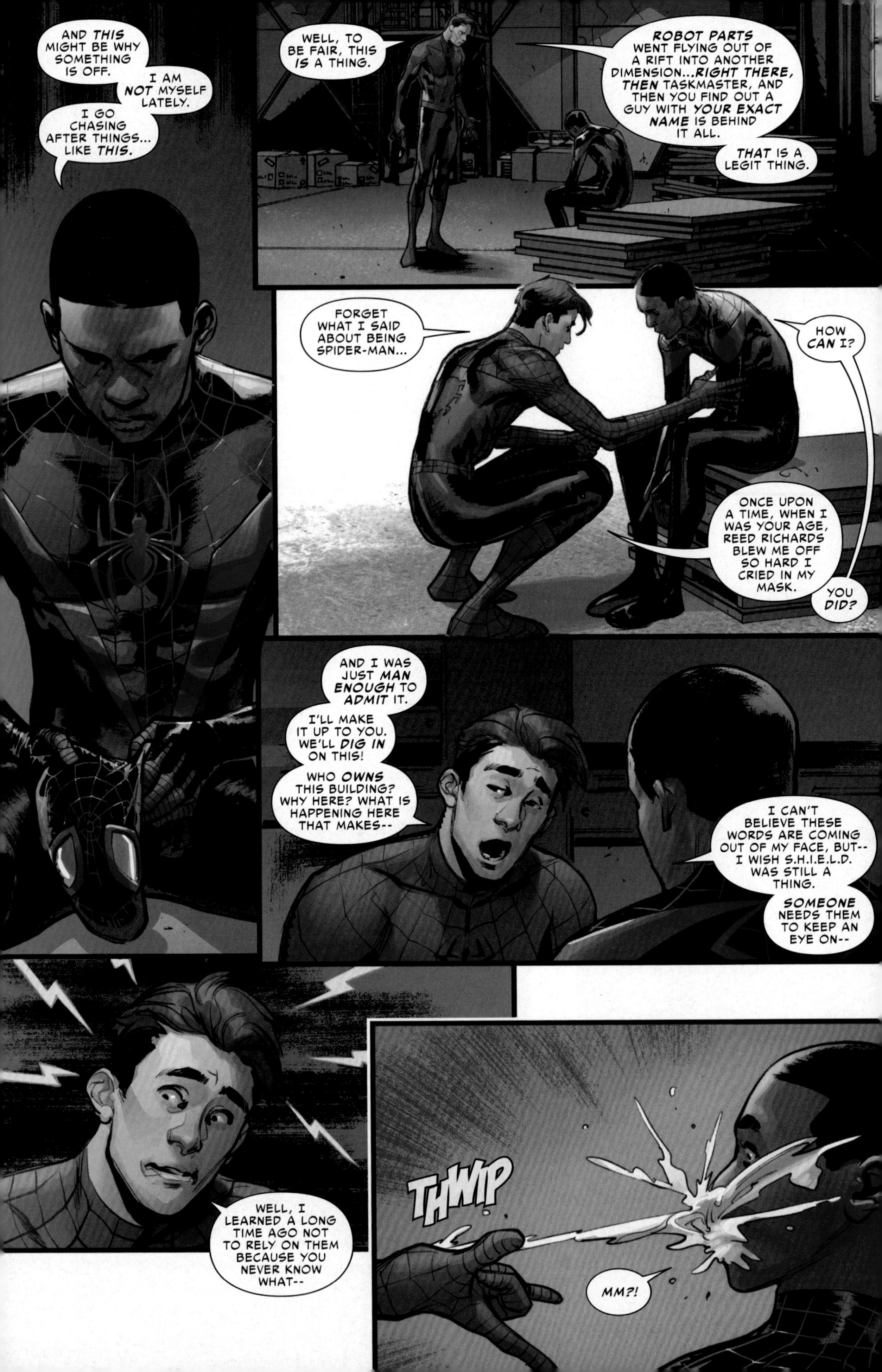
AND THIS MIGHT BE WHY SOMETHING IS OFF.
I AM NOT MYSELF LATELY.
I GO CHASING AFTER THINGS... LIKE THIS.
WELL, TO BE FAIR, THIS IS A THING.
ROBOT PARTS WENT FLYING OUT OF A RIFT INTO ANOTHER DIMENSION...RIGHT THERE, THEN TASKMASTER, AND THEN YOU FIND OUT A GUY WITH YOUR EXACT NAME IS BEHIND IT ALL.
THAT IS A LEGIT THING.
FORGET WHAT I SAID ABOUT BEING SPIDER-MAN...
HOW CAN I?
ONCE UPON A TIME, WHEN I WAS YOUR AGE, REED RICHARDS BLEW ME OFF SO HARD I CRIED IN MY MASK.
YOU DID?
AND I WAS JUST MAN ENOUGH TO ADMIT IT.
I'LL MAKE IT UP TO YOU. WE'LL DIG IN ON THIS!
WHO OWNS THIS BUILDING? WHY HERE? WHAT IS HAPPENING HERE THAT MAKES--
I CAN'T BELIEVE THESE WORDS ARE COMING OUT OF MY FACE, BUT-- I WISH S.H.I.E.L.D. WAS STILL A THING.
SOMEONE NEEDS THEM TO KEEP AN EYE ON--
WELL, I LEARNED A LONG TIME AGO NOT TO RELY ON THEM BECAUSE YOU NEVER KNOW WHAT--
THWIP
MM?!

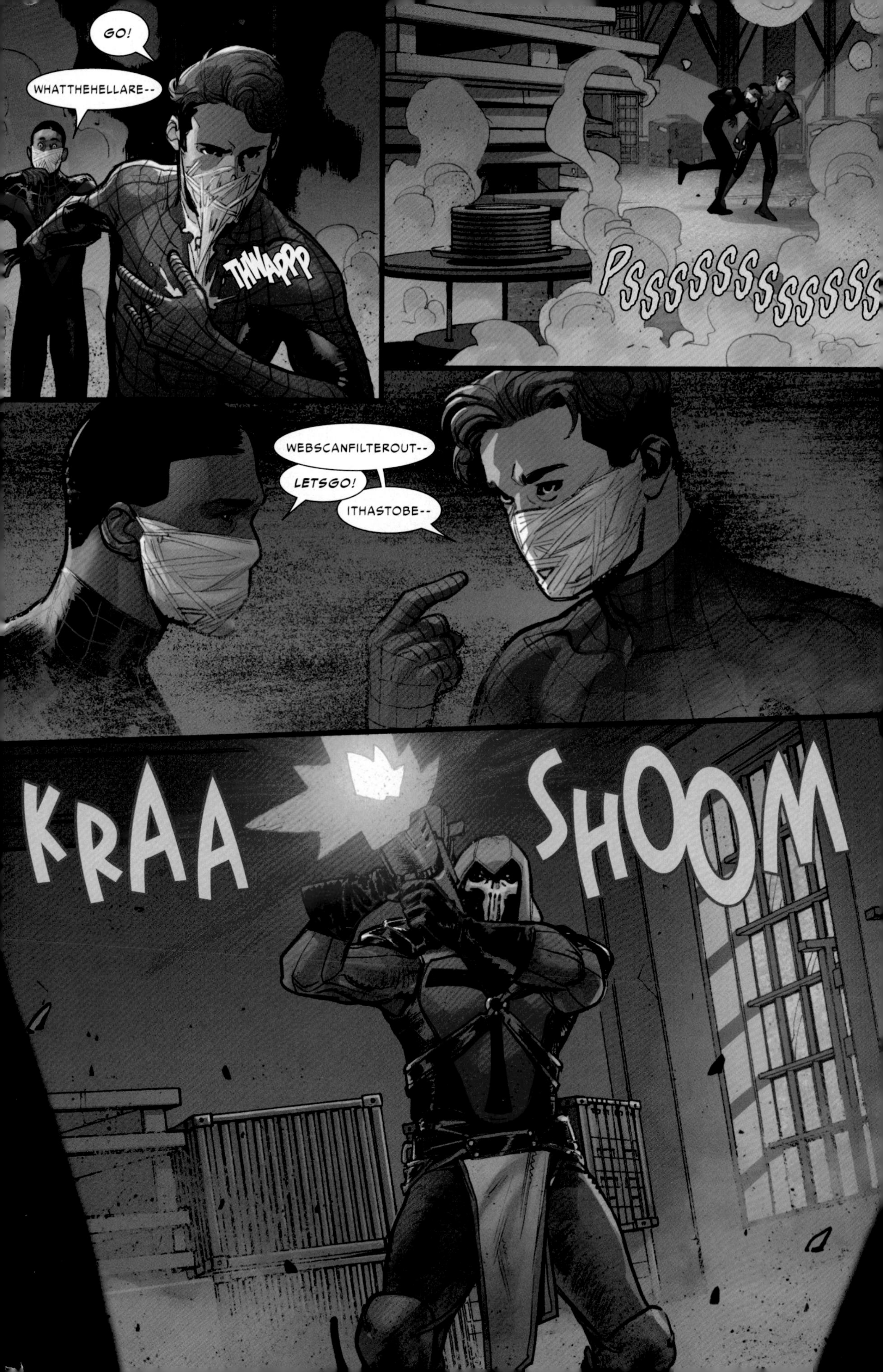
GO!
WHATTHEHELLARE--
THWAPPP
PSSSSSSSSSSSSS
WEBSCANFILTEROUT--
LETSGO!
ITHASTOBE--
KRAA
SHOOM

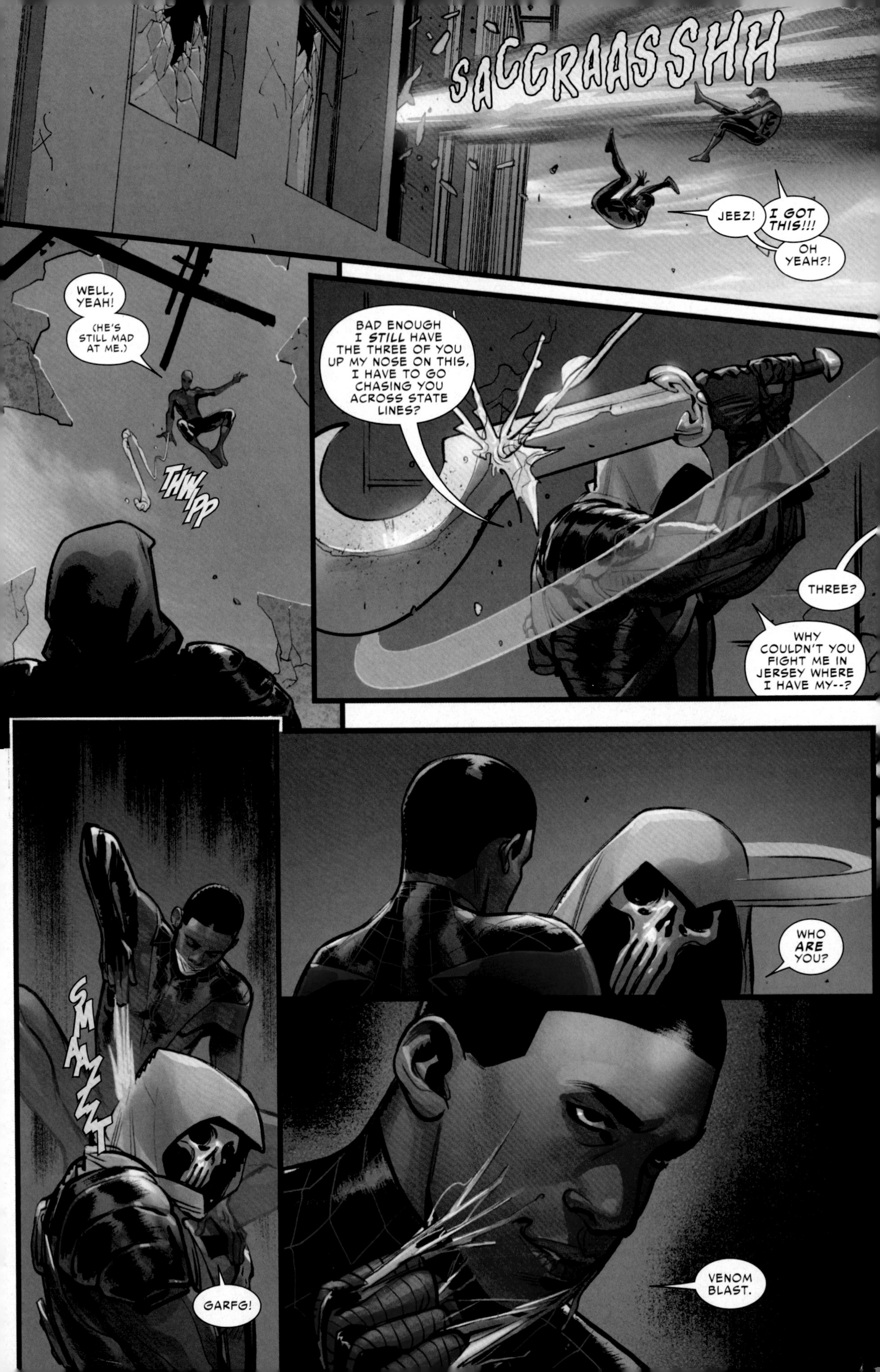
SACCRAASSHH
JEEZ!
I GOT THIS!!!
OH YEAH?!
WELL, YEAH!
(HE'S STILL MAD AT ME.)
THWIPP
BAD ENOUGH I STILL HAVE THE THREE OF YOU UP MY NOSE ON THIS, I HAVE TO GO CHASING YOU ACROSS STATE LINES?
THREE?
WHY COULDN'T YOU FIGHT ME IN JERSEY WHERE I HAVE MY--?
SMAZZT
GARFG!
WHO ARE YOU?
VENOM BLAST.

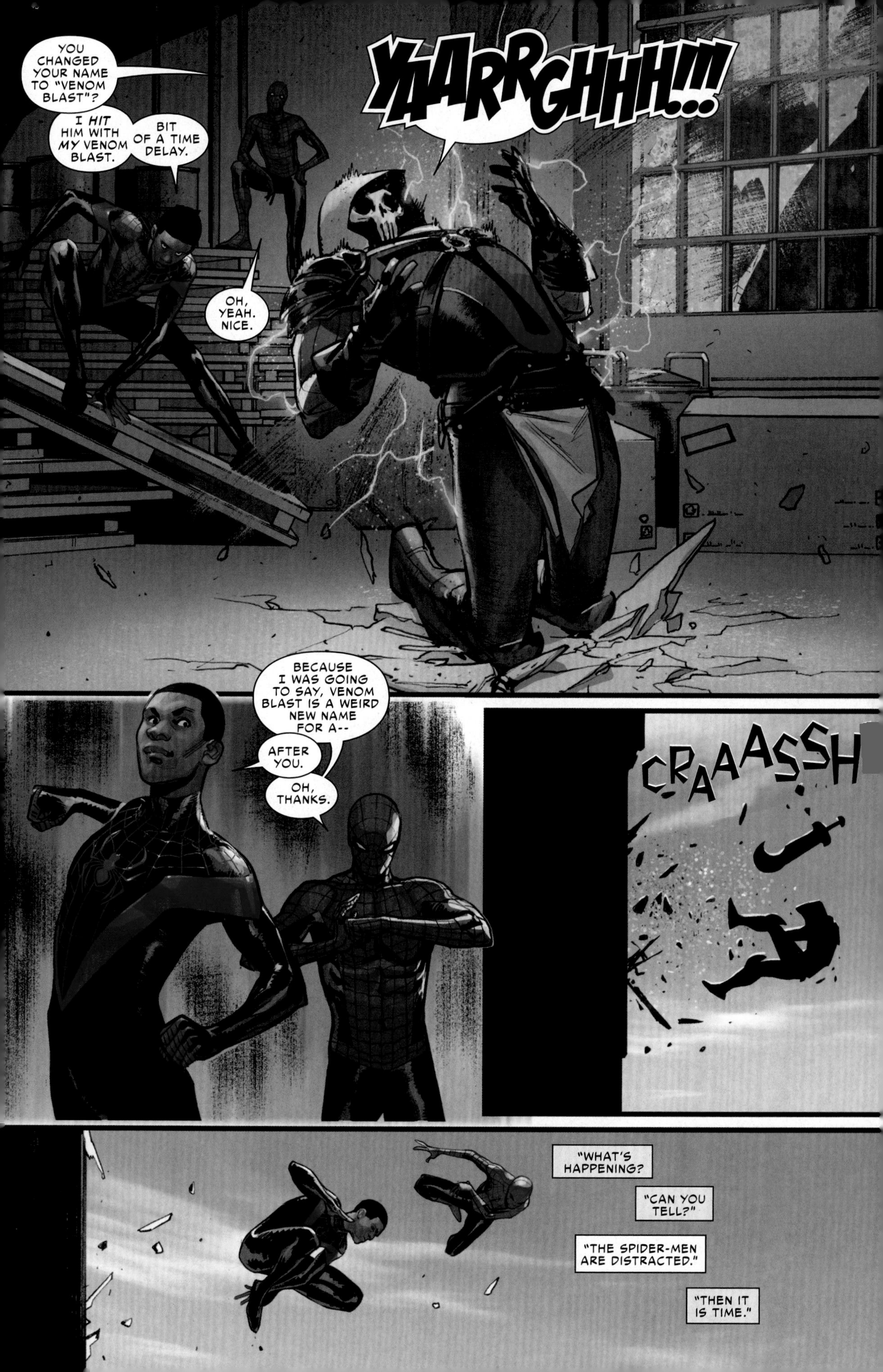
YAARRGHHH!!!...
YOU CHANGED YOUR NAME TO "VENOM BLAST"?
I HIT HIM WITH MY VENOM BLAST.
BIT OF A TIME DELAY.
OH, YEAH. NICE.
BECAUSE I WAS GOING TO SAY, VENOM BLAST IS A WEIRD NEW NAME FOR A--
AFTER YOU.
OH, THANKS.
CRAAASSH
"WHAT'S HAPPENING?
"CAN YOU TELL?"
"THE SPIDER-MEN ARE DISTRACTED."
"THEN IT IS TIME."

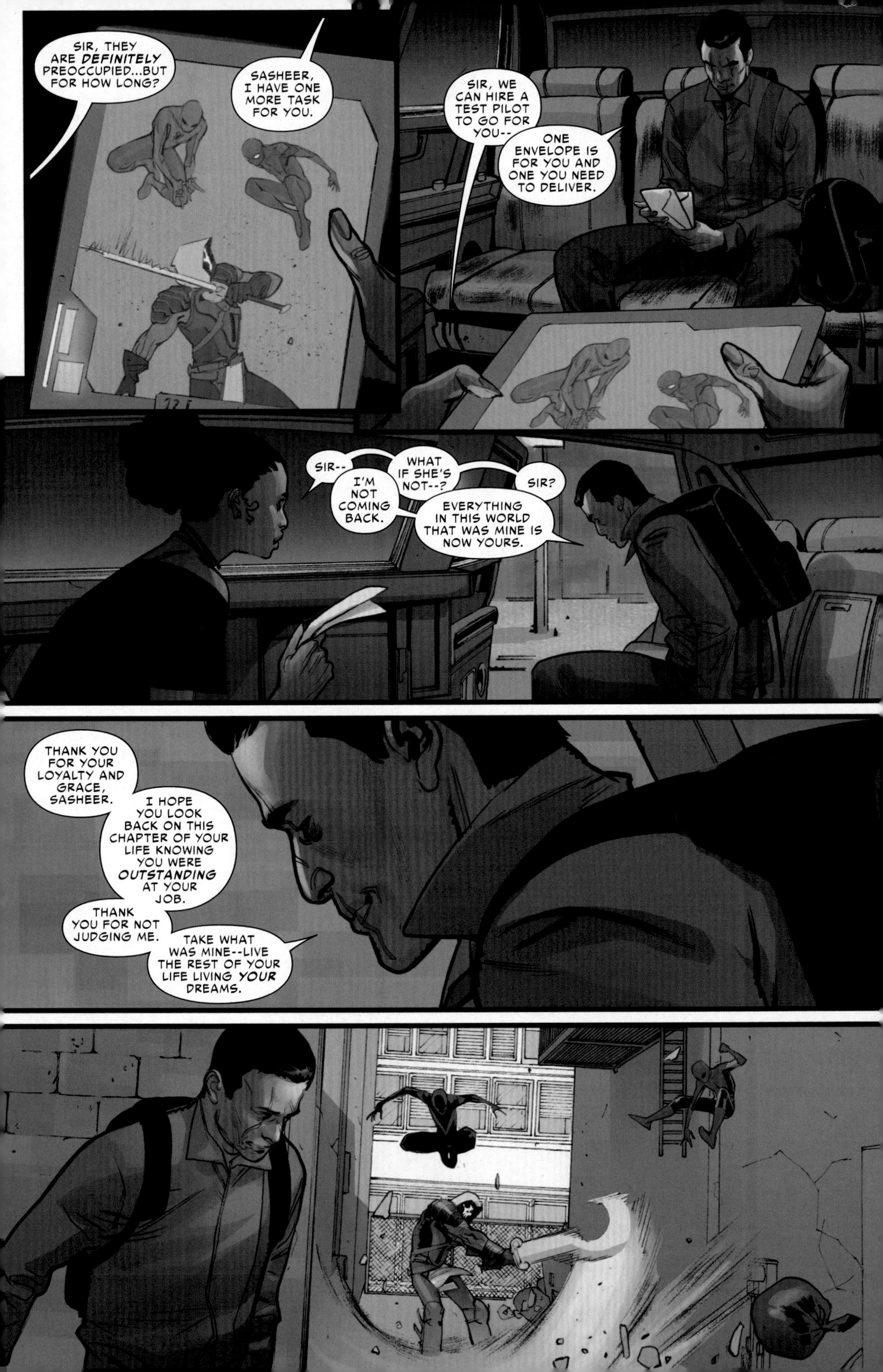
SIR, THEY ARE DEFINITELY PREOCCUPIED...BUT FOR HOW LONG?
SASHEER, I HAVE ONE MORE TASK FOR YOU.
SIR, WE CAN HIRE A TEST PILOT TO GO FOR YOU--
ONE ENVELOPE IS FOR YOU AND ONE YOU NEED TO DELIVER.
SIR--
I'M NOT COMING BACK.
WHAT IF SHE'S NOT--?
SIR?
EVERYTHING IN THIS WORLD THAT WAS MINE IS NOW YOURS.
THANK YOU FOR YOUR LOYALTY AND GRACE, SASHEER.
I HOPE YOU LOOK BACK ON THIS CHAPTER OF YOUR LIFE KNOWING YOU WERE OUTSTANDING AT YOUR JOB.
THANK YOU FOR NOT JUDGING ME.
TAKE WHAT WAS MINE--LIVE THE REST OF YOUR LIFE LIVING YOUR DREAMS.

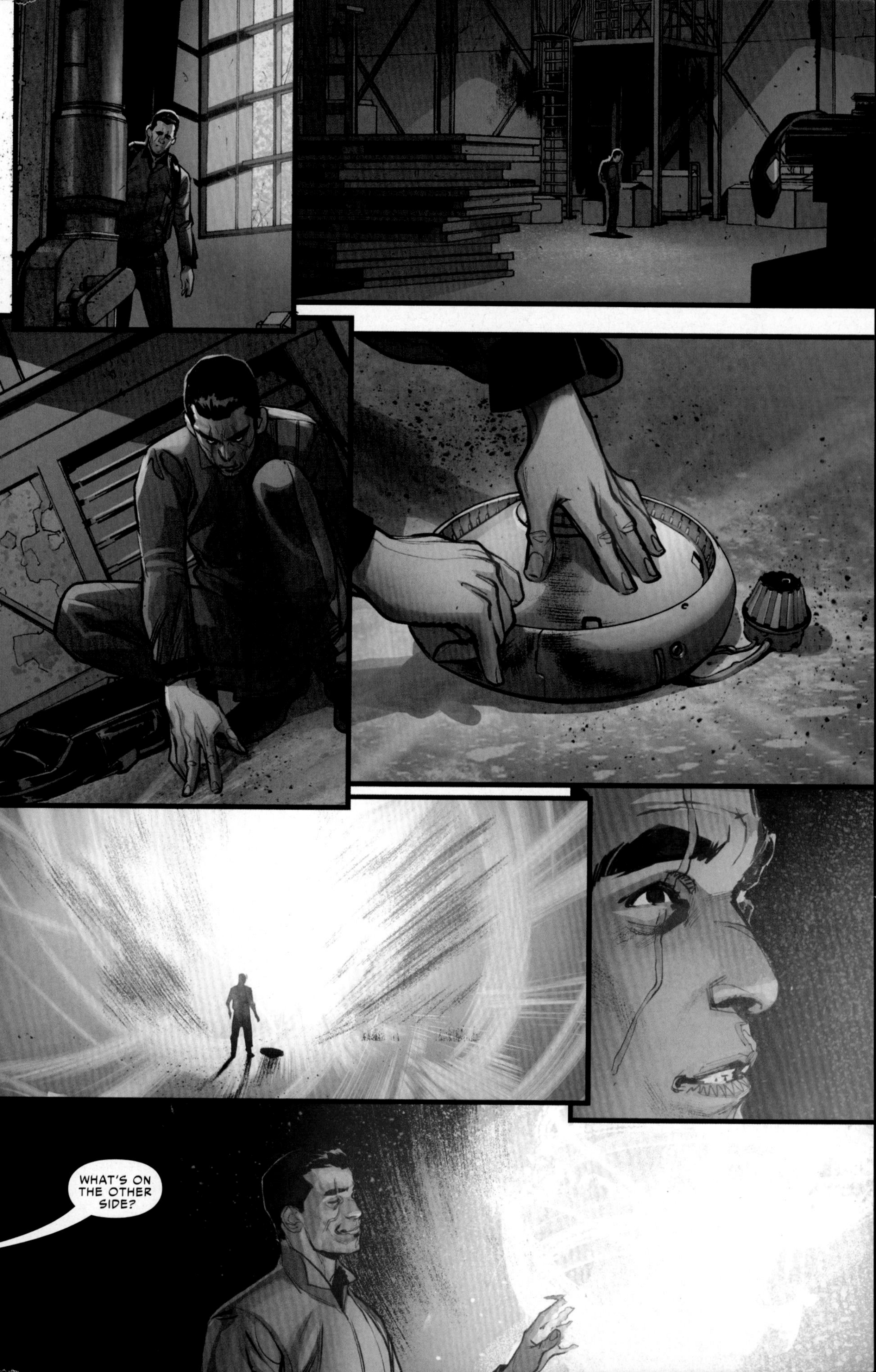
WHAT'S ON THE OTHER SIDE?

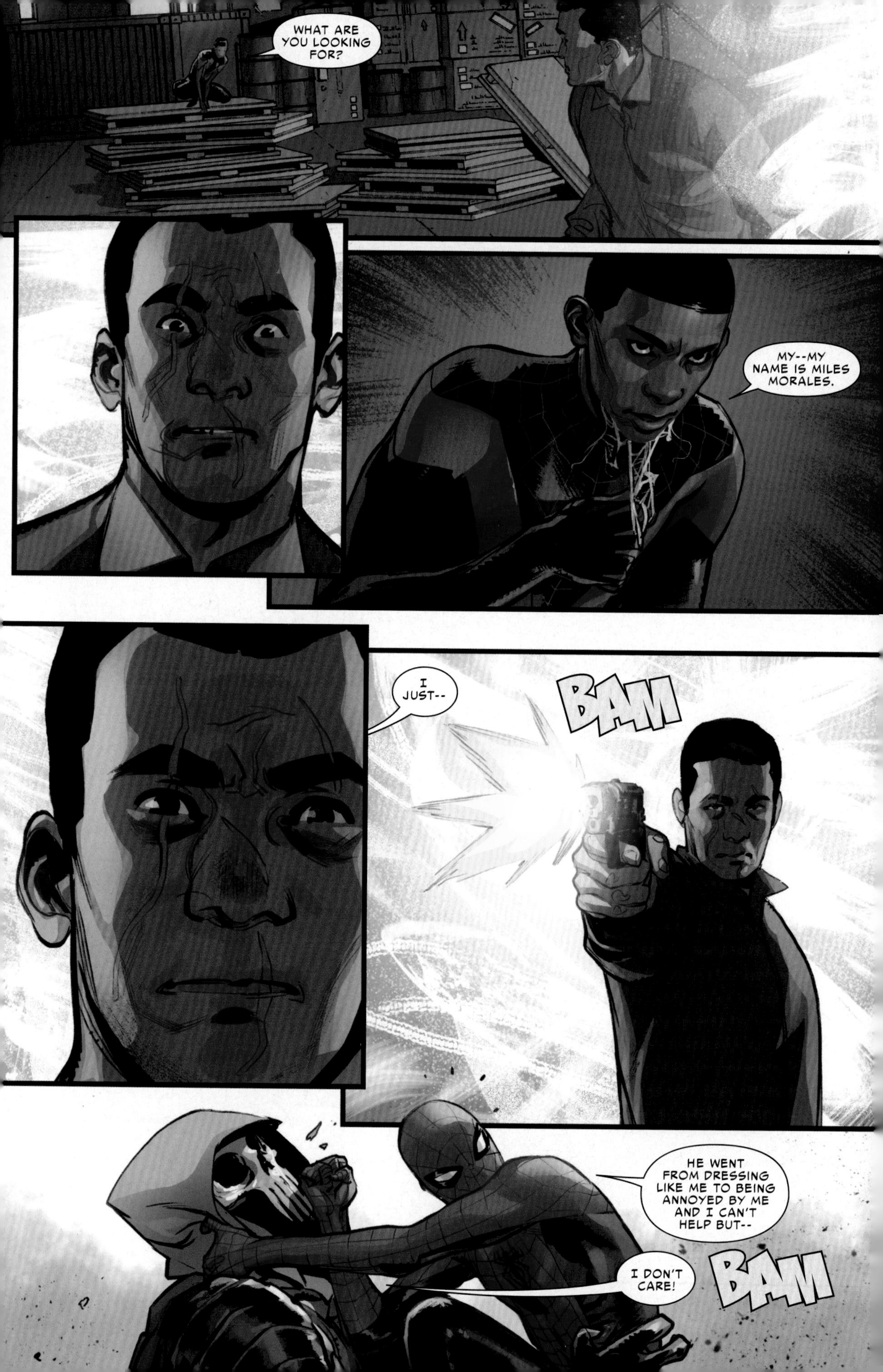
WHAT ARE YOU LOOKING FOR?
MY--MY NAME IS MILES MORALES.
I JUST--
BAM
HE WENT FROM DRESSING LIKE ME TO BEING ANNOYED BY ME AND I CAN'T HELP BUT--
I DON'T CARE!
BAM

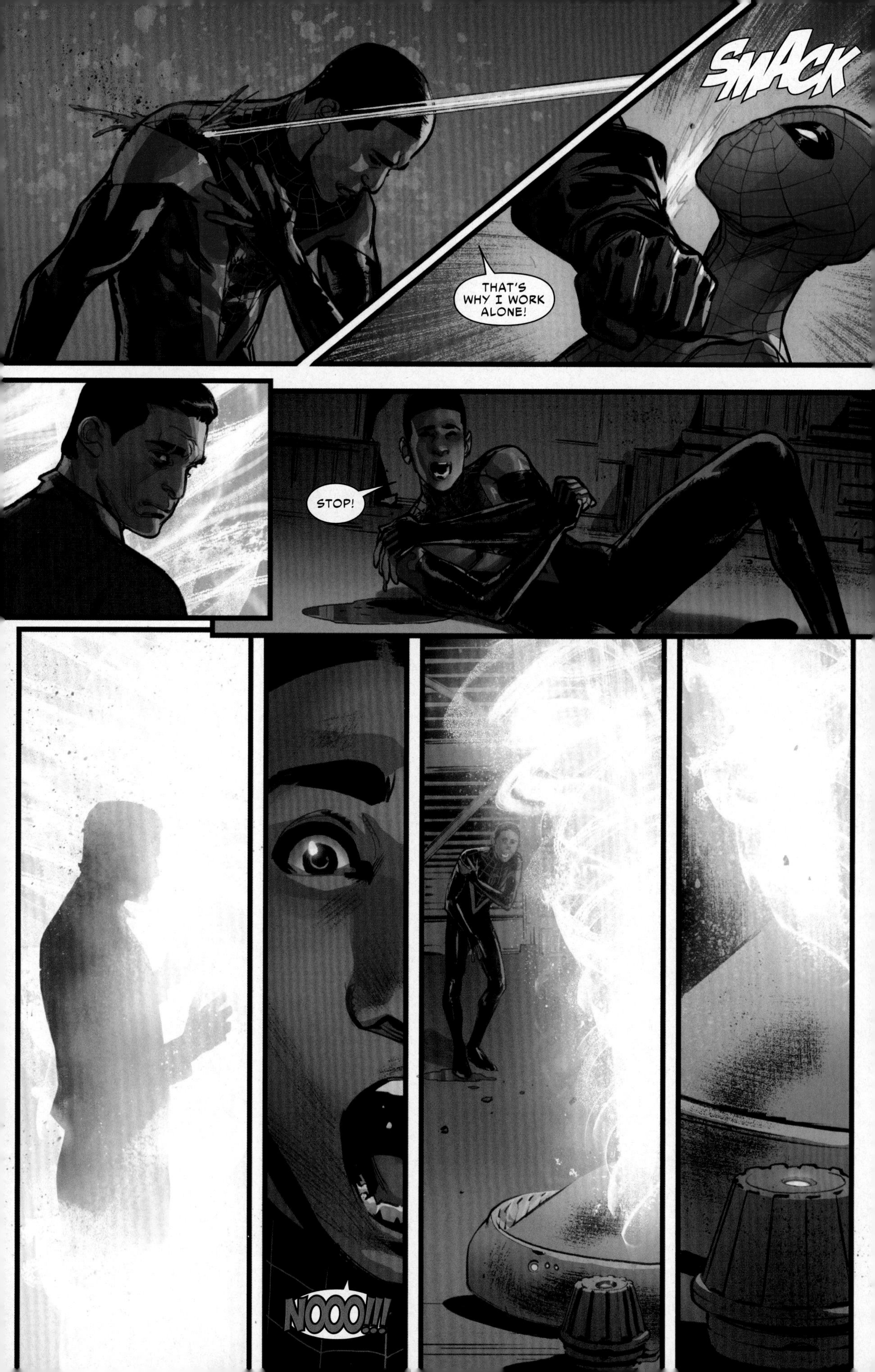
SMACK
THAT'S WHY I WORK ALONE!
STOP!
NOOO!!!

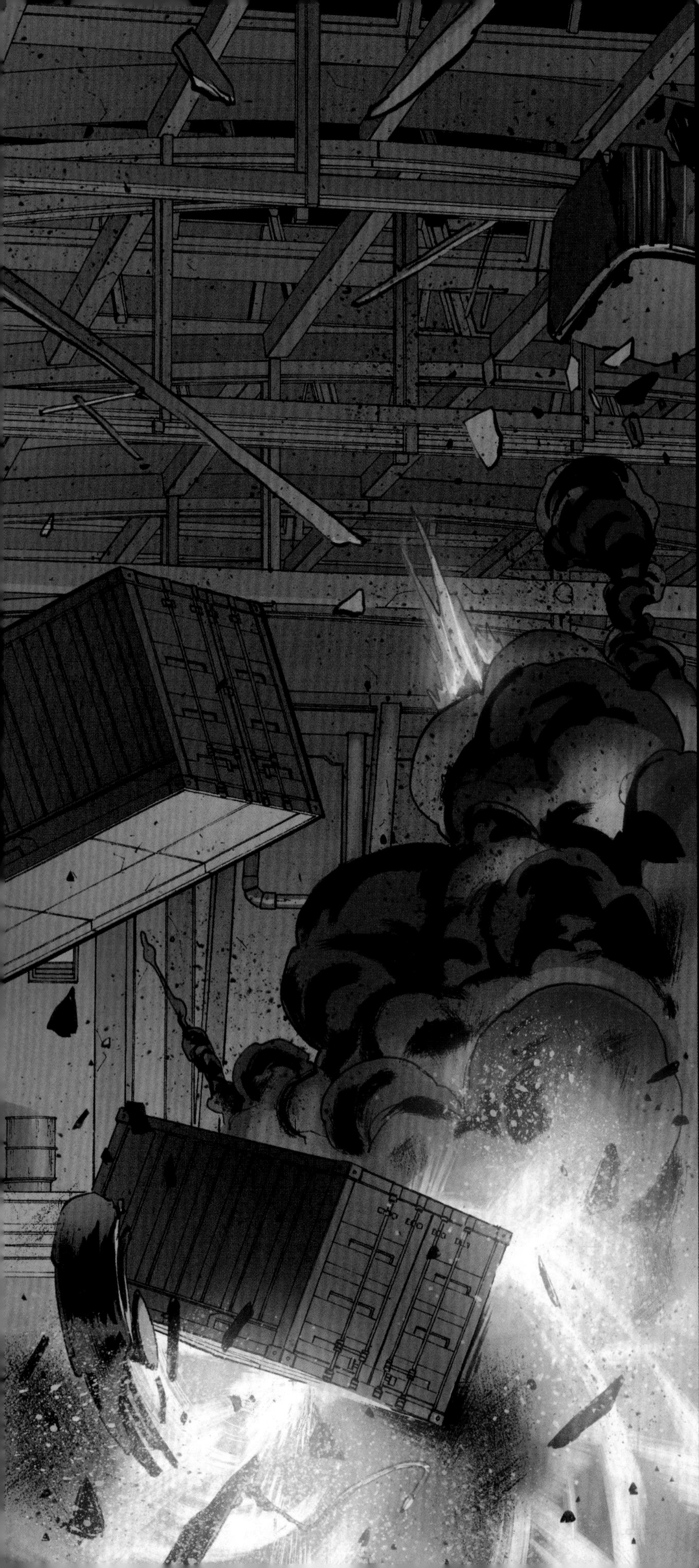
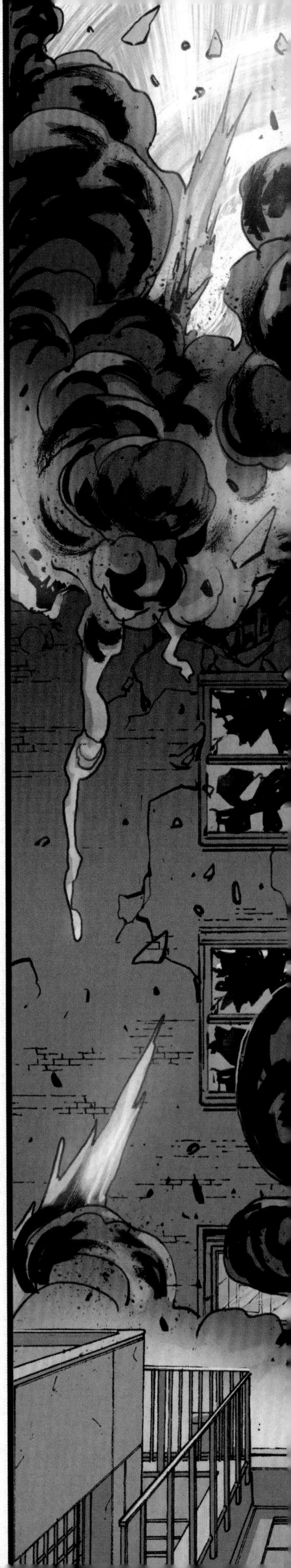

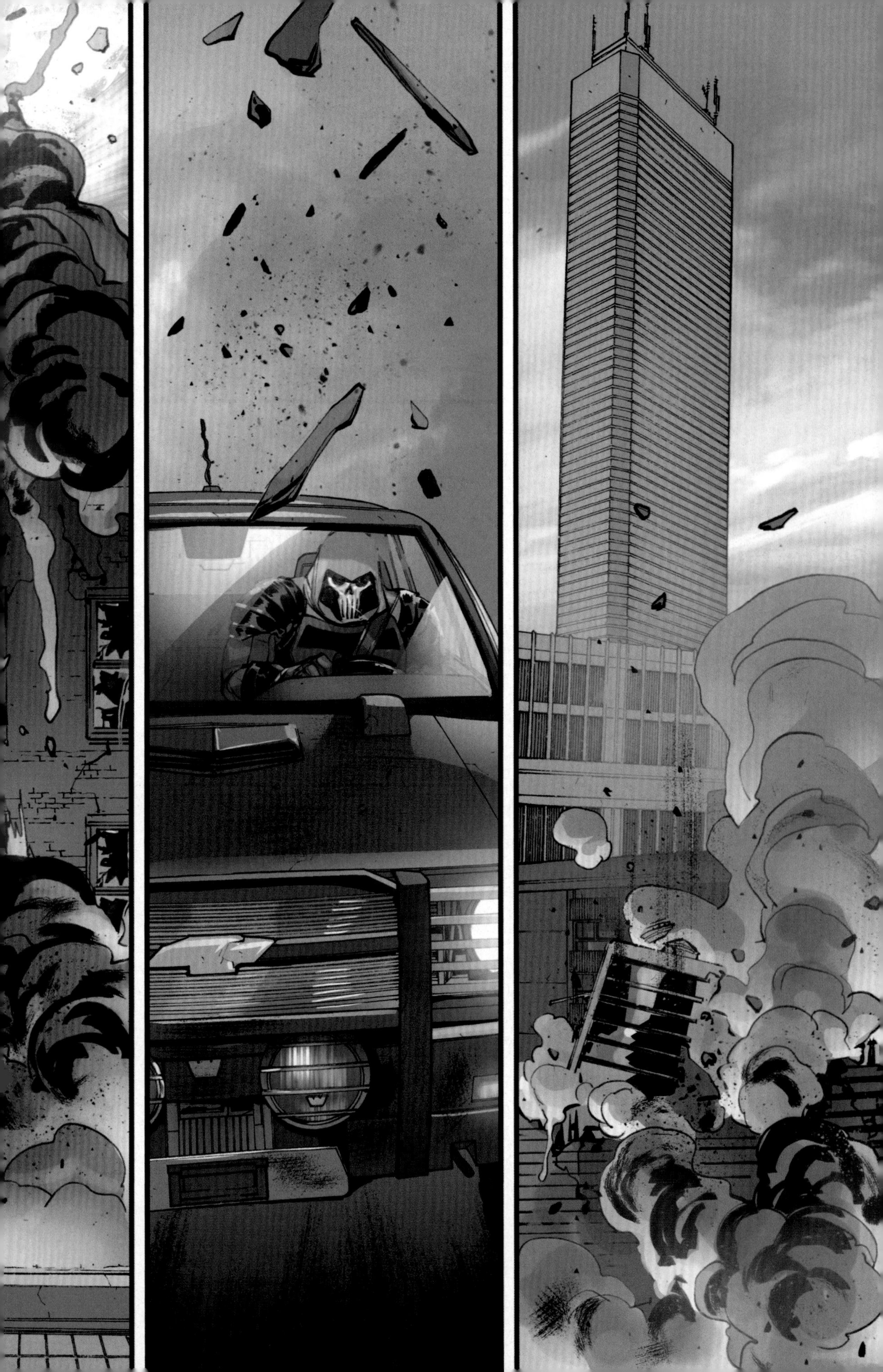

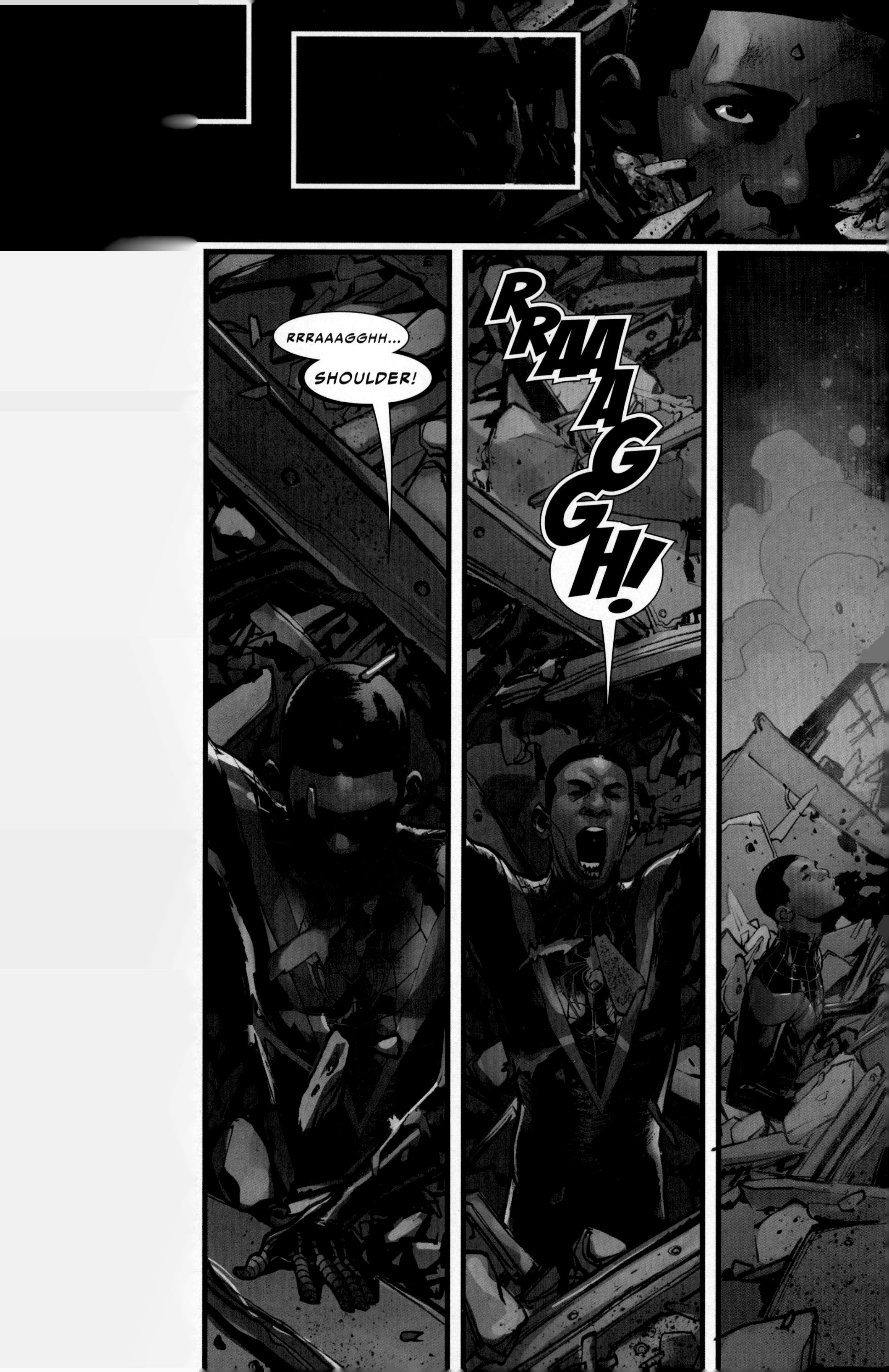
RRRAAAGGHH...
SHOULDER!
RRAAAAGGH!

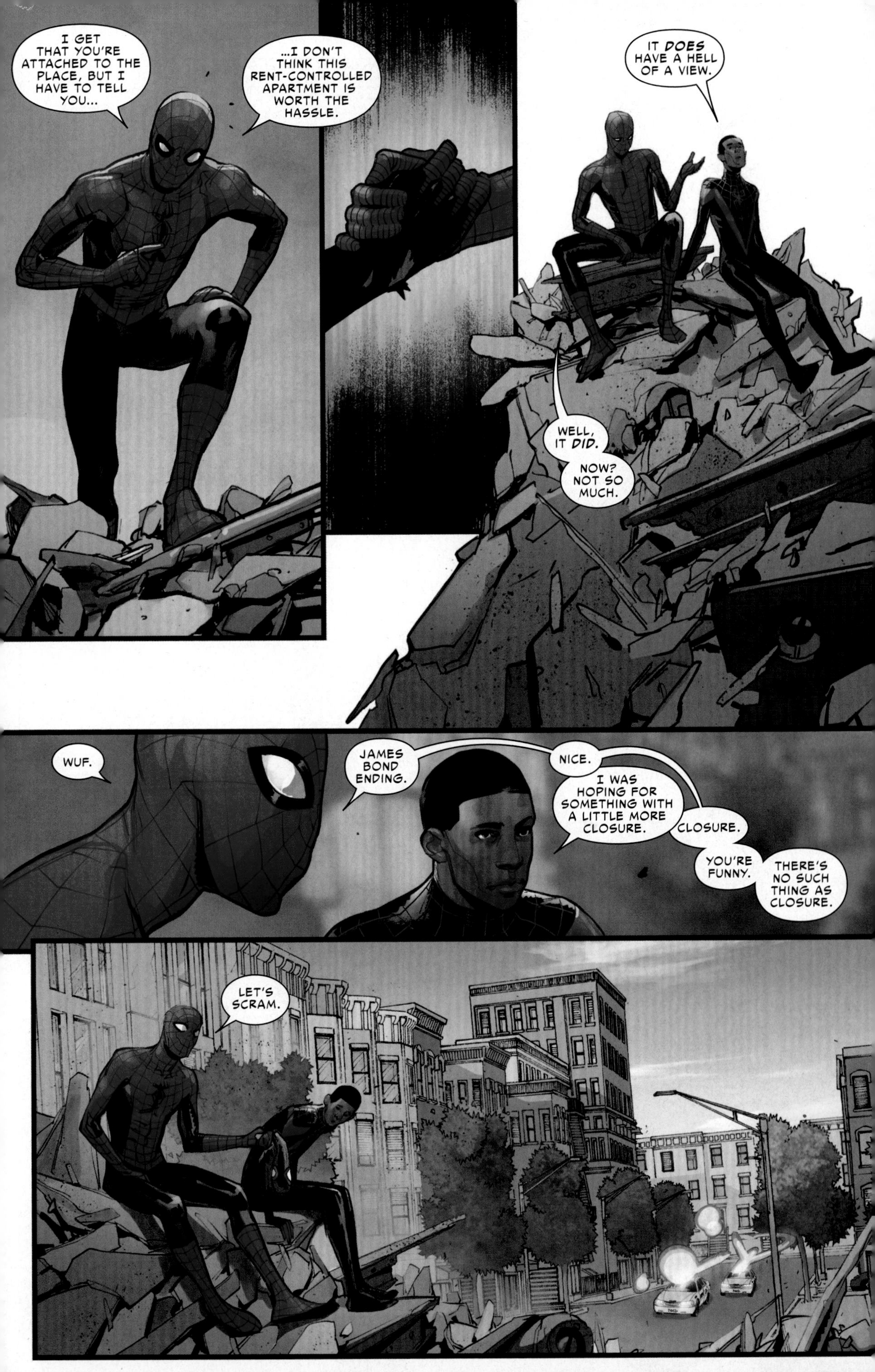
I GET THAT YOU'RE ATTACHED TO THE PLACE, BUT I HAVE TO TELL YOU...
...I DON'T THINK THIS RENT-CONTROLLED APARTMENT IS WORTH THE HASSLE.
IT DOES HAVE A HELL OF A VIEW.
WELL, IT DID.
NOW? NOT SO MUCH.
WUF.
JAMES BOND ENDING.
NICE.
I WAS HOPING FOR SOMETHING WITH A LITTLE MORE CLOSURE.
CLOSURE.
YOU'RE FUNNY.
THERE'S NO SUCH THING AS CLOSURE.
LET'S SCRAM.

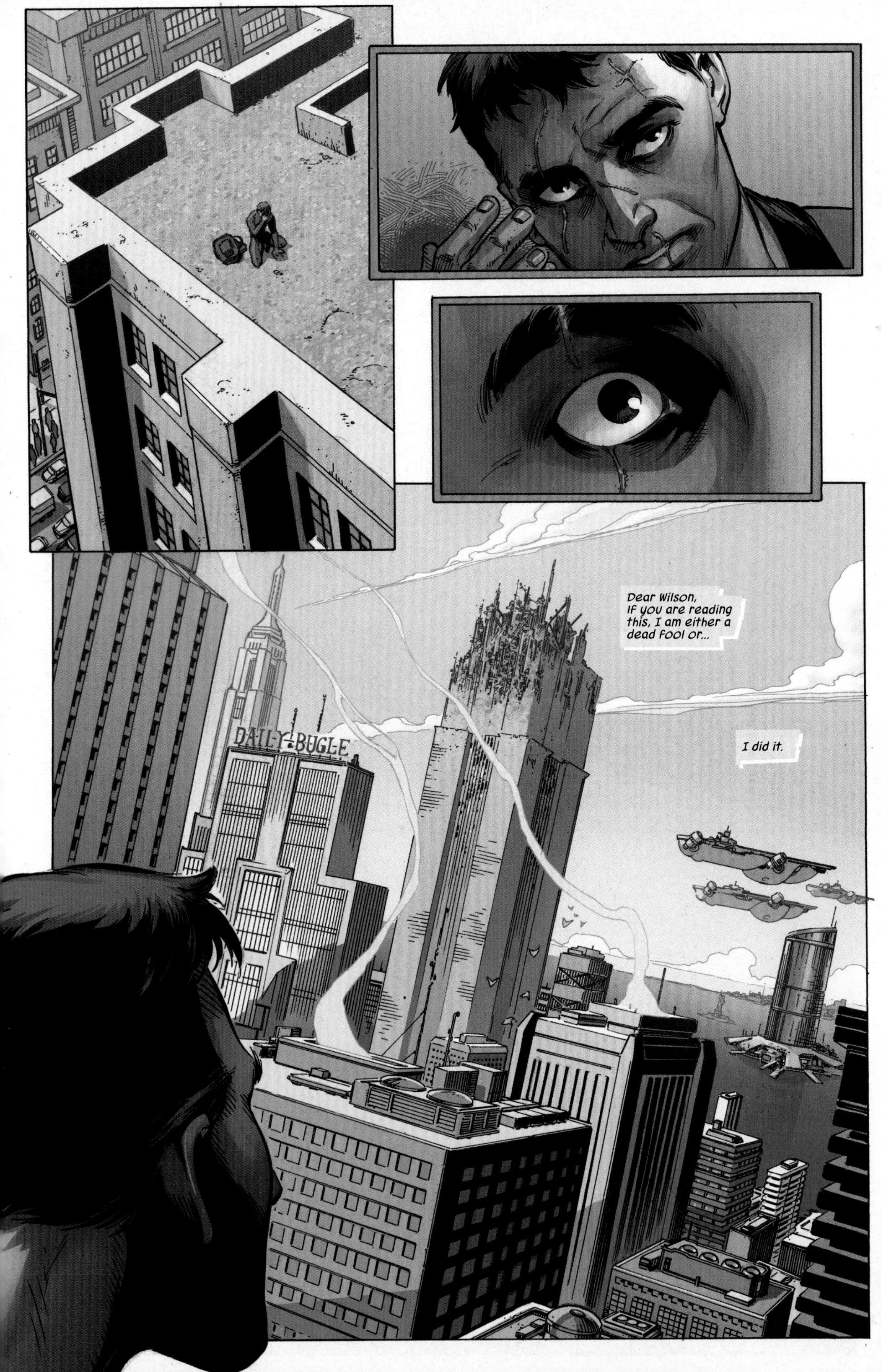
DAILY BUGLE
Dear Wilson,
If you are reading this, I am either a dead fool or...
I did it.

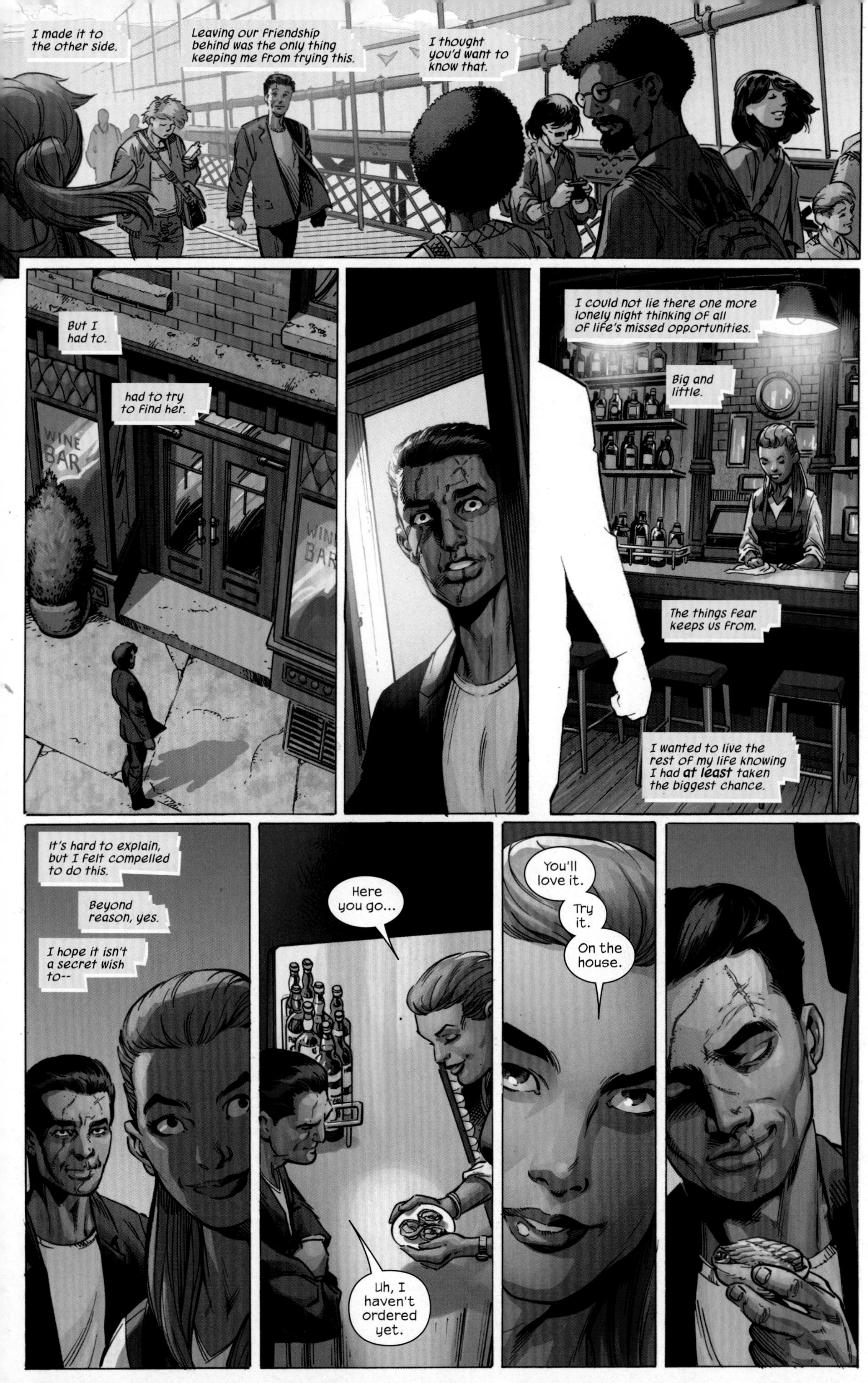

I made it to the other side.
Leaving our friendship behind was the only thing keeping me from trying this.
I thought you'd want to know that.
But I had to.
had to try to find her.
WINE BAR
WINE BAR
I could not lie there one more lonely night thinking of all of life's missed opportunities.
Big and little.
The things fear keeps us from.
I wanted to live the rest of my life knowing I had **at least** taken the biggest chance.
It's hard to explain, but I felt compelled to do this.
Beyond reason, yes.
I hope it isn't a secret wish to--
Here you go...
Uh, I haven't ordered yet.
You'll love it.
Try it.
On the house.

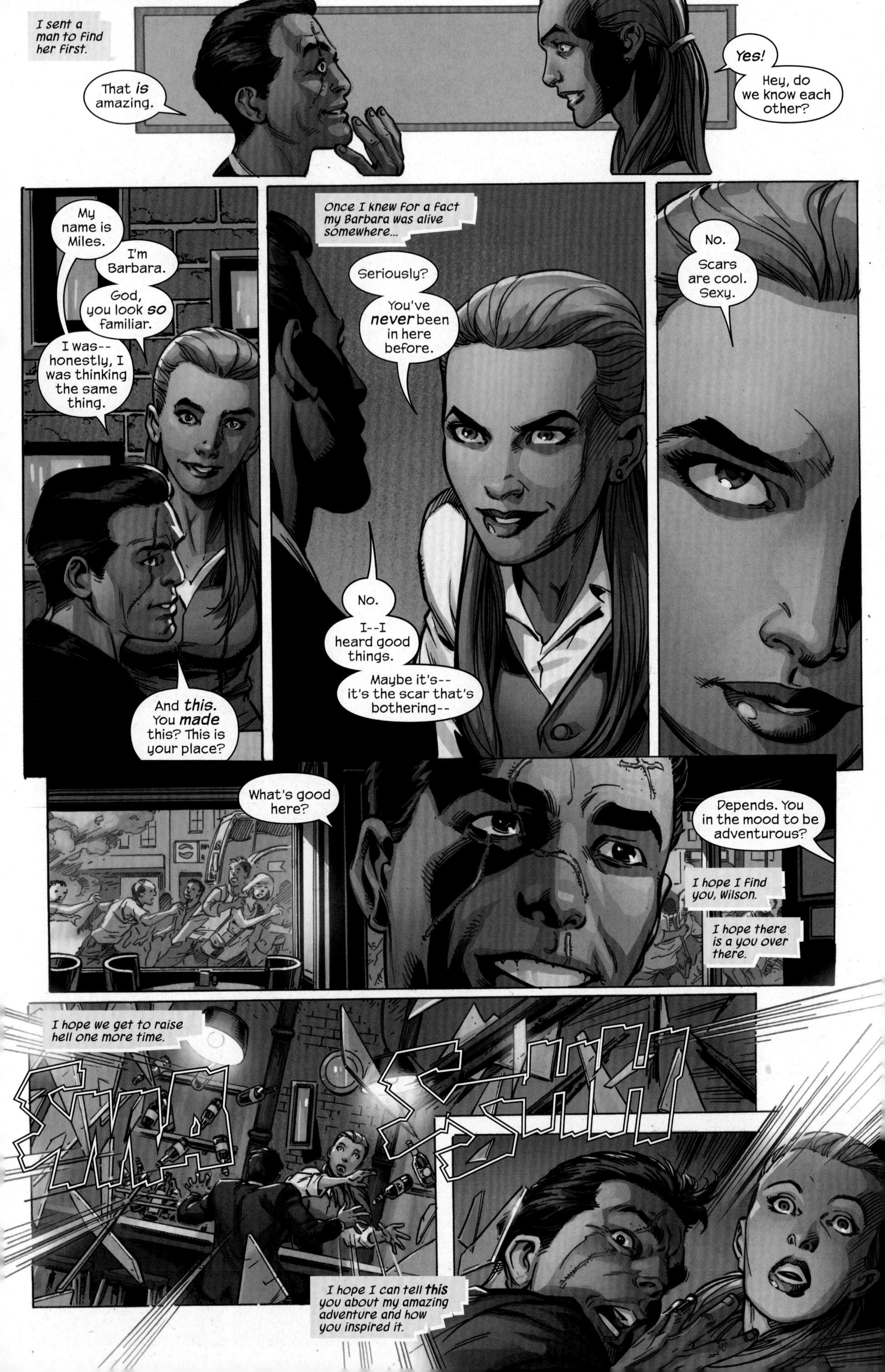
I sent a man to find her first.
That *is* amazing.
Yes!
Hey, do we know each other?
My name is Miles.
I'm Barbara.
God, you look *so* familiar.
I was-- honestly, I was thinking the same thing.
And *this.* You *made* this? This is your place?
Once I knew for a fact my Barbara was alive somewhere...
Seriously?
You've ***never*** been in here before.
No.
I--I heard good things.
Maybe it's-- it's the scar that's bothering--
No.
Scars are cool. Sexy.
What's good here?
Depends. You in the mood to be adventurous?
I hope I find you, Wilson.
I hope there is a you over there.
I hope we get to raise hell one more time.
I hope I can tell **this** you about my amazing adventure and how you inspired it.

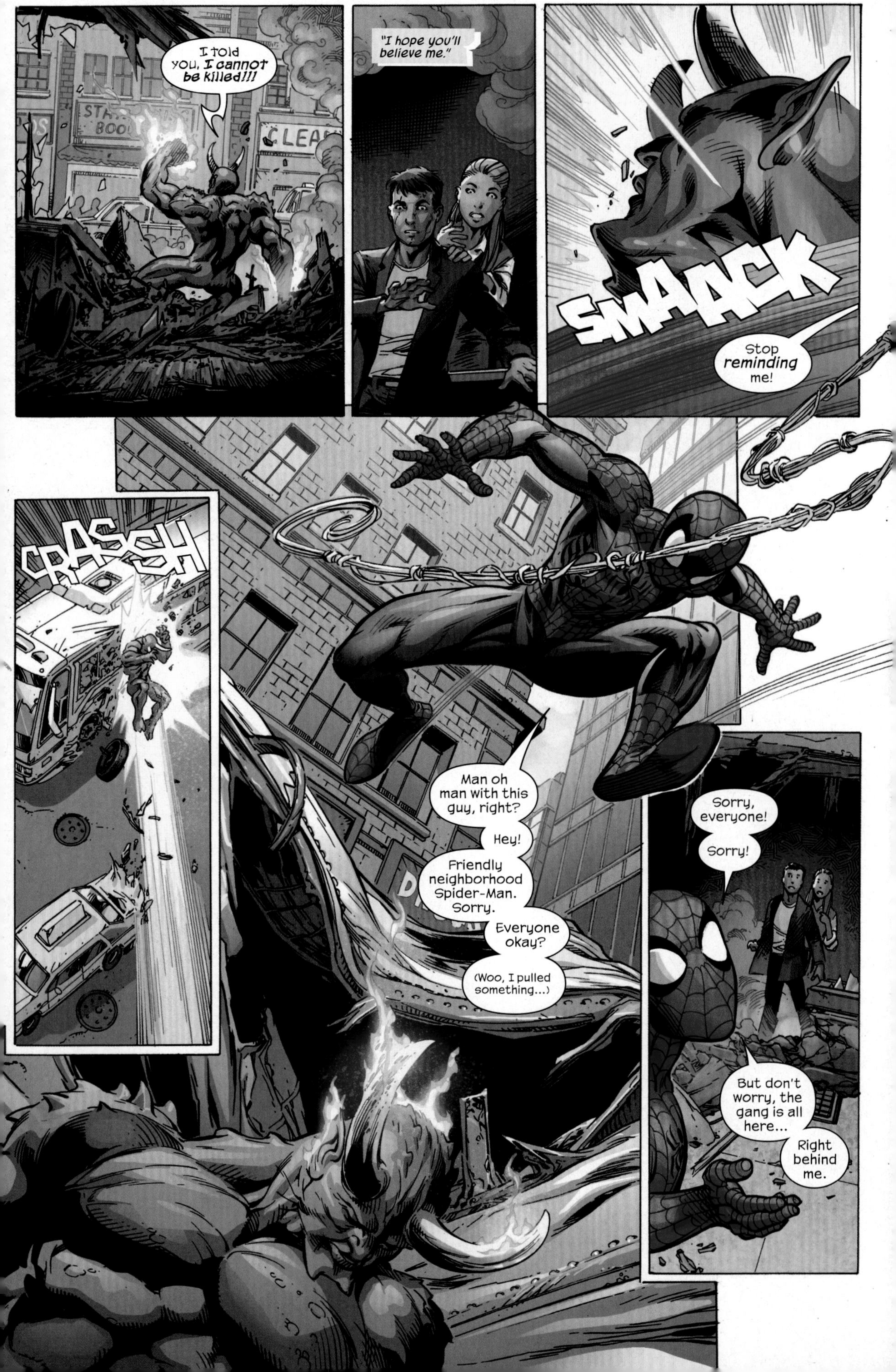
I told you, I cannot be killed!!!
"I hope you'll believe me."
SMAACK
Stop reminding me!
CRASSH
Man oh man with this guy, right?
Hey!
Friendly neighborhood Spider-Man. Sorry.
Everyone okay?
(Woo, I pulled something...)
Sorry, everyone!
Sorry!
But don't worry, the gang is all here...
Right behind me.

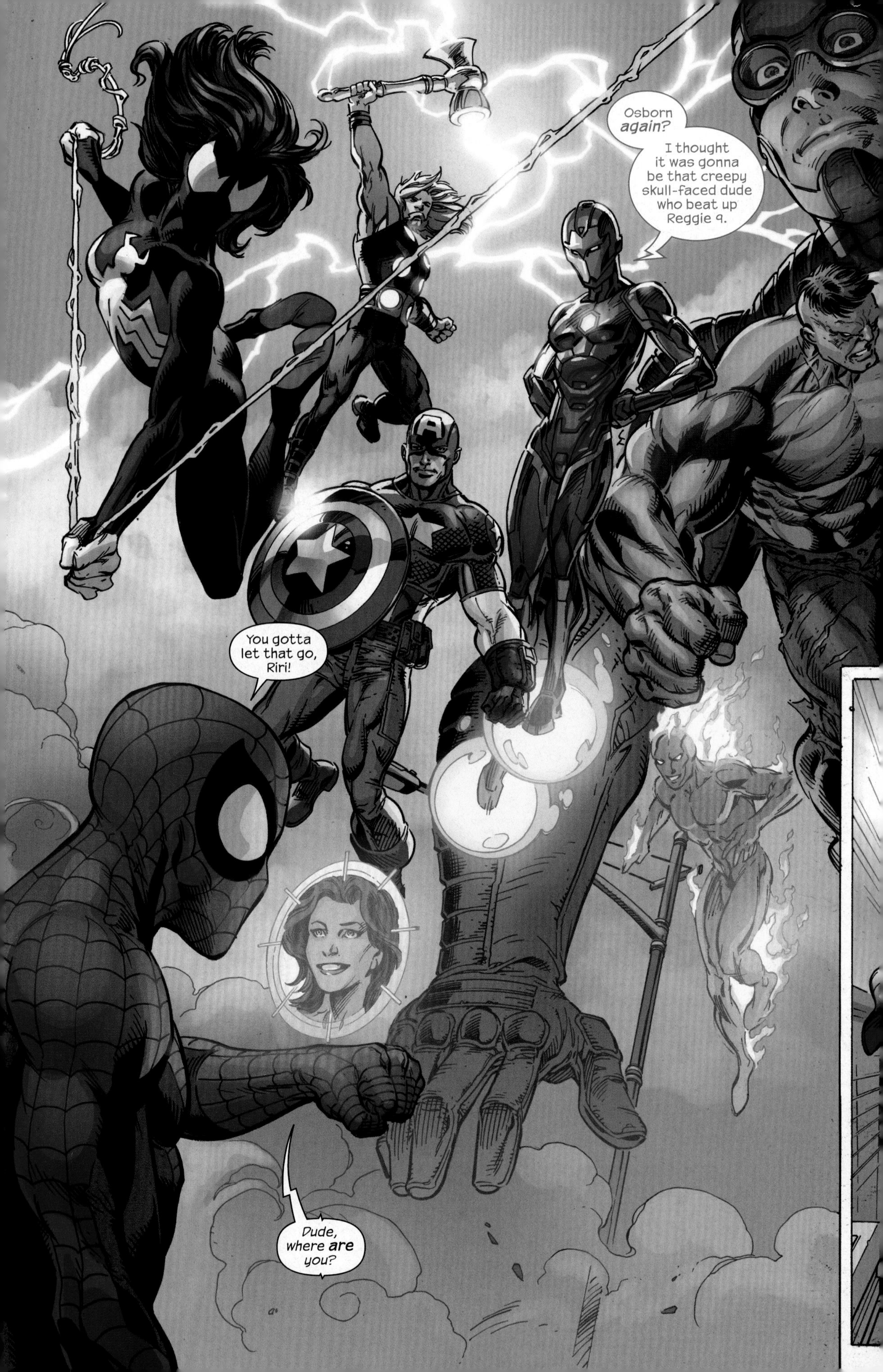
Osborn again?
I thought it was gonna be that creepy skull-faced dude who beat up Reggie 9.
You gotta let that go, Riri!
Dude, where are you?

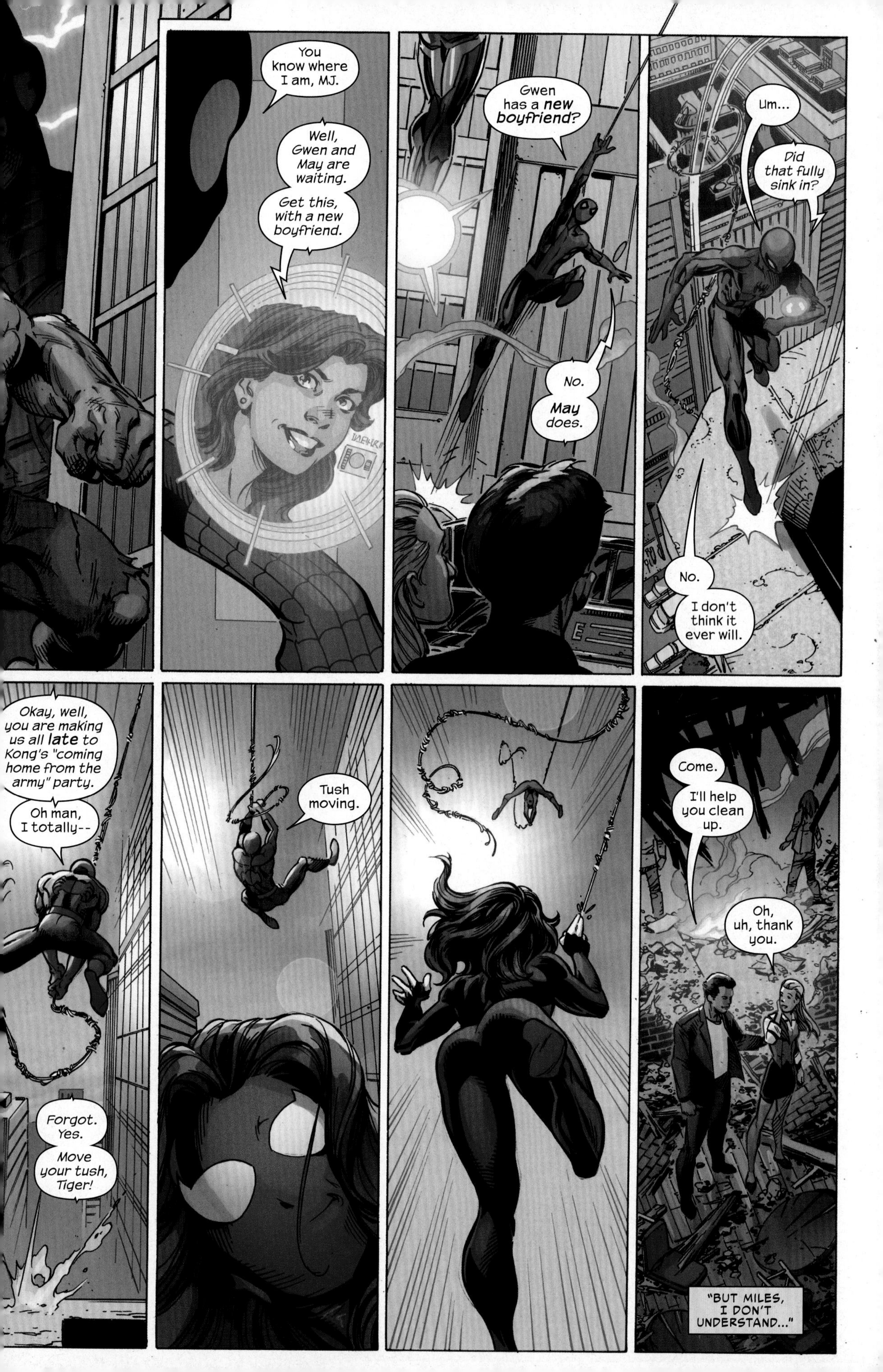
You know where I am, MJ.
Well, Gwen and May are waiting.
Get this, with a new boyfriend.
Gwen has a **new boyfriend**?
No.
May does.
Um...
Did that fully sink in?
No.
I don't think it ever will.
Okay, well, you are making us all **late** to Kong's "coming home from the army" party.
Oh man, I totally--
Forgot. Yes.
Move your tush, Tiger!
Tush moving.
Come.
I'll help you clean up.
Oh, uh, thank you.
"BUT MILES, I DON'T UNDERSTAND..."

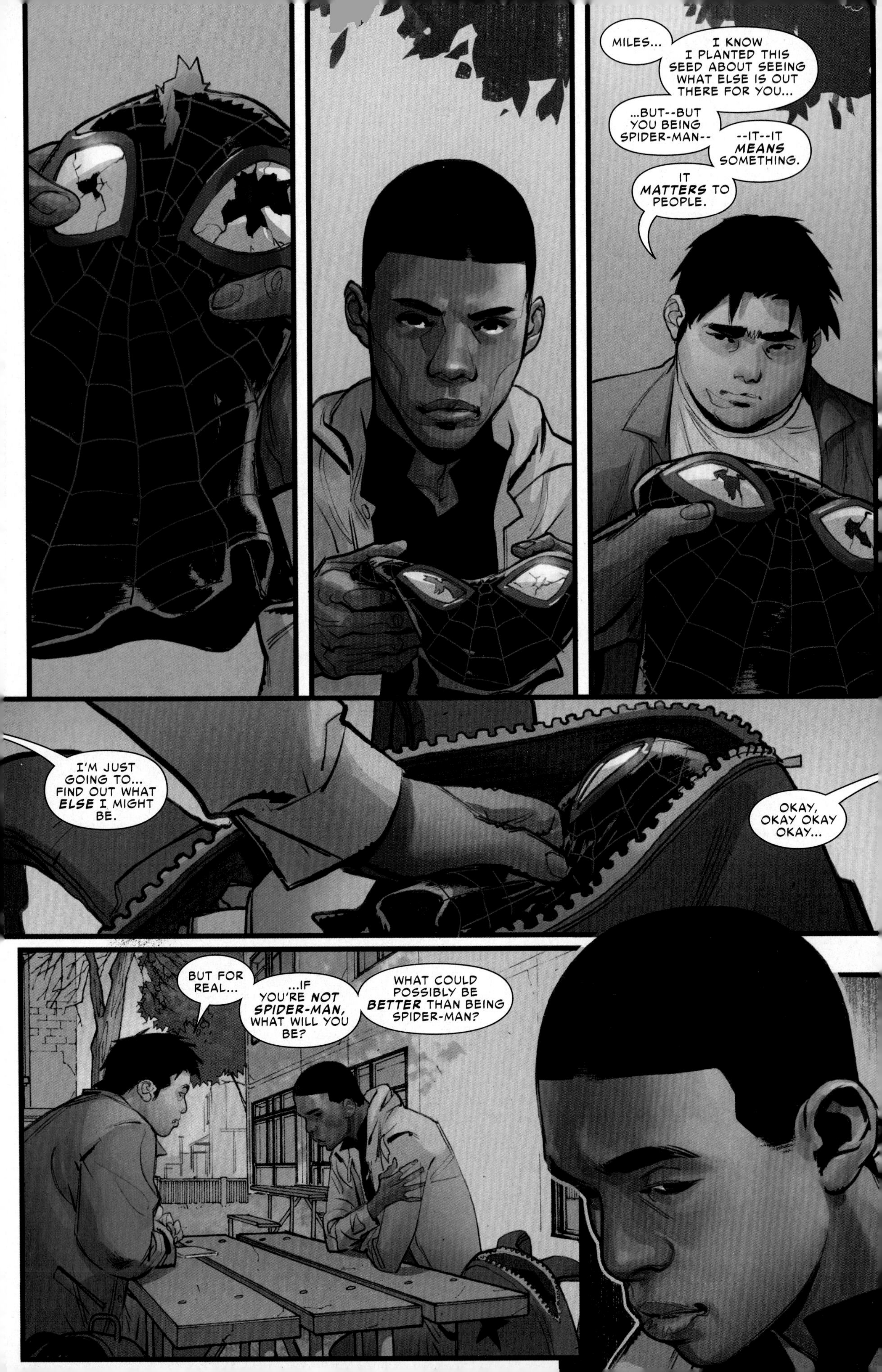
MILES...
I KNOW I PLANTED THIS SEED ABOUT SEEING WHAT ELSE IS OUT THERE FOR YOU...
...BUT--BUT YOU BEING SPIDER-MAN--
--IT--IT MEANS SOMETHING.
IT MATTERS TO PEOPLE.
I'M JUST GOING TO... FIND OUT WHAT ELSE I MIGHT BE.
OKAY, OKAY OKAY OKAY...
BUT FOR REAL...
...IF YOU'RE NOT SPIDER-MAN, WHAT WILL YOU BE?
WHAT COULD POSSIBLY BE BETTER THAN BEING SPIDER-MAN?

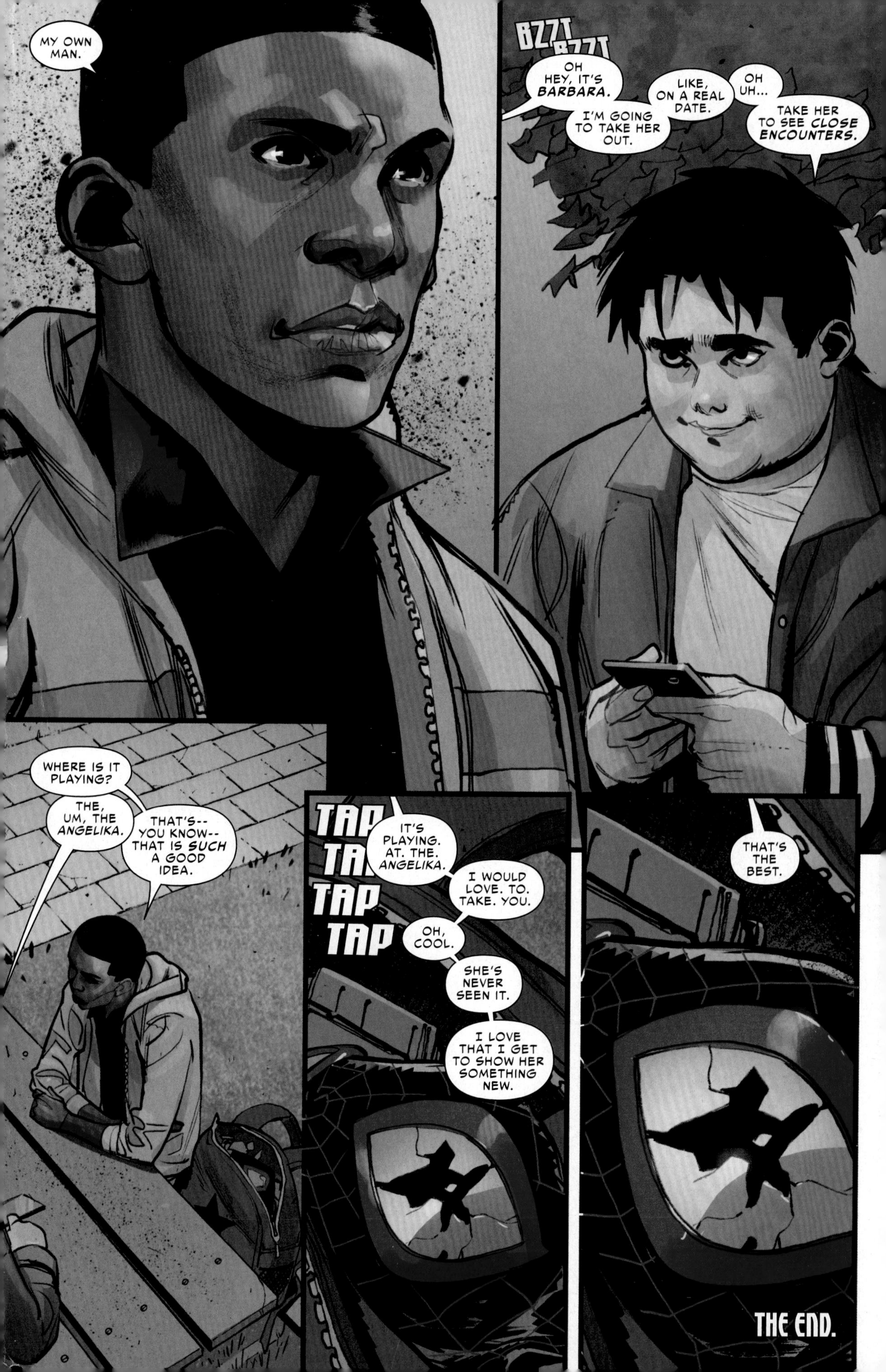
MY OWN MAN.
BZZT BZZT
OH HEY, IT'S BARBARA.
I'M GOING TO TAKE HER OUT.
LIKE, ON A REAL DATE.
OH UH...
TAKE HER TO SEE CLOSE ENCOUNTERS.
WHERE IS IT PLAYING?
THE, UM, THE ANGELIKA.
THAT'S-- YOU KNOW-- THAT IS SUCH A GOOD IDEA.
TAP TAP TAP TAP
IT'S PLAYING. AT. THE. ANGELIKA.
I WOULD LOVE. TO. TAKE. YOU.
OH, COOL.
SHE'S NEVER SEEN IT.
I LOVE THAT I GET TO SHOW HER SOMETHING NEW.
THAT'S THE BEST.
THE END.

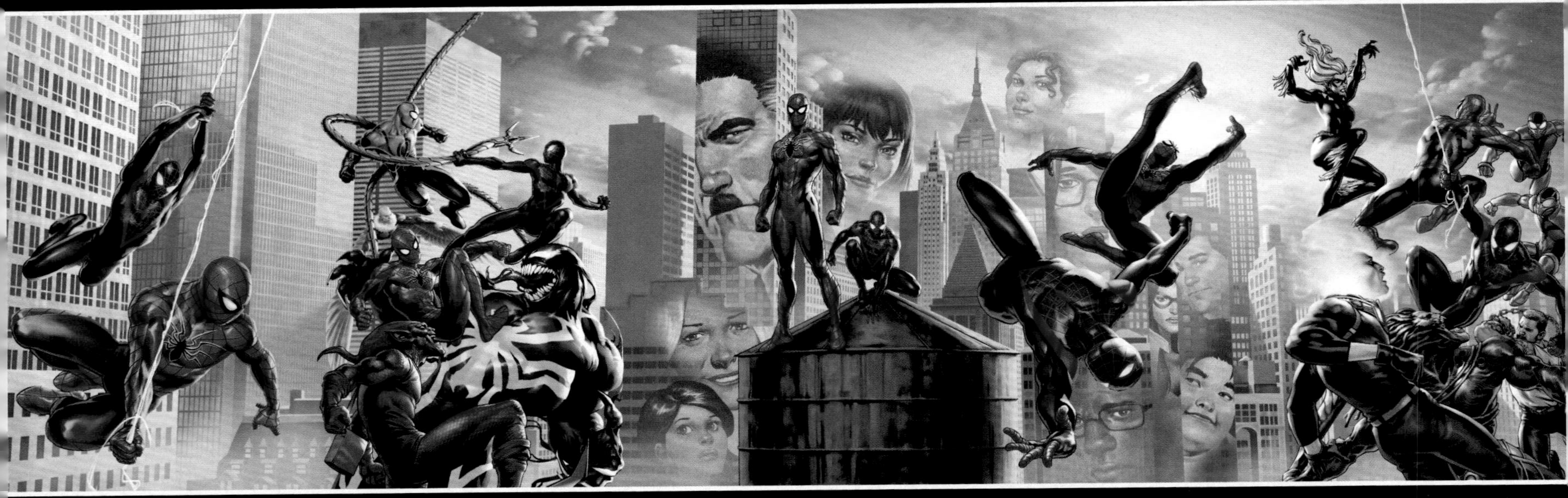

#1-5 CONNECTING VARIANTS BY **JESÚS SAIZ**